# War on Terror

BY THE SAME AUTHOR

*Militancy and Islam*

# War on Terror

Edited by

Maj. Gen. (Retd.) Afsir Karim

The Forum for Strategic and Security Studies (FSSS), New Delhi

HAR-ANAND
PUBLICATIONS PVT LTD

HAR-ANAND PUBLICATIONS PVT LTD
E-49/3, Okhla Industrial Area, Phase-II, New Delhi-110020
Tel.: 41603490 Fax: 011-41708607
E-mail: haranand@rediffmail.com
Website: www.haranandpublications.com



Published by Ashok Gosain and Ashish Gosain for
Har-Anand Publications Pvt Ltd

Printed in India at Ram Book Binding House

# Editor's Introduction

The articles published in this volume have been selected from *Aakrosh*, Asian Journal on terrorism and internal conflicts. *Aakrosh* focuses attention on transnational terrorism and internal conflicts in various parts of the world with special reference to Jihadi terrorism in South Asia, neighbouring regions and areas where there is a spillover affect. The activities of Islamic terrorist groups, trained and supported by al-Qaida and others fundamentalist groups are examined in-depth in regional and global context in *Aakrosh*.

*Aakrosh* has been analyzing various facets of the regional conflicts through well-researched and scholarly case studies. We, seek out scholars, academics, practitioners, and writers in this area of study to contribute to the journal.

Conceptuatlization of terrorism presents serious problems from the very outset because of divergent worldview of the phenomenon. It has not been possible to understand the nature of terrorism or to find a universal formula to combat terrorism because it is not easy to define or describe it with precision. Terrorism changes shapes and forms rapidly and this militates against attempts of forming a composite picture of the global manifestation of terrorism. It is now a well-organized activity that is spreading inordinatley brutal forms of violence and wanton destruction all over the world.

The objectives and the nature of terrorism may vary greatly in its several manifestations but terrorism occupies center stage as a vehicle of destruction and destabilization in various parts of the globe. Sponsored terrorism launched for achieving political objectives invariably assumes the shape of a protracted shadow war and it has become an organized form of violence for coercing targeted entities, forcing them to change their cultural ethos and political policies. It is designed to disrupt normal life by breaking social-economic and ethnic cohesion of targeted popualtions. The modus operandi of terrorist attacks have undergone a radical change with the availability of hi-tech weapons and means of causing catastrophic destruction, attacking a variety of targets with the aim of spreading chaos and instability is easier for terrorist groups now. suicide bombers are another dangerous weapon in the terrorist armory.

The primary aim of the Islamic fundamentalists grops based in South Asian countries has been destabilization and attacking of secular regimes by waging asymmetrical wars, wearing down and degrading their industrial resources and security infrastructure. South Asia is particularly vulnerable to Islamic terrorism becaue of the demographic composition of the region combined with the ethno-religious rivalries present in many parts of this region. There is qualitative difference between terrorist threats faced by Asian and western nations, Jihadi attacks in western nations are generally punitive in nature, while in Asia the aim of terrorists and fundamentalist activities is not merely destructive but change of regime and culture and religious ethos. It necessary to examine terrorist activiteis in Asia from this point of view.

India has been facing the challenge of terrorism of this kind for many decades. The fundamentalist organizations based in Pakistan, with the active connivance of the armed forces have mobilized vast resources of manpower, arms and finances, to carry out trans-border attacks on Indian targets. India faces multiple long-term threats to its territorial integrity and national unity by a kind of warfare in which sponsored terrorism and subversive activiteis are combined for achieving political and territorial objectives by encroaching on India's political and ideological space.

Aakrosh focuses attention on transnational terrorism and internal conflicts in various parts of the world with special focus on Jihadi terrorism in South Asia. Terrorism is having a deleterious impact in many regions and creating long-term security problems. Exposing these facts to the itnernational community, it is hoped, will reduce the dangers; as such exposures enhance the inherent capability of the target countries and societies to defend themselves.

We believe that it is useful to expose the true-nature of regional conflicts, for that could be one way of reducing the danger of permitting such conflicts to grow and multiply. We hope, such exposure will persuade agencies and governments that have been sponsoring these conflicts to reconsider their policies, and become aware that fomenting international and regional violnece is a seriously risky business.

The present status of international cooperation in countering terrorism is not particulrly encouraging because strategic interests of countries take priority over countering terrorism. Most collaborative measures at the global level taken so far are ineffective and disjointed. Indiscrimiante use of force by security forces invariably lead to conflict escalation, (comparative studies regarding relationship between harsh measures and escalation of) conflicts show that there is need of evolving better methods of using force that would not hurt non-combatants. *Aakrosh* has been highlighting various issues related to terrorism and itnernal conflicts for almost a decade now and emphasizing the fact that international cooperation in developing anti-terrorist institutions and enlarging and developing wider security network is necessary to combat terrorism. There is little doubt that we need to tackle the fountainhead of terorism, presently the entire effort seems to be directed to fight certain terrorist groups, mostly those that directly threaten us, and the so called war on terrorism has got totally lost in strategic agendas. A reorientation of global effort for combating terrorism is required, fundamentalism and terrorism must be countered in all its manifestations, as a narrow and selective approach can have little impact.

MAJ. GEN. AFSIR KARIM

# The Forum for Strategic & Security Studies [FSSS]

*The Forum for Strategic and Security Studies* is a well known think tank based in Delhi. The Forum for Strategic & Security Studies, a Independent, non-profit making, a non-political institution is designed to provide a platform for research, analysis, option formulation and evaluation of national security policies of, and security relationships between states, particularly those in South Asia and the Asia Pacific region.

The Forum was conceived and will remain dedicated to a better understanding of the multi-dimensional relevance of security on national, regional as well as global issues.

The Forum undertakes rigorous research and analysis of national security policies and strategic issues of relevance to India with a view to providing constructive inputs for policy development and to increase general awareness on issues impinging on formulation and implementation of national security strategies and policies. I may mention that the Forum accepts no foreign funding for its projects.

## Objectives

Its main objective is to create and harmonise the means to carry out a dedicated, rigourous and independent research and analysis of national security policies and strategic issues of relevance to India with a view to providing constructive inputs for policy development, promoting national security and strategic studies as an intellectual discipline, and to increase general awareness on issues impinging on formulation and implementation of national security strategies through the following instruments:

- Provide a independent forum to assimilate strategic issues from a wide range of specialist fields and to synthesise comprehensive solutions for a stable security environment in the South Asia – Asia Pacific, region.
- Initiate, co-ordinate and promote studies related to national security and strategy and formulation of national security strategies.
- Organise and facilitate the holding of seminars, symposia, lectures on national security policies and strategic issues concerning the region in general and India in particular.
- Assist in the development of post-graduate research and teaching on Asia Pacific strategic affairs and national security strategy related issues.
- Promote awareness and informed public debate on strategic and national security issues.
- Publish research papers (Agni and Aakrosh) put together by members and associates of the Forum and independent intellectuals.
- Provide constructive inputs for policy development to parliamentarians, ministries, public and private sector enterprises and academic institutions on strategic and national security related issues.
- Establish and award stipendiary and non-stipendiary fellowships.

# Contents

I

# Roots of Violence in Indian Punjab

*Vipul Mudgal*

*This paper presents an overview of the political and historical events leading to the spiraling of terrorism and counter-terrorism which claimed thousands of lives in over a decade. The issue of the genesis of terrorism in Punjab calls for rigorous research, particularly into the emergence of a collective ethnic consciousness in the century, and, more recently, the growth of Hindu and Sikh fundamentalism. There are many more philosophical and cultural processes—both Indian and global—which may have affected such processes. The attempt in the following paper is to build a bare framework of events leading to political violence. It begins from the final days of British colonialism, and moves on to a broad overview of Punjab's post-Independence and post-Partition turmoil, which gave rise to movements and disturbances culminating in social conflicts, terrorism and counter-terrorism in the late seventies and eighties. The paper draws on a large body of sociological and historical literature on Punjab, as well as on original papers/documents and reports concerning social/political conflict. It tackles the issues of the Sikh identity through India's independence movement, and later in the days of Jarnail Singh Bhindranwale. The paper is meant to be an exhaustive diagnosis of Punjab's conflict, and does not intend to offer solutions or judgements. The scope of the paper ends with the eighties, but the author has included a very broad sequence of events in the nineties in order to connect the historical overview with the present.*

## Introduction

The roots of the Sikh identity, as we know it today, run parallel to the 'renaissance of Hinduism' brought about by the Arya Samaj, a Hindu revivalist movement led by Punjabi Hindu nationalists. The Arya Samajis often criticized political actions of their Muslim counterparts, but some of their leaders also questioned the existence of a distinct Sikh identity. The more the Hindu revivalists claimed Sikhism to be yet another of Hinduism's many branches, the more the Sikhs insisted they had a separate identity.[1] The Government of India Census Reports of 1911 and 1921 show that out of as many as two dozen Sikh sects in Punjab in the beginning of the century, those which had varied identities moved towards a more unified and monolithic '*keshdari*' Sikh identity.[2] It was feared that the assertion of 'superiority' by the Hindus might absorb Sikhism into the wider stream of Hinduism, as happened with Jainism and partly with Buddhism in India. As a result of this fear, the expansion of the Arya Samaj gave impetus to the Singh Sabha movement, which organized the Sikhs much along the same lines.[3] Sensitive about the Hindus denying them a separate entity, the Singh Sabha was extremely suspicious about the multiplicity of the Sikh identity.[4] What was happening in Sikhism in the early century was not unique: it was something that many religions witnessed all over the world. A move towards an organized religion was replacing the older pluralist

[1] Singh, Khushwant, 1966. *A History of the Sikhs, Volume 2 : 1939–1974*, pp. 146-7, Delhi: Oxford University Press.

[2] Kapur, Rajiv A, 1987. *Sikh Separatism: The Politics of Faith*, pp. 31–2, New Delhi: Vikas.

[3] Malik, Harji, 1985. 'A Historical Legacy', in Amrik Singh (ed.) *Punjab in Indian Politics: Issues and Trends*, p. 2, Delhi: Ajanta Publications.

[4] Oberoi, Harjot, 1994. *The Construction of Religious Boundaries: Culture, Identity and Diversity in the Sikh Tradition*, p. 25, Delhi: Oxford University Press. Oberoi views the Singh Sabha as a new cultural elite 'which aggressively usurped the right to represent others within this singular tradition. Its ethnocentric logic subsumed other identities and dissolved alternative ideas… such as ascerticism under a monolithic, codified and closed culture'.

paradigm by a more uniform identity. The Sikh Gurudwara Act, 1925, passed by the British rulers after a long agitation, defined a Sikh as 'one who believes in the ten gurus and the *Granth Sahib* (the holy scriptures) and is not a 'patit' (apostate)'[5] The definition under the Act did not include most sects listed as Sikhs in the census reports in the early part of the century.[6]

A separate religious identity and consciousness was reinforced by the guiding principles of British colonialism in India: to create and intensify the wedge between different caste, class and community groups spread all over the country (substantial academic research is available on the subject). The colonial rulers were then natural benefactors of the emergence and consolidation of various religious identities all over India, including Punjab. They did their best to keep Hindus, Muslims and the Sikhs divided by administrative and legal means. The British administration passed the Land Alienation Act, specially in Punjab, whose declared aim was to prevent the money lender from exploiting the cultivator. In practice, the Act heightened communal tensions in the erstwhile Indian Punjab.[7] It

[5] Cole and Sambhi, 1978. *The Sikhs: Their Religious Beliefs and Practices,* p. 160 , New Delhi: Vikas.

[6] The definition helped the Singh Sabha gain its objective of evolving one unified Sikh identity as only of those who believed in the Guru Granth Sahib as their scripture and eternal guru, the gurudwara their place of worship and observed the five K's of Sikhism, each beginning with the letter *K* in Punjabi (uncut hair, comb, sword, steel bracelet and undershorts). Many sects follow Sikh tenets to varying degrees and often in combination with other beliefs. Some of the most common sects are: *Hazuris, Nanakpanthis, Udasis,* specified and unspecified *Sahajdharis* and *Radha Soamis*. A more comprehensive list of sects cited in the 1911 and 1921 census reports is given by Rajiv A. Kapur (1987), and Harjot Oberoi (1994) has discussed the multiplicity of the Sikh faith.

[7] Satya, M. Rai, 1965. *Partition of Punjab: A Study of Its Effects on the Politics and Administration of the Punjab (I) 1947–56,* p. 27. London: Asia Publishing House. According to Rai, many other apparently progressive measures were passed in such a way that the mainly Muslim and Sikh cultivators were at loggerheads with predominantly Hindu moneylenders. The author includes among these measures the following Acts: The Punjab Limitation Act, 1904; The Transfer of Property Act, 1904 and; the Punjab Pre-Emption Act, 1905. The main effect of the laws was that the 'peasants now could not be evicted by a civil court without the intervention of the revenue authorities' (p. 28).

was felt by the predominantly Hindu moneylenders that it had been enacted to favour the Muslim and Sikh cultivators. The introduction of a communal electorate in Punjab further complicated the problem.[8] The Cripps Mission of 1942 widened this divide and gave impetus to the demand for Pakistan, a course which later affected the Sikh leadership in its own way.[9]

As a reaction to the possibility of the Muslims getting Pakistan in the forties, the Akali Dal issued a pamphlet proposing a Sikh-ruled 'Azad Punjab' (free Punjab).[10] In 1944, when the Congress leader Rajgopalachari published his controversial formula which suggested, among other things, that areas of Muslim dominance be demarcated, Akali leader Master Tara Singh stated for the first time that the Sikhs were a separate nation. Many scholars thought that this demand was more of a reaction to the demand for Pakistan. In July 1946, about a year before Independence, Jawaharlal Nehru, who later became the first prime minister of free India in 1947, promised to set up an area in the north wherein the Sikh could experience the 'glow of freedom'.[11]

Punjab's worst time of the century came when it had to be partitioned between India and Pakistan in 1947. The aftermath of freedom and the process of partition saw unparalleled violence and massacres of all three communities: Hindu, Muslims and Sikhs. The violence was unprecedented in history. Khushwant Singh (1961) has quoted Moon (1961) as having given the 'some-what inflated' figure of 200,000 Hindus, Muslims and Sikhs killed on both the Indian and Pakistani sides.

[8] Kumar, P., M. Sharma, A. Sood and A. Handa, 1984. *Punjab Crisis: Contexts and Trends.* Chandigarh: Centre for Research in Rural and Industrial Development (CRRID). The authors maintain that 'Constitutional developments such as the Morley–Minto reforms of 1909, The Montague–Chelmsford Reforms of 1919 and the Act of 1935, incorporating principles of separate electorate and communal reservations, perpetuated and intensified (in as much as they necessitated competition for limited elected seats) the communal problem' (p. 33).

[9] Kapur, *op. cit.,* n. 2 above, p. 205.

[10] Ibid., p. 206.

[11] Malik, *op. cit.,* n .3 above.

Subsequently, in 1950, when the Constitution of India was finalized, the Akali leadership did not find Nehru's promise reflected in it. The draft so provoked the two Sikh members of the Constituent Assembly, Hukum Singh and Bhupinder Singh Mann, that they refused to endorse the Constitution, pleading that it was against the minorities' interests.

## THE SIKHS AND THE INDIAN CONSTITUTION

The overall framework of the Indian Constitution (1950) was democratic and secular. A quasi-federal structure with a union government at the center and several state governments in the provinces offered an opportunity of limited self-rule to the states, with their own elections, cabinets and governments. A secular foundation to the nation's political system also kept religious and sectarian politics at bay, at least in the formative years. The first government of independent India abolished communal electorates and other legal provisions which were seen by the nation's leadership as British tools for dividing the people. In the first decade, political parties like the Akali Dal, Muslim League and the Hindu Jana Sangh backed by its militant front organisation, the RSS, had little success in the elections. In the 1952 general elections, the Congress party got an overall majority on a secular, social democratic programme. It returned to power in the next two successive elections in 1957 and 1962. (Interestingly, the Akalis did not fight the 1957 election as a political party, as it had got merged in the Congress in 1956. The merger lasted for a very short while.) A large section of the Sikh community supported the Congress, even though it was not completely satisfied with its political programme. Its grievances resurfaced over a decade later during the '*Punjabi Suba*' movement led by Master Tara Singh and Sant Fateh Singh. They demanded a new state out of the unified Punjab, with Punjabi as its official language.

The movement succeeded in rallying a cross-section of Sikhs behind it, and among the campaign's sympathizers was a section of

Congress leaders in New Delhi. After Mrs Gandhi became the prime minister of India in 1966, she proposed the division of Punjab. All major political parties of the opposition, except the Hindu Jana Sangh, supported her proposal. In 1966, what was left of Indian Punjab after partition was further divided into Punjab, Haryana and Himachal Pradesh. The *Punjabi Suba* was a major victory for its leadership which fought the Congress party in the subsequent elections in 1967 and 1969 with the help of other opposition parties.

In the first general election after the state's division, a highly unlikely coalition consisting of the Akalis, the Jana Sangh and the Communist Party of India defeated the Congress. The coalition government could not complete its tenure mainly due to the Akali s' internal bickering, its own contradictions and en masse defections from the Akali Dal to the Congress. In the next two general elections in 1969 and 1970, Akali-led coalitions came to power twice, but each government lasted for a little over a year, instead of the full term of five years. Throughout these years, the Akalis were using gurudwara (Sikh temple) politics and the office of the Shiromani Gurudwara Prabandhak Committee (SGPC) for political and electoral gain s.[12] Although politically the Akali party was closer to the Congress than to its two coalition partners (the Jana Sangh which opposed the Punjabi Suba movement and the communists who were against religious parties), it declared the Congress to be its main enemy.[13]

[12] The SGPC (Shiromani Gurudwara Prabandhak Committee) is a statutory elected body which is more like a religious parliament for the Sikh community. It was established under the British-promulgated Sikh Gurudwara Act, 1925, for the purpose of running gurudwaras.

[13] The Akalis had supported the Congress in the national movement, barring some reservations, and the party got merged with the Indian National Congress twice, in 1948 and 1956. Detailed accounts of the Akali Dal's relationship with the Congress party have been given by P.S. Verma (1985), 'The Akali Dal: History, Electoral Performance and Leadership Profile', in Gopal Singh (1985), Kumar et al. (1984), and Khushwant Singh (1966).

The Akalis were upset with the Congress for various reasons. The Sikh leadership felt betrayed when the Congress government in New Delhi, instead of helping out, chose to impose Presidents' Rule each time its coalition government was in crisis. (The same mistrust would be deepened after the anti-Sikh riots of 1984, in the aftermath of Mrs Indira Gandhi's assassination by her Sikh bodyguards.) Another bone of contention was an Akali political programme called the 'Anandpur Sahib Resolution'. The Congress party, as also many other opposition parties including the Hindu Bharatiya Janata party (a new incarnation of the old Jana Sangh), opposed the programme as anti-national. Passed in 1978 by the general house of the Akali Dal in Ludhiana, the resolution has been interpreted in many different forms. Mrs Indira Gandhi saw seeds of separatism in the Akalis' demand for more autonomy for Punjab, within a federal polity, even though the Communists and many more regional parties were raising the same demand.

## THE RISE OF BHINDRANWALE

A Congress chief minister, Giani Zail Singh, who came to power in 1972, abandoned the party's secular programme to a large extent and used sectarian politics to fight Hindu and Sikh communalists. During his tenure as chief minister of Punjab, Giani Zail Singh followed the policy of appeasement of extremists, with New Delhi's blessings. In his fight against the Akalis, he openly used the Sikh fanatics, who were beginning to gain ground in the seventies.[14] A good number of observers believe that the Congress party was responsible for the emergence of Sikh fundamentalists in Punjab (Patwant Singh and Harji Malik, 1985; Mark Tully and Satish Jacob, 1985; Kumar et al., 1984). Tully and Jacob have noted that Mrs. Gandhi's younger son, Sanjay Gandhi, who had become an extra-constitutional authority in the party, hand-picked Jarnail Singh Bhindranwale, a priest of the landowning class (*jat*) on the

[14] Kumar et al., *op cit.*, n. 8 above, p. 71.

*giani's* advice. Bhindranwale, who was known for his fundamentalist views, was encouraged to stand up to the Akalis with the help of an extremist platform, the Dal Khalsa, Bhindranwale piqued the Akalis with his demand for 'Khalistan' on one hand, and on the other actively campaigned for Congress candidates in 1980, a charge Mrs Gandhi partly admitted in an interview given to the BBC's Panorama programme.[15]

In 1977, when Mrs Gandhi returned to power after her post-Emergency debacle, her loyal supporter Giani Zail Singh was made the federal home minister. By then, Bhindranwale's extreme views and his abhorrence for the Akali leadership had become common knowledge. It is debatable whether Bhindranwale was still being used by his earlier mentor, Zail Singh, or he was acting on his own, but one of his avowed aims was to counter the Akalis politically. In his religious congregations held inside the Golden Temple, he often ridiculed and challenged the Akali Dal president, Harchand Singh Longowal, a leader of considerable stature and repute. In August 1982, Longowal started a peasants' movement,' *Dharmyudh Morcha* (crusade), in order to strengthen his party. Thousands of the campaign's supporters courted arrest during the agitation. Their demands included both political ones, such as a fair share of river water for the farmers, and religious ones, like holy city status to Amritsar and the broadcast of Sikh religious hymns on All India Radio. New Delhi had several rounds of talks with the Akali leadership, but no compromise formula emerged on their charter of 15 demands. This gave Bhindranwale and his supporters more opportunity to ridicule the Akalis.

Bhindranwale shared a part of the more moderate Akali leader Longowal's methods and his political constituency. Longowal championed farmers' rights; Bhindranwale talked about injustice to the rural Sikhs; Longowal wanted Amritsar to be a holy city and

[15] Tully, Mark and Jacob, 1985. *Amritsar: Mrs. Gandhi's Last Battle,* pp. 60–2, London: Jonathan Cape.

'*gurbani*' broadcast on radio; propagation of Sikhism was one of Bhindranwale's cardinal missions. Both operated from the Golden Temple and launched their actions and movements from there, and inside the Golden Temple, both leaders had the support of armed followers who often challenged each other for battles of supremacy. However, Longowal's long-drawn-out 'crusade' was slipping out of his grip in the early eighties around the same time when Bhindranwale's influence was increasing. For the orthodox, Bhindranwale was emerging like a symbol of Sikh revivalism. In his congregations inside gurudwaras, he often challenged skeptics and heretics among the Sikhs, and sects like the Nirankaris which still followed a living guru instead of the holy scriptures.[16] He had also started a campaign against those in the faith who trimmed their beards or consumed tobacco or alcohol,. Banned by the Sikh gurus. Bhindranwale was the national headlines in April 1978 when he led a procession of his angry supporters, right after a fiery speech, to a Nirankari convention a few miles from the Golden Temple.[17] This resulted in a clash between the Nirankaris and the Khalsas in which 12 of Bhindranwale's supporters and a Nirankari were killed. A Nirankari agitation followed, which became a major crisis for the ruling Akali Party in Punjab.

For the next two years, Bhindranwale used this incident as a reminder to his followers that the true Sikhs were being persecuted. When the Nirankaris put on trial were acquitted as they were found to have acted in self-defence, Bhindranwale swore vengeance. About two years after this clash, his supporters in Delhi gunned down the Nirankaris' supreme leader, their guru, Baba Gurbachan Singh.

[16] Juergensmeyer, M. 1988, 'The Logic of Religious Violence', in Rapoport (ed). *Inside Terrorist Organisations*, pp. 174–5. New York: Columbia University Press.

[17] According to Tully and Jacob, Bhindranwale himself shouted in front of a gathering of his supporters: 'We will not allow this Nirankari convention to take place. We are going to march there and cut them to pieces' (p. 59). Juergensmeyer (1988) says, '... for some reason he [Bhindranwale] seemed to have been fixated on the Nirankaris: his fiery sermons condemned them as evil' (pp. 174–5).

Fearing action, Bhindranwale shifted to one of the rooms inside the Golden Temple.[18] It was curious that Home Minister Zail Singh told the Indian Parliament that the *sant* had nothing to do with the murder, while Bhindranwale declared that the killers deserved to be honoured, and he would weigh them in gold if they came to him.[19] Later, Bhindranwale was accused of bringing out a 'hit list' of his enemies, who were proclaimed as enemies of the Sikh religion. Apart from dissenting politicians and critical journalists, the 'hit list' carried names of several Sikh bureaucrats and intellectuals, or virtually anyone who stood up to Bhindranwale.

Among the first few target killings by Bhindranwale's supporters were two prominent journalists. In 1981, chief editor of the Hindi paper *Punjab Kesari*, and proprietor of the Hind Samachar group of Publications, Lala Jagat Narain, were killed. 'Lalaji', as the editor was known, was one of the most committed opponents of Bhindranwale. About a year later, armed men struck again, killing his son, Ramesh Chandra, who had taken over as chief editor and had continued his father's aggressively pro-Hindu editorial policy. It was fairly well known that the names of both these journalists as well as that of the Nirankari Guru had figured on Bhindranwale's hit list. After several cold-blooded murders in the next two years, of priests, prominent people in gurudwara politics and high-ranking police officers, the pattern of violence slowly began to adopt a more indiscriminate nature.

It was indeed intriguing that Bhindranwale was never tried for fomenting violence. He was once arrested from a gurudwara near Amritsar on his own conditions, which included a chosen time and place and permission to address a congregation before he gave himself up to the police. His supporters got violent when he was being taken and attacked the police. In the ensuing clash, 11 people were killed. Bhindranwale was let off without charges in a few

[18] Tully and Jacob, *op. cit* n. 15, above p. 65.

[19] Ibid., p. 66.

weeks.[20] Several academics and journalists believe that the preacher was released from custody on the then Prime Minister Mrs Indira Gandhi's orders.[21]

The aftermath of Bhindranwale's arrest witnessed a convulsive spurt of violence. Within days of his arrest, Sikh gunmen killed four people and injured about 12 in an incident of indiscriminate firing on Hindus in Jalandhar. In a similar incident in Amritsar district the next day, one Hindu was killed and 13 injured. Apart from sporadic shoot-outs and incidents of sabotage like derailment of trains, an Indian Airlines plane was hijacked to Lahore in Pakistan. In another daring incident in Patiala, a bomb explosion took place inside the office of the deputy inspector general of police who was sent to arrest Bhindranwale. The officer escaped unhurt, but the blast exhibited Bhindranwale's penetration of the police force. In the next few months, Bhindranwale's supporters made headlines either for their utterances, or actions varying from bomb blasts to bank robberies. In January 1983, bombs were thrown at two Congress leaders' houses, one of them a minister, and a few weeks later a Sikh DIG of police was killed while coming out of the Golden Temple after offering prayers.

One of the early massacres took place in October 1983, when armed men struck on a bus in Dhilwan village near Jalandhar. They singled out six passengers and shot them because they were Hindus. This pattern of killing Hindus was to later become the most notable method of violence in Punjab with the advent of several new organisations. Apart from the Khalistan Liberation Force (KLF), Khalistan Commando Force (KCF), Babbar Khalsa, Dashmesh Regiment, and All India Sikh Students' Federation(AISSF), at least two dozen other pro-Khalistan organisations were floated in the mid- and late-eighties. The Panthic Committee, a coordinating

[20] Ibid., p. 69.

[21] Singh, Devinder, 1993, *Akali Politics in Punjab (1964–1985), p. 183,* New Delhi, National Book Organisations, Tully and Jacob, p. 71.

body of these organisations, was later formed which itself got divided into several factions towards the end of the eighties. The violence perpetrated by these groups could be easily divided into two distinct phases. The first phase was contiguous with the rise of Bhindranwale. It began in the late seventies and continued till June 1984, when the Indian Army conducted an armed operation at the Golden Temple. Bhindranwale was among hundreds who were killed during the operation. The second phase began in the aftermath of the operation and continued with its ups and downs till the end of the eighties. The violence subsided in the nineties, particularly after 1992, though sporadic incidents still continue.

The first phase of terrorism in Punjab was marked by Bhindranwale's undisputed command over almost all armed organisations.[22] A large number of killings in this phase were of the 'targets' whose names would appear on the notorious 'hit list'. Bhindranwale was the fountainhead of power and the biggest living source of inspiration for those committing violence. In his many speeches at the Golden Temple and other gurudwaras, he quoted examples of martyrs from Sikh history and mythology to inspire his followers to take to arms. Bhindranwale's religious discourses offered his followers logic for using violence as a matter of right in their struggle against what was seen by him as injustice. Juergensmeyer (1988), who has analysed Bhindranwale's speeches made at his famous congregations, argues that all such violent actions which had religion's moral sanction were essentially political actions. According to him, 'By putting the right to kill in their own hands, the perpetrators of religious violence are also making a daring claim of political independence.'[23]

[22] The only exception was the Babbar Khalsa, which opposed Bhindranwale in the pre-Bluestar days and the relatively small Akhand Kirtani Jatha, which did not obey Bhindranwale. Babbars supported Bhindranwale's cause after his death, while the Kirtani Jatha got completely marginalized in post-Bluestar politics.

[23] Juergensmeyer, *op. cit.*, n.16 above, p.183.

## OPERATION BLUESTAR

In December 1983, when pressure was mounting on the central government to arrest Bhindranwale, he and a large number of his armed supporters moved to the Akal Takht—one of the most sacred buildings inside the Golden Temple complex.[24] After the entourage had shifted to what was considered then a safe haven, a spate of 'punishments' inside the complex and other 'actions' all over Punjab started to take place. Several people who apparently disagreed with Bhindranwale and his supporters were severely tortured and their bodies thrown into the drain.[25] Such was the state of lawlessness all over Punjab, that between 1 October 1983 and 31 May 1984, as many as 24 banks were robbed. Millions of rupees were looted in thee incidents and several officials and guards killed. In the month of April, 39 railway stations, mostly unmanned ones, were burned down in a three-day campaign by the movement's supporters.[26] Several politicians and many Sikh priests were among those killed. Hardly any day passed during this time without a few killings being reported. While these incidents carried on all over Punjab, those inside the Golden Temple fortified the turrets and walls of the sprawling complex and placed sandbags at strategic points. Arms and ammunition were brought to the temple in *kar sewa* (voluntary service) trucks. The militants also hired private houses around the temple and forcibly occupied some in order to consolidate their

[24] The Akal Takht is the seat of Sikh spiritual and temporal authority and is situated in a gold-domed white building in front of the main door leading to the Darbar Sahib, the sanctum sanctorum.

[25] Government of India, 1984. White Paper on Punjab Agitation, p. 29. 10 July, New Delhi. The paper was tabled in Parliament after Operation Bluestar. Several academics, journalists and politicians have criticized the White Paper as inadequate. The main complaint is that it does not answer many questions about Operation Bluestar and the build-up towards it. Its legality and inadequacites have been discussed in detail by A.G. Noorani in Patwant Singh and Harji Malik, 1985, *Punjab: The Fatal Miscalculation*, pp. 145–61, New Delhi.

[26] Ibid., p. 31.

position.[27] The Government's White Paper claims that the 'terrorists in the rural areas were instructed that in the event of any government action, they should go ahead on their own to kill Hindus and Central Government employees and to move in large numbers to the temple'.[28]

The temple was fortified with the help of expert former army personnel (under the leadership of a former major general, Shubheg Singh), who also imparted weapons training to armed Bhindranwale supporters. The White Paper notes: 'Battle plans had been drawn up with ingenuity, maximizing the advantages provided by the basements, underground passages, niches, winding staircases, lockouts and towers in the temple complex.'[29] The biggest advantage of those inside the temple was that they had the sanctuary of the precincts, considered inviolable till then. The operation started in the early hours of 4 June 1984. According to Subhash Kirpekar, one of the very few journalists who witnessed the whole operation from a building close by, light and medium machine guns, grenades and a variety of other guns were used by both sides. The militants also used rocket launchers, anti-personnel mines, and according to the government's claim, some anti-tank missiles and other heavy weapons were also recovered form their possession. The Army troops used tanks, helicopters and several types of artillery shells in the operation which lasted for over two and a half days.

Many journalists and academics believe that the official death toll during the operation was underplayed. Khushwant Singh has come to a final figure of 379 dead and 2,000 wounded. Singh has quoted the 'Akalis' figure' as well over a thousand. Subhash Kirpekar puts the toll at 2,000, quoting unconfirmed reports and rumours in Amritsar. The operation caused an enormous degree of hurt in the minds of all Sikhs, whether in the Congress party, the defence

[27] Ibid., pp. 30–47.
[28] Ibid., p. 33.
[29] Ibid., p. 47.

services or in the opposition. Some scholars believe that the operation and the November riots in Delhi and elsewhere united the Sikhs, as their different identities like *jat, bhapa, mazhabi, khatri,* tended to merge into one single Sikh identity.[30]

## MRS GANDHI'S ASSASSINATION AND THE CARNAGE OF SIKHS

The immediate aftermath of the operation saw great discontentment among Sikhs in the Indian Army spread in different cantonments all over the country. Over 1,400 army men revolted at the Ramgarh Sikh Regimental Centre and deserted barracks with their service rifles and ammunition. There were protests by Sikhs all over the world, and some Khalistan supporters abroad threatened revenge. The Indian High Commission in London protested to the British Foreign Office against an interview given by a Khalistan leader in the UK, Jagjit Singh Chauhan, in which he reportedly said that Mrs Gandhi and her family members would be beheaded by the Sikhs.[31] New Delhi took up this opportunity to reassert its claim that a 'foreign hand' was conspiring to divide India.

In Punjab's recent political history, 1984 was like a watershed. The sequence of events after Operation Bluestar changed the entire face of Punjab's—and perhaps India's—politics for a long time. Within less than five months of the operation, two Sikh bodyguards shot Prime Minister Mrs Indira Gandhi on 31 October 1984. Within hours of the assassination, mobs went berserk, burning and

[30] Gupta, Dipankar, 1985, 'The Communalism of Punjab, 1980–85', in Patwant Singh and Harji Malik, p. 211. This was also reflected in the fact that the *majhabi* Sikhs, whose leadership called Bhindranwale's movement a campaign by the upper caste *jats*, later joined many underground organisations in the aftermath of the operation and that the two assassins of Mrs Gandhi belonged to this caste. Devinder Pal Sandhu (1992) maintains that Operation Bluestar, Operation Woodrose and the anti-Sikh riots of 1984 together 'had a direct bearing and an everlasting impact on a separate and distinct identity of Sikhs as a minority as well as on their psyche, thereby further strengthening the already existing "sense of persecution" among a section of the community' (p.124).

[31] *The Times of India*, 14 June 1984.

rampaging shops and businesses owned by Sikhs. In the following two days, a large number of Sikh men, women and children were killed on roads, inside trains and buses and even in their own houses and gurudwaras. The violence also spread to other towns and cities in India. The incidents were referred to as the 'Delhi riots' or the 'November riots' by the media, but the reports brought out by India's human rights organisations and citizens' fora labelled them as a 'carnage' or 'massacre' of the Sikhs.[32] They had a point because at most places Sikhs were picked up and killed without any signs of a sectarian conflict.

Charges of official complicity, in at least ignoring violence and not deploying the army soon enough and with strict orders, gained currency after human rights organisations held some Congress-I leaders responsible for inciting the rioters. The death toll estimates by various non-official agencies is put at between 4,000 and 5,000 in Delhi and the nearby areas. The atrocities included abduction and rape of women, most of which could not be documented in a proper manner because of taboos among the victims and the fear of ostracism by their own community.[33] Several commissions were appointed by the government in the subsequent years, and one of them even implicated, though not charge-sheeted, several ruling party members. The process of bringing the 'culprits' to book is still on after more than 10 years of the carnage. Meanwhile, underground Sikh organisations shot down many of those thought to be behind the carnage and also killed ordinary people in residential colonies and public places. In one single day, over 100 residents of Delhi slums

[32] The Citizens' Commission, headed by a former chief justice of India, S.M. Sikri, has specifically noted that 'it was not a communal riot'. The report brought out by the Peoples' Union for Democratic Rights (PUDR) and the Peoples' Union of Civil Liberties (PUCL) entitled 'Who are the Guilty', has called the violence an act of 'organised massacre'.

[33] Madhu Kishwar, a voluntary organisation activist and editor of a New Delhi-based feminist magazine, has compiled many such cases and their circumstances in her articles. She has discussed the reasons for which several such cases could not be documented in 'Gangster Rule' in Patwant Singh and Malik Harji (eds.), pp. 177-9.

and hutments were killed by planting bombs concealed in transistors. Incidents of terrorism continued in Delhi and Punjab throughout the eighties in a big way, and to a lesser extent in the early nineties.

### THE RAJIV-LONGOWAL ACCORD

The first signs of a settlement emerged in July 1985 when the Central government headed by Mrs Gandhi's son Rajiv, who was appointed prime minister after his mother's assassination in 1984, but who won the subsequent election with a convincing margin, negotiated with Akali Dal President Longowal. Subsequently, an accord was signed by Mr Longowal and Mr Gandhi on 24 July 1985, which was followed by an election which the Akalis swept. The main provisions of the accord included the transfer of Chandigarh to Punjab, an inquiry into the November incidents, compensation to the innocent persons killed, and the withdrawal of the Armed Forces Special Powers Act.[34] The Government of India also agreed to enact an All-India Gurudwara Act. Among other important aspects of the accord was the understanding that the claims of Punjab and Haryana regarding the sharing of river waters would be referred for adjudication to a tribunal to be presided over by a Supreme Court judge. It was agreed that the decision of the tribunal would be binding on both sides. The transfer of Chandigarh was to take place on India's Republic Day, 26 January, the following year, simultaneously with the transfer of certain areas in lieu to Haryana, Punjab's adjoining province. Many other demands were not conceded immediately, but the government agreed to consider them.

The Longowal Accord was welcomed by Sikhs in Punjab and all over the country and this was reflected in his party's landslide victory after the accord. He followed a two-pronged strategy after the accord. First he got his detractors in the party to unanimously endorse the agreement. Subsequently, he started a mass contact

[34] Government of India Document 1: Text of the Pun jab Accord, Reproduced in Gopal Singh (ed.), 1987, *Punjab Today*, pp. 383–6, New Delhi: Intellectual Publishing House.

programme all over Punjab, particularly in the countryside, to win acceptability for his agreement. However, Longowal himself did not live to see that unprecedented victory in the elections which he had converted into some kind of a referendum on the accord. He was shot by armed extremists in less than a month after the accord was signed. His party was led to elections by his deputy, Surjit Singh Barnala, who became the Akali chief minister of Punjab. However, Chandigarh was not transferred to Punjab on the appointed day, which suggested that the government's view on the accord had changed after Longowal's assassination. The new-found shift in the government's attitude became handy to justify terrorist violence. It gave a nice opportunity for the dissidents in the Akali party to start a campaign against the chief minister.

## The Second Phase of Violence

Barnala's truncated tenure as chief minister witnessed an unprecedented upsurge in terrorist violence. Hundreds were killed in less than two years. This was just the beginning of the second phase of violence, characterized by a clear lack of leadership. In this phase, the number of terrorist organisations was multiplying and the pattern of violence was fast becoming more indisc riminate and unpredictable. In 1981 and 1982, civilian killings were 13 each year, while only two police officials had been shot. In 1983, the figure of civilian killings went up to 75 and that of police officials to 20. The figures generated concern all over the country. But the indiscriminate phase of violence which began from 1985 onwards witnessed a completely disproportionate escalation of violence. The number of civilian killings in 1986 and 1987 were 520 and 910 respectively. IN 1988, it came close to 2,000, and in the next two years the figure touched 2,500.[35] This means that more than 200 civilians were being killed every month, or around seven every day.

[35] The statistics were provided by K. P. S. Gill, DGP, Punjab, to the author in October 1993.

The five-member Panthic Committee, before it got splintered into several groups, announced the formation of Khalistan on 26 January 1986. The announcement was made at a dramatic meeting which took place in front of the Akal Takht and was given the historically sanctimonious epithet of '*Sarbat Khalsa*'[36] According to the declaration made on the occasion, the five members were also 'nominated' by the congregation, which then announced the formation of Khalistan.[37] A demand was made in the declaration to the UNO and its member states to recognize Khalistan. [38] The KCF, one of the several insurgent organisations, was declared as 'the nucleus of the future defence organisation of Khalistan ', under its 'commander-in-chief'.[39] The declaration directed Hindus not to put 'hurdles in the way of [the] Khalsa Panth' and announced that 'no particular community or sect will be allowed to impose [its] selfish will arbitrarily upon others through the medium of press, writings, education or other media of publicity.[40]

The government condemned the declaration and pointed out that it eulogized terrorists and that it also expressed gratitude to neighbouring countries which were sympathetic to the activities of the terrorists. It fitted in with the Indian Government's overall threat perception that certain external forces were out to destabilize India. Several Sikh organisations, many of them underground, did not approve of the declaration because they were not consulted, and, moreover, it declared the supremacy of the KCF over other insurgent

[36] *Sarbat Khalsa* is a name for the Sikh *sangat* or congregation, which is treated as a general body meeting of the sect inside the Golden Temple, and important announcements about political and social life are made in it. Oberoi (1994) maintains that one of the earlier gurus had exalted the status of the congregation by pronouncing that God resided in the *sangat*.

[37] Document of the Declaration of Khalistan (reproduced from Punjabi magazine *Sant Sipahi* and translated in English by Manjit Ahluwalia, Nazar Singh Brar and Gopal Singh et al.), further reproduced in Gopal Singh, 1987, p. 387.

[38] Ibid., p. 388.

[39] Ibid., p. 391.

[40] Ibid., p. 390.

organisations. These differences were not made public, but they were soon reflected in the way the Panthic Committee itself got divided into several camps. Many underground organisations stepped up violence in order to prove their worth in the struggle. Chief Minister Barnala was forced to send his police inside the Golden Temple, and the declaration prompted the government to intensify the counter-terrorism offensive.

Underground organisations were so strong in Punjab during this phase that they were able to frame their own laws. During 1986-87, they brought out a list of 13 do's and don'ts as a part of their 'social reform movement' aimed at 'reforming' the Sikh masses. This included boycott of tobacco, liquor, meat and barber shops. Hundreds of barber shops were burned down or forcibly closed during the campaign. A dress code was announced for Sikh men, women and school-going children. The campaign called for killing those members of the sect who visited Radha Soami *deras* (camps).[41] The dictat also 'prohibited' giving or accepting dowry and ostentatious displays during weddings. Many newspapers printed news to this effect and held editorial discussions on the movement's 'merits' and 'demerits', thereby keeping the issue in the news agenda. Many other Punjabi dailies, including *Aj Di Awaz*, regularly carried such news items attributed to press releases received by post.[42]

## COUNTER-TERRORISM: THE OFFICIAL VIOLENCE

Soon after the army's operation at the Golden Temple, the security forces launched Operation Woodrose, a concerted counter-terrorism campaign, in July and August 1994. The operation was conducted all over Punjab by the army, police and paramilitary forces (including the BSF, CRPF and ITBP) covering practically every important village and gurudwara. A Delhi-based human rights organisation, Citizens for Democracy, has noted in its 'Report to the Nation ' that

[41] Dang, Satyapal, 1988, *Genesis of Terrorism*, p. 26, New Delhi: Patriot Publishers.
[42] *Aj Di Awaz*, 29 May 1991 (quoted in the Press Council of India Report, p. 198).

the civil administration was replaced by virtual army rule during Operation Woodrose.[43] The report has cited a case in which a junior commissioned officer of the army disobeyed a chief judicial magistrate's order inside a court and threatened to shoot him.[44] The report has also presented copies of affidavits submitted by people illegally arrested and tortured by the security forces.

Complaints o f excesses and torture of ordinary people by the police and the use of undercover and vigilante organisations continued in the subsequent years, though the situation improved after the Akali government led by Barnala came to power. There is little evidence to suggest that the people of the minority communities ever formed vigilante organisation in Punjab. However, a large number of such organisations were operating in Punjab in mid-eighties. It was being alleged that the police were using unauthorized spotters and undercover agents to fight insurgents, passing them off as vigilantes.

Towards the end of eighties, the Punjab police were being helped in their anti-terrorism operations by several undercover organisations which operated in an extremely low-key fashion and never issued an y press releases. When press reports about them appeared in the regional and national press, the police top brass either denied their existence completely, or called them vigilante organisations which were operating without their permission or concurrence.[45] Two of the most notorious leaders of such vigilante organisations were Dalbir Singh and Santokh Singh Kala, both former employees of the state's police.

The police never officially conceded that they had backed or armed them until Dalbir Singh went astray and killed two senior police officers.[46] The operation was completely exposed when Chaman Lal, an inspector general of police commanding operations

[43] The CFD Report to the Nation , p. 33.

[44] Ibid., p. 34.

[45] Mudgal, Vipul, 1988, *India Today*, 15 September, pp 74–7.

[46] Ibid.

in the border areas, fell out with the top brass and publicly criticised such unlawful activities. The officer's disclosures corroborated human rights organisations' allegations that the police were using questionable methods in their fight against terrorism. Two of Punjab's best-known police officers, Julio Ribeiro and K.P.S. Gill, have justified these methods and from a police point of view, and both have found the role of the judiciary not up to the mark.

The security forces argued that they were being made to use ruthless methods because the judiciary was u n able to perform normally. Between 1981 and 1986, the terrorists managed to kill as many as 69 police officials who were put on the 'hit list', but the government could not succeed in getting a single conviction for the policemen's murders.[47] Those arrested by the police were easily granted bail by the intimidated local courts. The insurgents killed several judicial officials, including judges, in various parts of Punjab for failing to grant bail to their comrades.

In the meantime, Rajiv Gandhi's Congress party government was following the policy of tougher actions. He appointed Sidharth Shankar Ray, who is often accused of illegally liquidating Naxal ties in the sixties, as governor, and J.F. Ribeiro, a tough officer from Bombay, as the police chief of Punjab. Ribeiro and his deputy, K.P.S. Gill, who later took his place, were following a 'bullet-for-bullet policy', ignoring allegations of fake encounters and human rights abuses. In 1989, the security forces conducted their second major operation at the Golden Temple in Amritsar, where, after a 10-day siege, several wanted men surrendered to the paramilitary forces. Ribeiro has denied ever having used the phrase 'bullet for bullet', but he has justified the substance of this alleged quote in his recent book, which incidentally bears the same title.[48]

[47] Kohli, A, 1990, *Democracy and Discontent: India's Growing Crisis of Governability*, revised edn., p. 373, Cambridge: Cambridge University Press.

[48] Ribeiro, Julio, 1998, *Bullet for Bullet*, Delhi: Viking Penguin Books India.

Punjab's police officers often complained that while the judges demanded strict procedures from the police, they were often lenient with the terrorists. Besides making police work difficult by granting bail to the most wanted men, the judges routinely questioned the methods used by the police in combating terrorism. The security forces also had a similar complaint against the press. Senior police officers expected the media to impose self-censorship on matters which gave publicity to the terrorists and publicly demand ed their cooperation in combating terrorism. The state and its security forces' logic was that since they were fighting a 'war' against terrorism, they should be above the norms of civil security.

## BEANT SINGH AND THE RETURN OF THE AKALIS

The badly splintered Akalis decided to boycott the state assembly elections scheduled for November 1991. Initially, even the Congress was against participation, but it later changed its min d. All Akali parties, except the Shiromani Akali Dal (Panthic), led by Capt. Amarinder Singh, boycotted the polls. Nobody was surprised when the Congress party swept the election s. Unlike the Akalis, Congress Chief Minister Beant Singh did not need to mix politics with religion. Nor did he ever consider it necessary to appease the hardliners. Having come to power through an election in which less than one-fifth of the electorate participated, Beant Singh was not even accountable to many political lobbies of Punjab. His DGP complimented him for giving a 'free hand' to the police, and for the first few years of his tenure, the army stayed in control of the countryside.[49]

Many analysts believe that the Indian state's victory over terrorism in Punjab would not have been a reality without 'unconventional'

[49] The most high-profile operations during this time were Operation Rakshak I and II. Many large-scale search operations were conducted during this phase, and towards the end the army even took up a public relations exercise, repairing schools and hospitals in the countryside. With the help of the army, DGP K.P.S. Gill started Operation Night Dominance, with surprise checks on suburban roads and canal junctions.

methods. Hardly any documents or other primary material is available on this. It is hardly surprising that the two DGPs, Gill and Ribeiro, who pioneered these methods and established an operational chain of command for encounters, both real and fake, have blacked out this crucial information in their recently-released books on Punjab. However, some light is thrown by the cases brought before the Supreme Court of India and the National Human Rights Commission. The court had, on the basis of some writ petitions, directed the Central Bureau of Investigation (CBI) in 1995 to investigate allegations of mass cremations of victims of police action. The court observed on the basis of the CBI report that there had been flagrant violations of human rights on a mass scale in Punjab. Some of these cases are still pending in various courts, and many police officers fear reprisals for acts which they believe they committed in the national interest, mostly between 1984 and 1994.

The police in Punjab conducted some of its most successful counter-terrorism operations during the early nineties. The list of terrorists killed in police encounters during this period included such big names as Gujrat Singh Budhsinghwala of the KLF, Gurbachan Singh Manochal of the Panthic Committee, and Sukhdev Singh Babbar of the Babbar Khalsa. One of the reasons for this success, according to DGP Gill, was an unprecedented flow of information that the police was beginning to get in the nineties from common villagers.[50] Besides, an unusually large number of underground militants surrendered to the police during the early nineties. By the mid-nineties, the terrorist operations had become fewer and more far between. The last major terrorist operation was the massacre of Hindu bus passengers between Moga and Ludhiana in 1993. One of the last major assassinations took place two years later when Chief Minister Beant Singh's car was blown up outside his office in Chandigarh, most probably by a suicide bomber.

[50] Author's interviews with DGP Gill in Chandigarh, Delhi and London.

Punjab was largely peaceful when the Akalis, most of their important factions united, and backed by the Bharatiya Janata Party, swept the next round of assembly elections in 1997 under Prakash Singh Badal. Apart from the Congress, the electorate comprehensively rejected hardliners like Simranjit Singh Mann, who had sought a virtual referendum for Khalistan. Within two years of taking power, the Akalis are once again divided into the moderate and extremist camps. Perhaps judging the mood of the common Sikhs, the extremists are no longer talking about an independent Khalistan.

II

# Terror and The Indian Subcontinent Analyses, Anomalies and Answers

*Shabnam Mallick and Rajarshi Sen*

*The Indian subcontinent provides a unique combination of trends and incidences that cumulatively make the region particularly interesting in terms of researching the root causes, development, effects and control of terrorism and related violence. As it is, any academic concentration on a topic such as terrorism is "fraught with dangers on all sides."*[1] *Among other things, it must be clear at the outset that there are problems of accurately defining the term 'terrorism' on account of the various commonsense ways it is used in everyday life; there are value judgments to consider that are associated with the various definitions of terrorism, and accordingly, are to be factored in through simultaneous construction-deconstruction of the phenomena of terrorism so as to allow a dispassionate scholarly treatment of the subject. Then again, notwithstanding the 11 September 2001 attacks on the United States, in most seats of higher learning, academic cultivation of terrorism as a discipline is conspicuous by its rarity, thus leading to restrictive deliberation and dissemination of associated knowledge. Original, dedicated, diachronic information related to terrorism is, therefore, sporadic – a reality that has impacted on the attempts in this paper.*

[1] See, Shashi B. Sahai, *South Asia : From Freedom to Terrorism*, New Delhi: Gyan Publishing House, 1998, pp. 97-98.

This paper has focused on relevant information culled from and used in various sources that originally had different intent and use. The selection of those pieces of information is, then, based only on their incidental relevance to the topic at hand. So, the pieces of information used here are not of a topically dedicated genre. This approach is thus indicative not comprehensive, and the following arguments are, consequently, hypothetical not conclusive. However, an attempt has been made to be systematic and rigorous in the treatment of the subject, and it is hoped that the efforts highlight the complexity of the context in which terrorism may be situated – a factor so essential for its proper sociological appreciation.

In this paper, the focus will be primarily on India – the largest entity in the subcontinent, and tortured by far by the most varied blend of terrorist activities. Reference to the other countries in the subcontinent will be brought in too, in order to qualify India-specific analysis. This is useful since, for obvious reasons of geographic proximity, many separate social phenomena across the subcontinent display common bearings on developments in India. Given the commonality of cultures among peoples in the subcontinent, it is hoped in this exercise that just as events in India's neighbourhood are able to referentially qualify India-specific analyses, so can the results of such analyses find relevance in counter terrorism policy prescriptions relevant to those neighbours.

## HISTORICAL BACKGROUND

During the period of independence and receding of colonial occupation following World War II, the British colonial overlords left behind a geopolitically subdivided and fractious subcontinent. In essence, the British largely undid the cohesion which they had painstakindly achieved over two centuries of colonial presence in the region. Before the arrival of the European colonial age, the Indian subcontinent existed in atomistic, feuding entities. It was the presence of the British and their effective administrative glue that unified this diverse region in order to ensure effective service to the colonialists' vital economic and trade interests.

In the wake of independence, the various bases of diversity in the subcontinent —religion, linguistics, caste, ethnicity, class, creed and so on—became manifest, particularly in the division of India, along religious lines. The final products, of course, were: a secular socialist democratic India; a theocratic Pakistan (West and East); and a politically ambivalent, secular democracy of Sri Lanka.

Striking anomalies marked the unfolding events in those geo-political creations at independence, albeit within an otherwise broad meta-structure of uniformity, in the sense that they have always shared many common cultural traits by virtue of their geographic proximity, an also the fact that they were freed fro m a common ruler. India and Pakistan had had mature nationalistic political movements in place well preceding the transition to independence. In the case of Sri Lanka, a nationally representative political party was formed only very nearly after independence, born out of the need to fill the political/administrative vacuum left by the departing overlords.[2] Moreover, Sri Lanka, as opposed to India and Pakistan, experienced virtually no independence-related violence immediately prior to, or post independence. There is a further oddity to consider; the relative pause in organized violence in the public domain in both India and Pakistan during the decade of the 1950s, and its curious resumption during the 1960s and continuance thereon (Sahai 1998, de Silva 2000).

The above facts in combination underscore the disparate causal mechanism behind the separate versions of terrorism that have emerged in countries of the Indian subcontinent, thereby arguing against a 'one size fits all' law enforcement counter terrorism policy.

## CURRENT REALITIES

India's current reality is that it experiences a culture of quasi-organised violence in daily social life. That is not to suggest that

[2] Ibid, p. 114.

Indian society is in any greater turmoil yet, for any more or less esoteric causes beyond the extent of certain causal factors unique to this region, than any other typical third world country. The portentous concern, however, is that the cultivation of a respect for the rule of law is not encouraged in India's society at large, and therefore there is a tendency to respect the law only in the exception. In other words, there is a regular acceptability in the employment of violence, even if largely at the fringes of society, although steadily burgeoning fringes to achieve socio-political ends, and often for naked economic ends too.

Such a culture engenders at least three outcomes: first, the passively tolerant attitude towards violence tends to reduce socio-legal costs of indulging in isolated violent activities; second, the employment of violence surreptitiously gains a desensitizing precedence in the body politic at large; and finally, the nascent t presence and implicit legitimacy of violent tendencies in society, on occasion, congeals into larger-scale quasi-organised public violence.

As we see, if the sparks of violence that cause terrorism are primarily due to social factors, then there must logically be corresponding sociological remedies and resolutions too. Clearly, treating terrorism merely as a law and order problem may not suffice. What is this phenomenon and what are the identities of its causal mechanisms? What are the factors that aid restorative forces in society against the culture of violence? What policy prescriptions may evolve from their identification that may supplement conventional counter terrorism measures?

## Analysis of Violence

Most of the quasi-organised or impromptu collective violence in the sub-continent is directed indiscriminately against the state, authorities, or the establishment; often without valid grounds, habitually, and even symbolically. As such, the symbolism is deemed a way of 'getting back' at the state, which is usually viewed as a 'big brother'. Such trends may be considered as rough continuation of a certain quality of heroism, currently often misdirected, which nonetheless was once associated to violence committed in protest against the state during days of the British *Raj*.[3] Now, of course, continuation of those practices provide unhealthy companionship for the civil code, and make the job of administration of law and order that much less legitimate.

To be sure, however, such explanations are not infallible. Attempts at explaining the present scale of violence in Sri Lanka, for instance, certainly runs into an anomalous inexplicability if we keep in mind the absence of any tenor of indigenous, pre-independence culture of violence in the island, that could perchance become established and mutate post-independence into terrorism.[4] Indeed, therefore, any prediction that a community's current propensity to violence may be a function of its violent antecedents must be restricted in terms of its explanatory and/or representative validities, especially considering that there could not have been ex ante knowledge of today's secessionist violence in Sri Lanka at least at the time of her independence.

More generally, however, given the (1) impoverished conditions of large sections of the teeming populace in the subcontinent, the systematically entrenched oppression of the socially disadvantaged classes – along various lines including caste, creed, linguistic, religion, ethnicity; and (2) coupled with the populist vote-bank brinkmanship by politicians and various popular leaders along those very fault lines

[3] Having said that, it must be reasonably assumed that colonialist-perpetrated violence was prevalent as fairly standard administrative practice meted out to native populations. The point, therefore, is that Sri Lankans were in no way uninformed of violence.

[4] For an excellent analysis bridging the gap between individual violent behaviour according to the frustration-aggression (FA) hypothesis and group behaviour along the relative depravation (RD) syndrome, see, Nehemia Friedland, 'Becoming a Terrorist: Social and Individual Antecedents' in Lawrence Howard (ed.), *Terrorism: Roots, Impact, Responses,* Praeger, 1992, (pp. 81-93).

or some combination thereof, only serve to accentuate the collective perceptions of relative depravation[5] among the impoverished.

In the sequence of events, an incompetent socio-political leadership is often found to stoke factors like religion or caste, which are far removed fro m the real causes of frustration of the masses – causes that usually have more pertinent economic or material origins. Such abetting accelerates the propensity of those extraneous factors to gravitate to the fore in social agendas. The scenario constructed in the above few lines represents the social characteristic of 'displacement of responsibility' and 'shifting of blame'. Even as mass hysteria seizes the unreal situation so constructed, collective self-delusion obliges that hysteria, perhaps in the futility of a subconscious recognition that the *real* causes remain intractable; the elevation, therefore, of the recourse to violence to norm.

In such a milieu of tolerable perspectives to violence and stubborn socio-political tensions, (1) cross-border instigation to terrorism (a trend that has its &&& origin in the Cold War days) and, (2) a section of marginalized, disgruntled elite who unhesitatingly lend political/ideological spin to violence, create the enabling conditions for serious terrorism and insurgent activities to become entrenched. A vacillating politico-legal establishment inexperienced in dealing with asymmetric threats such as insurgency and terrorism further facilitates their entrenchment, especially once the intensity of violence successfully crosses a certain threshold, thus compelling the government to turn to negotiations. The opportunity costs of negotiations are usually loaded in favour of the terrorists and insurgents, as they tend to confer on them quasi-legal status and create a precedence of 'successful' violence.[6]

[5] On the folly of negotiating with terrorists in the South Asian context, see, KPS Gill and Dr Ajay Sahni, The J & K Peace Process: Chasing, the Chimera view edonlineat http://www.satp.org/faultlines/Faultlines8/Article1.htm>

[6] Those two words representing the suggested change in what was originally named, 'Operation Infinite Justice' by the US government in its new war.

## CORRECT RESPONSE?

In his seminal work, (How the Weak Win Wars: A Theory of Asymmetric Conflicts, *International Security*, vol. 26, no. 1, Summer 2001, pp. 93-128), Ivan Arreguin-Toft argues persuasively with Andrew Mack and others that the gap in relative powers in a conflict between unequal parties is often inversely proportional to their respective resolve. It is this asymmetry of resolve, and, surprisingly, not power or armed might, that in an atmosphere of disproportionate stakes assumes decisive proportions. And the weaker party, usually, is the repository of infinite stakes against its perceived possibility of losing an asymmetric conflict, and hence retains greater resolve for winning such conflict, than are the cases with more powerful democracies, which typically have lesser stake and wavering resolve.

Arreguin-Toft qualifies his synoptic analysis of why big states lose small wars by advancing a strategic interaction thesis that calls for the employment of massi ve force and barbarism as the correct strategy in counter-insurgency operations on the part of governments, in order to degrade those social bases of support so vital for sub-state actors, insurgents or terrorists for waging their campaign of terror and resistance. But he recognizes that barbarism may not be an appropriate strategy when the objective of governments is not merely military defeat of the insurgents, but political control of the region in conflict, or an approximate source of it. In the Battle of Algiers in 1957, for example, the French military learned that lesson quickly, when, although it had won a military victory against Algerian insurgents by resorting to large-scale brutality, public knowledge of that barbarism quickly eroded any French claim to political legitimacy and forced her to abandon residual control – a classic case of winning the war, but losing the peace!

Correct strategic interaction thesis, therefore, involving surgical/expeditionary counter –insurgency operations, and requiring a foundation of sustained, carefully nurtured public opinion within the stronger nation for such campaign, is more apposite as an instrument of foreign or military policy. Just as it is now the unraveling case in the United States, evident in the nearly 90 percent high approval ratings reported by recent CNN-Gallup polls for President George W. Bush and his conduct, in the quest for *enduring freedom*.[7]

Also, given the situation facing the US today of having to project overwhelming force in a possible limited/surgical campaign in Afghanistan, it is gradually becoming evident that the conduct of that campaign may veer towards barbarity, especially in light of recent reports that the US, borrowing on lessons from the earlier failure of the Soviets as they faced the hurdles of terrain in Afghanistan, may consider using 'cave busters' or similar ammunition. The suspicion of possible barbarity is similarly supported by the inclination of US Secretary of State General Colin Powell to follow his own doctrine (Powell doctrine) that entails using overwhelming force in a context of defined objectives.[8]

In a situation such as India's, however, where governments have to contend with essentially home-grown constituency of insurgency, any adopted strategy may not be nearly as non-judgmental and asociological; because no matter how much foreign support terrorists inside India's borders may receive from across, it has to be realized that many critical causes of terrorism are local, as is all politics, and it is locally – that terrorism will have to be routed. Pertinent analysis, therefore, must patiently penetrate the socio-economic circumstances that trigger a violent culture of the type expounded earlier.

## FAULTY METHODS

For embarrassing reasons, analyses in India, however, are rarely patient and seldom correct. Strategy, therefore, is the casualty.

[7] The apparent restraint in US military reaction thus far to 11 September 2001 terrorist attacks by suspected al-Qaida terrorists might also be understood in light of the above inclination, requiring, first, building of sustained public support that ought to be unwavering in the face of employment of overwhelming force, if the military objectives so require.

[8] Ved Marwah, *Uncivil Wars: Pathology of Terrorism in India*, (Centre for Policy Research), New Delhi: Indus/Harper Collins, 1995, pp. 50-64.

There is a serious flaw in (the Indian) policy-planning and decision-making system. It has resulted time and again in major blunders on important national security issues. With both the generalist civil servants and politicians depending on their intuition to steer them through the complex problems, the chances of making major policy decisions on wrong premises become high, because important inputs from the experts and those who have more experience and knowledge are frequently missing. Policy makers suffer from the illusion that they are experts on every subject on earth and, therefore, have no need to consult anyone else. This prejudice against professionals and experts is so overwhelming in system that even the specialists try to imitate the generalists rather than further developing their own expertise.

The persons who advise the political leadership on policy formulations, even on vital security matters, themselves have little or no experience of the subject. One set of blind men merrily lead another set of blind men. The political leaders, at least, have no pretensions to be experts on security matters of the game of giving the advice which politicians would like to receive. These pseudo-experts strut around the corridors of power and ensure that those who know the subject and have experience in dealing with these problems are kept out of the decision-making process. The top police advisers in the (Indian) Ministry of Home Affairs, who generally advise the government on security matters are frequently theoreticians with little field experience. Most of these 'police advisers' have never handled any law and order situation in their entire career and certainly not terrorism and proxy wad situations. There are officers who have not put on a uniform in their entire police service, but are found suitable for heading a paramilitary force of 89,000 men in the last year of their service. Should we then be surprised, if these 'paper tigers' fail to provide inspiring leadership to the force?[9]

[9] For an excellent analysis of the underlying issues, see, for instance, F. Tomasson Jannuzi, *India In Transition: Issues of Political Economy in a Plural Society*, Boulder: Westview Press, 1989.

Even when expert help is sought, it is usually from a broad, and due care is not taken to ensure that, prior to application, imported techniques be adapted to local contexts or conditions. This was, notably, the case with foreign aid during agrarian reforms – a crucial phase in India's social dynamics. Throughout that phase, there were misleading attempts to implement agrarian reforms without regard to the core agrarian relations that underpin agriculture in vast swathes of the subcontinent.[10]

Admittedly, such contextlessness in implementation of developmental agenda in the third world is not unique to the subcontinent, but near universal, as may be gleaned from the historical analysis in a recent article by Jessica Einhorn, former managing director of the World Bank, (The World Bank's Mission Creep, *Foreign Affairs*, New York: Council on Foreign Relations, Sep/Oct 2001, vol. 80, no. 5). Einhorn argues that there is no one certain way toward development across countries and regions, and details how the World Bank gradually warmed to the idea that development is serendipitous, and accordingly, how that knowledge has incrementally informed many of World Bank's policies so that eventually nuances of local contexts began to be taken into account

[10] One recent evidence comes to mind; typical of a democracy being run on undemocratic principles and institutions, this is the latest in a series of daily anecdotes exemplifying criminalization of politics and politicization of criminals: Some hardened criminals with alleged links to a ranking government functionary long accused of utilizing extra-legal methods to influence the outcome of elections were apprehended from a government facility in a city in Eastern India, where they were apparently in sanctuary, under the auspices of the said functionary. Although this nexus is not unprecedented, and long tolerated, the brazenness of such *flagrante delicto* apprehending brought forth healthy demands from across the society and within the parent political party of that functionary for his temporary suspension lest there be any let or hindrance during the course of investigations. The implications for this illustrative situation to go either way will surely be immense for posterity. My point is not only that instances like these contain the germinating potential of serious terrorism, but the very fact that that germination may go either way suggests a moral tug- of-war and hope for balance. (Review the last few issues of any news media published from Eastern India for details) http://www/telegraphindia.com/archive/1010629/index.htm (accessed 7/9/01 3:44:53 AM)

more carefully. Sadly, however, such wisdom is usually to be had in retrospect, and after much damage is already done.

## FORCES TO HOPE

Yet, there are empirical restorative forces[11] that tend to counteract the centrifugally inclined culture of terrorism. It may be argued that the peculiarities of conservative social life in the subcontinent, comprised of traditional, god-fearing 'elders' still commanding hierarchical obeisance in a culture of consensus, tend to weigh in favour of social cohesion, and politics peaceful status quo. However, the rapid anachronism of the institution of the 'elderly' – the gentry of tradition – is contributing to social *anomie*, consequently providing violent direction to pent-up social frustrations too.

A brief relative respite in the level of terrorist activities and quasi-organized public violence in general in both India and Pakistan, for about a decade immediately after 1947 is, again, one of the more curious aspects of the pattern of violence peculiar to the Indian subcontinent (Sahai 1998, de Silva 2000). Mounting political ineptitude resulting from the eclipse of national leaders of independence-struggle stature, the increasing vernacularization and provincialism in the remnants form the *Raj* days of the 'steel frame' of administration – the civil services, as well as other factors, may have contributed to the rekindling of violence around the 1960s.

Synoptically, it may be argued that due to a combination of socio-economic factors, (a) the '50 beheld the concluding dynamics in an erosion of social authority commanded by the traditional familial hierarchy, and consequent disregard of the directive balance and wisdom reposed in its top echelons; and (b) the concurrent influence of exogenous anti-establishment and other destabilizing ideological movements spanning the globe (Russel et al 1979). All these

[11] See, Dr. Sachin Sen, 'Aspects of Conflicts and Tensions in Contemporary Indian Society', (pp. 25-34) in L.P. Vidyarthi (ed), *Conflict Tension and Cultural Trend in India*, Calcutta: Punthi Pustak, 1969.

contributed to a resumption of violence in the '60s after the lull o the '50s. Adding fuel to the conflagration, certain sections of the traditional social authority decided to retain their social status quo by 'being traditional in the traditional way' (Murray 1988). This released fresh fundamentalist forces, many of which are unraveling even to this day by way of religious fundamentalism and associated vote-bank.

## DESTABILIZING CHANGES

Social flux out of whose churnings the seeds of terrorism emerge can be traced back to the days of transition from colonialism to national autonomy. The transfer of power from colonial rulers to Indians involved changes in the *modus operandi* to determine the fates of the people in India. The transfer of power bestowed, relatively suddenly, immense authority into the hands of hitherto inexperienced Indian politicians. These leaders, who, until now had been practicing political protests and similar activism against the British establishment, were now operating in a different orbit, and with a misunderstanding that gripe and governance are often antithetical concepts. Only the best politicians are able to tread the fine line between the two.

Many, of course, were unable to make that transition seamlessly, and in their zeal to control the destiny of India, they often extended the ambit of state control the destiny of India, they often extended the ambit of state control and interference from strictly political and economic spheres, as was hitherto the case, to now include social and religious spheres too. The unshackling of the government's role, thus, unlike any earlier instance, also meant that the old concepts of government neutrality in the realms of social reforms could not be strictly maintained.[12]

[12] See, George Rosen, *Democracy and Economic Change in India*, Berkley: University of California Press, 1966, especially chaps. 2-4.

## Caste Factors

Social strain attendant in social reforms, however, was definitely not a monopoly only of Indian rulers and administrators. Two hundred years of British rule ensured that the paradoxical bedrock of social stability in India – the caste system, which often served as the determinant of relative ritual and social hierarchy and status among social groups and individuals, was disrupted. This disruption further ensured that the culturally embedded passivity of people in the various social strata, due largely to the traditionally slow prospects of socio-hierarchical change granted by a society operating within the restrictions of the caste system, was gradually abandoned in favour of more 'modern' concepts of class mobility. The introduction of prospects of mobility increased aspirations even among those of the lowest social stratum. While these new developments on the one hand contributed to social progress, on the other hand they disrupted social stability and encouraged a culture of general non-compliance,[13] especially in light of the fact that, … the cast system provides a remarkable example of a long-lived social organisation. It performed many services. In association with Hinduism it provided a framework for stability of village life and custom that made it possible for the Indian village to exist as a unit in the periods of great political upheaval that have characterized so much of the Indian history, and during periods of natural disaster that have been even more prevalent. At the same time it tied the village into a larger communal and national set of relationships, that provided a supravillage unity.[14]

The unraveling of the caste system ran seriously aground when typical third world resource constraints and India's population explosion skewed the demand-supply relationship of village economics, with consequent overlapping effects on overburdened

[13] Ibid., p 22.
[14] Ibid., p 25-6.

cities, even as people throughout Indian began to confront serious hindrances in their newly unbridled aspirations and desires for faster social mobility.

> The British provided new opportunities for advancement in all castes to those members able to take advantage of them. …But there were also more chances for decline: the breakdown of communal responsibilities for village members, which accompanied the introduction of private property in land; the breakdown of customary village occupations and services, which accompanied the spread of the market place and urbanization … all contributed to the rise of a large group of landless labourers. These were usually of the lower castes, who now received not an annual share of the village's output as a matter of custom, but only a daily wage when their services were required on the land, and they frequently sought additional earnings in the new cities. In almost all cases, both for high and low castes, the relation between a traditional occupation and caste either greatly widened to include not just a single occupation but a whole range of work or broke down entirely. Thus at both ends of the caste hierarchy…castes were less willing to accept the sancti ons of the system, since the system's support for them weakened…. [15]

The above scenario released divisive forces that contributed to the misbalancing of social equilibrium in India in particular, as well as spread generally over the entire subcontinent. Those forces were reinforced by further factors: failure of agrarian reforms, effects on the political economy, and the failure of political leadership.

## AGRARIAN REFORMS FAILURE

Beginning with the early 1950s, government intervention through land reforms and similar schemes changed the immutable tradition relationship of the rural poor to land. It is important to clarify here that the term rural poor does not necessarily denote people of low income, but, consistent with Amartya Sen's (1981) and F. Tomasson

[15] Jannuzi, n.9, p. 91.

Jannuzi's (1989) definitions, people of tenuous or no legal rights to land, and thus of low status in the agrarian hierarchy, where secure rights to land have strong bearing on people's capacity to fulfil many basic needs. The point, therefore, is that the rural poor, in traditional South Asian context, may belong, materially, even to the lower middle class yet feel insecure about their social status. It is thus also an issue of perception.

'...government interventions in rural India, and the worsening of the man-to-land ratio in the countryside as a derivative of the doubling of India's population in the same period, have made plain to increasing numbers of peasantry that traditional agrarian systems and the relationships shaped by them are not immutable. Government initiated agrarian reforms – even when drafted consciously to minimize change in traditional, hierarchical relationship in the countryside – have produced direct and indirect change sin agrarian structures, contributed to disputes over rights in land, and have fueled tensions between those having securing rights in land and those who, while dependent on agriculture for survival, do not. Attempts by government...have gradually transformed old patterns of interaction between established authority and the peasantry, and have spread awareness in the countryside that change in the traditional order is inevitable...'[16]

The manifest inevitability of change, regrettably, was belied when agrarian reforms largely failed to resolve the problem of rural poverty, primarily since it failed to confer land to the tiller. Half – baked reforms would never really overcome the legal loopholes.[17]

The attempts at reform, however, managed to revolutionize, at an ideational level, the aspirations of the vast majorities of partial-beneficiaries or non-beneficiaries of the failed reforms. Ideationally

[16] Like land-holding ceiling on individual not family holdings, allowing *zamindars* and related interests (often referred to as 'middle land owning groups), to redistribute holding titles among family and friends thereby largely allowing the 'old order' to retain functional/operational control of land resources.

[17] Ibid., p 96.

unshackled of time-honoured constraints and traditions of deference to the social status quo, many now disgruntled partial/non-beneficiaries began forming coalitions to politically challenge the old order of landholding elites. The minority gentry of the land fought back, with the result now that, "Those at the bottom of India's agrarian hierarchy – roughly categorized here as the rural poor … are less subservient to authority…"[18] Such disruption of the old equilibrium of reciprocal obligations to the social hierarchy and obeisance to social relationships have "weakened the nexus between those having superior and inferior rights to land… (and have thus provided) basis for the emergence of new standards of behaviour, and for conflict between the traditional elites and the marginal people in the countryside who were, in some instances, partial beneficiaries of reforms…. "[19]

Even the much-touted agricultural revolutions, with their accent on greater productivity and new technologies, but without concern for social equity, merely widened the already acute income inequality and human insecurities absolutely. This was so because technical and agronomic techniques, often imported directly from abroad, notably the United States, were implanted without sensitizing them to local contexts, the peculiarities associated with historical landholding patterns in South Asia, and the hierarchy of social interests. Therefore, the assumptions in which these imported techniques were meant to be successful (what experts, like Jannuzi, contend) – that farmers would be rational profit-maximizers – were contradicted, thus leading to their failure.

Recurring agrarian violence in the 1960s in Purnia, Bhagalpur, Darbhanga, Champaran, Monghyr, Gaya and Chapra districts of Bihar, and Naxalbari in West Bengal, for instance, may be considered result of the situation described above, and a precursor to the establishment of a violent future.

[18] Ibid., p 95.

[19] See, among others, Jann uzi, n.9, pp. 64-5.

Social upheaval becomes even more unmanageable in the event of stagnation of the political economy, coupled with buckling of the political establishment in a country. In the case of India, those are exactly what happened, not necessarily in any particular order.

## ECONOMIC DECAY

It became readily apparent by the end o the 1950s that the annual ballpark four percent rate of economic growth, often despairingly referred to as 'the Hindu rate of growth', combined with declining rate of increase in agricultural output, even with encouraging procurement price policies in place, would not suffice for India's long-term goals of poverty eradication and infrastructure development. India's failure to utilize capital efficiently, and with a consistently high incremental capital to output ratio, even higher than those of both Pakistan and Bangladesh in the 1980s, meant an excessive reliance on capital intensive development trajectories. Rarely any effort was cultivated to mitigate India's shortage of capital with compensatory development of relatively abundant land and/or labour resources.[20] Capital intensive development technologies tend to extract a high social price for capital, especially when labour resources, and project-related time management are neglected, leading to cost escalations in an already cash-starved economy. With the need for more cash revenues arising, as happened in India's case, governments typically ratchet up revenue collection efforts as well as taxation rates. These efforts operating in a climate of price escalations, quickly tend to exhaust a nation's taxable capacity, leading to more serious damages than just the tendency on the part of the population to withhold taxes; it results in an inevitable neglect of developmental expenditure, which is a 'slippery-slope' course of action as it perpetuates the situation that brought about such a course of action

[20] For a cogent analysis of the problems afflicting Indian economies, see, Prem Shankar Jha, *India—A political Economy of Stagnation*, Bombay : Oxford University Press, 1980.

in the first place, even as the government struggles with raising more real revenues in an absence of generative possibilities, faster than rising national incomes reflected by demands for increasing dearness allowance to keep pace with inflation. Unemployment figures rise in the absence of development.[21]

'Government emphasis on, … a given investment of capital in heavy industries gives an expanded stream of future benefits … depending on how far back in the production process one has gone. The drawback with this reasoning is that the further back one goes, the longer does one defer the enjoyment of the final benefits. …'

The choice of where to break into this production chain thus depends crucially on the government's ability to persuade people to postpone the satisfaction of their needs, in other words not to discount future benefits too heavily in relation to present ones.

The root cause of the failure of planning in India is that the rate at which the government has been prepared to discount the future in relation to the rate at which the people have been prepared to do so.[22]

Some have even pointed out that there has been the rise of an entire constituency among the population that has not only been prepared to discount the future, but also promote its own immediate gratification and develop vested interests in the economic stagnation to their own ends. This is the 'parasitic, intermediate class'[23] that thrives on the shortages and deficiencies of the system and has captured clout in both rural and urban regions. These are the people significant in their accent on the prevention of change and surplus[24]

[21] Ibid., p 74-5, (emphasis mine).

[22] Ibid., pp. 120-121.

[23] Middle landlords in rural areas are not necessarily in favour of success of land reforms to prevent passage of land to tillers; and, small businessmen in urban areas are also not necessarily in favour of big manufacturers hiking their production capacities lest they acquire monopolistic clout. These are examples of two typical subsets of the intermediate class, and why they would resist change and plenty.

[24] George Rosen, *Democracy and Economic Change in India*, Berkeley: University of California Press, 1966, pp. 68-9.

often cause political repercussions in those who are adversely affected by the strategy and proclivities of this intermediate class.

### POLITICAL ALIENATION

Concurrently with implosion of social institutions, political direction to social churnings was conspicuous by its absence as the main political parties in India suffered the pangs of post-independence transition. The taste of power of political parties after independence increased infighting, factionalism, defections, and one-upmanship. In the Congress party, for instance, membership profile shifted from 'have not groups' ...to attract the 'haves,'[25] because being in power meant the capacity to affect the fortunes of those who ordinarily held the reins of influence in society, the very people, who, prior to independence often sided with the British; thus, "What had been a movement representing the nation became a party representing its members and those who voted for it."[26] Political leadership thus became divorced from India's social mainstream.

### STRATEGIC HAZARD

It may be surmised from the above treatment of socio-economic developments in India and its neighbours since independence that the erosion in the performance of a number of significant socio-economic factors, which traditionally contributed to a stable culture of society, such as caste, political, agricultural (a person's relation to land), economic administrative and other systems, have ironically served to thwart the prospects of general progress that the decades immediately succeeding independence beheld. The collective sense of frustration that such convergence of desperation generated led to

[25] Ibid., p 69.

[26] When law enforcement agencies seek authority for electronic surveillance on a highly itinerant suspect, for instance, proposed changes in legislation may allow a judge to grant authorization for such surveillance that shall be considered to remain valid even after the suspect will have exited that judge's geographic jurisdictional limits.

conditions of latent accumulated aggression, approximating the frustration-aggregation/relative depravation syndromes hypotheses. Conditions of abject poverty, violent historical precedents, tendency to desensitize violence, or a peculiar public propensity to the dismissive about it, have all contributed to the context in which respect for nonviolent values are no longer considered virtuous. Certain innately violence-prone catalysts, like certain individuals, or some religious and ideological factors, have played critical roles as they have managed to transform that latent aggression into manifest threats, by further corrupting the conscientious restraints to action (passivity) that are natural to cultures of the Indian subcontinent. A superstructure of a lethargic government administration that does not extract a price from its subject for usurping its monopoly on violence, perhaps due to corruption or other weaknesses in its institutions of authority, promotes the dismal scenario, by reducing the 'legal sanctions' threshold between latent and manifest violence.

## CONVERGENCE OF FACTORS

Identifying the enabling conditions of violence, as above, does not necessarily mean that their mere presence will automatically translate to terrorism. Although any statistical correlation requires further research, what we are trying to argue is that (a) the probability will be high for the occurrence of terrorism whenever enabling conditions of the type illustrated above shall be present; and (b) conversely, wherever presence of terrorists is suspect, comparable combination of enabling conditions shall be present.

The preceding hypotheses have important ramifications: presence of enabling conditions of the types identified in our analyses imply 'strategic hazards', bearing not only on a nation's internal security, but also on its external security. If present within the boundaries of a state, such strategic hazards may be capable of destablilizing what is already probably a badly governed state; if present without, it may raise the prospects of asymmetric threats for which defense forces have to prepare. In other words, in this day and age, since no country is safe sanctuary or insulated from the penetrating reach of terrorism, order in one's own house does not necessarily mean on should be unconcerned about the state of others. Logically, concern for others' state of affairs implies a potential erosion, or interference, in their sovereignty. Developments of a similar vein are already afoot in the wake of the recent attacks on the United States, with stringent law enforcement requirements calling for legal reforms implying extra-jurisdictional application of law.[27]

We have to remain aware that the sword cuts both ways, in that external jurisdiction may be extended into holding the United States accountable, too. Another uncertainty about such developments is the degree of public backlash these new resultant regimes of government intrusiveness is likely to breed in the long run.

## POSSIBLE RESOLUTION

The redeeming aspect about those enabling conditions or strategic hazards is that they are not unique, but that most of their causes are due to bad governance; and this synthetic quality infers that efforts can be mounted to undo them.

While specific policy prescriptions directed towards individual or a combination of factors, or enabling conditions, of violence and/or terrorism need to be devise, discussing them in detail is beyond the scope of this paper. What is indispensable, though, in most conflict situations is a mechanism of conflict resolution. Accordingly, we wish to focus on the institution of the *panchayat*.

The *panchayat* is an extant, indigenous, time-tested conflict resolution forum, well entrenched and acclimatized in the subcontinental social context. A system of local self-government common in rural India, *panchayats* operate with the logic of consensus qualified with the prevailing wisdom of tradition. After

[27] For detailed accounts, see, among others, Henry Maddick, *Panchayati Raj : A Study of Rural Local Government in India*, London: Longman, 1970.

independence, India experimented with granting a more official status to *panchayats*, by electing members of the institution through adult suffrage, and structuring a three-tiered body characterized by hierarchical complexity and pyramidal flow of command. The value of the *panchayat*, however, is best comprehended through its distilled, unceremonious version as being a deliberative body of 'five elders'.

It was the British, in their own interests of unified administrative and tax appropriating machinery, who first violated the authority of the *panchayats* by bypassing the traditional clout that these institutions commanded. For the sake of uniformity in application of laws, in Roman traditions of non-discriminating, overarching jurisprudence, the British eroded a pristine mechanism that effected devolution of power right to the grass roots. Accessibility and sense of fairness with which the *panchayat* conducted itself conferred a feeling of empowerment among people who chose to partake of its proceeds, and the contextual embeddedness of the institution afforded it local legitimacy.[28]

The *panchayats* facilitated dispute resolution in a personalized setting, by fairly democratic means, to the extent that consensus was operative among the members of the body, and their agreements were allowed to prevail. Even the number of constituents or members of the body was novel and beneficial, because in the event of a decisional impasse, the odd fifth member cast the tiebreaker. Since any honorable member could potentially find him/herself in the tiebreaker role, the system encouraged mutual compromise and reciprocity among the local powers-that-be.

Although, occasionally, the consensual nature of democracy practiced through the *panchayats* proved insensitive to the minority, or un/under-represented factions in society, weight of age or maturity of the functionaries and wisdom of their tradition ensured a benign nature of their public discourse. Thus, the nature of that

[28] Ibid., p 20.

discourse obviated the need for tyranny of the majority on the minority to realize the majority's ends.

Historically, the end of the relative isolation of the 'village republics' (as described by Lord Metcalfe in the Report of Select Committee of House of Commons, 1832, and cited in Maddick's *Panchayati Raj*) signaled the beginning of intrusions of politics and external interests (those not native to the village) that impinged on the functioning of *panchayats*. In India, notwithstanding intentions, the first large-scale interference with the autonomy of *panchayat* occurred on behalf of the cause of independence during the Swaraj movement in the first quarter of the twentieth century.[29] Thereafter, the course of development managed to change the composition, functioning and utility of *panchayats*, to the point that in their modern renditions, "old…men…are giving way to younger, more energetic candidates. These are a new breed of politicians – with a different approach to politics and power, to problems and their resolution, not so easily charmed by bland words."[30]

The rise of aggression of youth and sidelining of traditional wisdom of the elderly are more than coincidental when considered in perspective of the overall socio-economic uncertainties that have been detailed earlier. Societal flux resulting in increasing inability to confer the assurance of social security to the community has eroded the traditional legitimacy and command of custodians of the *panchayats* – the elders; the vacuum has been filled by forces of inexperience – the immature youth, (inexperience ascended, because the domain of experience in the gentry of traditions seemingly proved so useless). These forces of inexperience, riding on immature disgruntled youth, have sought to cope with social flux and attendant insecurity by the obvious way known to youth –

[29] Ibid., p 309.

[30] Santibhusan Nandi, 'Resolution of Conflicts in Bengal Village' in L.P. Vidyarthi (ed), *Conflict Tension and Cultural Trend in India,* Calcutta: Punthi Pustak, 1969, p. 272.

forcefulness. Force mutated to violence, violence to terrorism; catalysed along the way by many of the triggers and enabling factors described above.

Yet, feelings of security-insecurity are rarely based only on the objective calculus, they are also more a matter of perception. The remaining legitimacy of the *panchayati* system is precisely because of it sutility in being able to mould that perception.

> '... although the capability of the *panchayats* to resolve conflicts has waned significantly, there are some ultimo ate situations when elders of the caste or locality, if they can act in cohesion among themselves, make their sanctions really meaningful and effective. It is by dint of such residual power that the *panchayats* are still capable of resolving some of the conflicts'.[31]

Therefore, the sociological value of an institution such as the *panchayat* cannot be ignored. It is obvious now that government policy must address the causes that have resulted in erosion of the capacity of those allegorical 'five elders' to restore perceptions of security—material (*i.e.*, economic, food, health, physical etc.), and socio-cultural (status, legitimacy, etc.)—to the public through their deliberations. The emphasis may even be proactively and expeditiously restore some of that capacity in advance of rectifying the underlying causes that resulted in their reneging in the first place. Such a course of action is justified in light of the obvious strategic and national security interests clarified in the analysis.

## CONCLUSION

It can be easily surmised from the above account and also, notably, from the recent realities that terrorized America, that terrorism is an

[31] For accounts on 'thick' or 'dense', and 'thin' webs of interests and their differences in the context of national and international communities, see, notably, Emmanuel Adler and Michael Barnett (eds.), *Security Communities,* Cambridge, MA: Cambridge University Press, 1998.

asymmetric threat of national and international magnitude. What is unique about such a threat, and we wish rather to err on the side of caution here, is that it may not be seen in a manner similar to how any other national security issue would be – through the lens of 'Realism'. Threats like terrorism, even of the transnational variety, require and thrive on domestic communities or societies. Realism, on the contrary, is a more appropriate response to the 'thin' web of international communities or societies, not the 'thick' domestic ones in which terror is prone to habituate. The strategy against terrorism, therefore, should also be communitarian, as it were, and devoid of asociological bias.

In the culture of the Indian subcontinent, we find embedded mechanisms uniquely suited to deal with conflict – the precursor to terrorism. In order to nip the malaise of terrorism in the bud, then such mechanisms and institutions need to be reinforced to mitigate conflict and restore perceptions of safety and security among the populace, with the same urgency as one would approach a national security issue.

III

# Terrorism, Freedom and Institutions: Reconstructing the State in Afghanistan

*William Maley*

*The 11 September terrorist attack, and the subsequent war in Afghanistan to crush Osama bin Laden's al-Qaida organization and the Taliban movement which supported it, have raised some important questions for those interested in the architecture of a free society. In the United States, serious questions have surfaced about the freedom of aliens, the judicial review of executive action, and even the extent to which cherished freedoms might need to be compromised for the higher good of preventing terrorist networks from conducting their nefarious activities. In Afghanistan also, some important questions for liberals have surfaced. One set relates to the possibility, disturbing for anarchists that the weakness of the state was indispensable to the flourishing of the al-Qaida network. But another relates to the question of how new institutions should be designed in the post- Taliban period. The State in Afghanistan collapsed many years ago, and the results have not been very pleasant: civil society, historically quite robust, found itself pillaged by decidedly uncivil forces. In the current situation, there is strong international support for rebuilding the state. In this article, I shall suggest that liberal political theory offers some guidelines as to how to proceed.*[1]

[1] This is a revised and updated version of a paper presented at the Special Asian Regional Meeting of the Mont Pelerin Society, Goa, 27-30 January 2002.

What we call 'the state' actually has number of different levels. Migdal has usefully distinguished four. First are the *trenches,* consisting of 'the officials who must execute state directives in the face of possibly strong societal resistance'. Second are the *dispersed field offices,* that is, the 'regional and local bodies that rework and organize state policies and directives for local consumption, or even formulate and implement wholly local policies'. Third are the *agency's central offices,* the 'nerve centers' where national policies are formulated and enacted and where resources for implementation are marshaled. Fourth are the *commanding heights*, the 'pinnacle of the state' where the 'top executive leadership' is to be found.[2] Afghanistan had extensive experience with a centralized state (*hukumat-e mutamarkiz-e qawi*) during the long era of Muhammadzai rule from 1929 to 1978, but at the 'trenches' and 'dispersed field offices' level it was inefficient,[3] and at the commanding heights was one of the most corrupt on the face of the earth. It displayed an unhealthy combination of weakness and strength. Writing twenty-five years ago, Hasan Kakar observed that 'Afghan civil servants are probably among the lowest paid in the world. It is impossible for them to live decently on their salaries unless they supplemented by other sources of income. Corruption and embezzlement are accepted facts of Afghan bureaucratic life and are objected to only when excesses are committed'.[4] Problems of financial corruption were compounded by widespread *nepotism*, which saw patron-client relations overwhelm competence and dedication as routes at advancement. In the

[2] Joel S. Migdal, 'The state in society: an approach to struggles for domination', in Joel S. Migdal, Atul Kohli and Vivienne Shue (eds), *State Power and Social Forces: Domination and Transformation in the Third World* (Cambridge: Cambridge University Press, 1994) pp.7-34 at p.16.

[3] Thomas J. Barfield, 'Weak Links on a Rustry Chain: Structural Weaknesses in Afghanistan's Provincial Government Administration', in M. Zazif Shahrani and Robert L. Canfield (eds), Revolution and Rebellions in Afghanistan: Anthropological Perspectives (Berkeley: Institute of International Studies, University of California, 1984) pp. 170-184.

[4] Hasan Kakar, 'The Fall of the Afghan Monarchy in 1973', *International Journal of Middle East Studies,* vol.9, 1978, pp.195-214 at p. 200.

military, this had deadly consequences, as young non-elite members of the Pushtun ethnic group in the officer corps 'found their road to promotion and choice assignments blocked by the old inner circle of Pushtuns with close connections to the royal family'.[5] No one in his or her right mind would want to return to such a situation, but there is more to stabilizing a state than just avoiding corruption.

A state, which enjoys generalized normative support, is likely to be more stable in the long run than one, which needs resources to fund either bribery or coercion. But the legitimacy of the state can be compromised in a number of different ways. One is through processes of state decay. States can be overly dependent on foreign aid, or on rentier income at levels, which are not sustainable. External shocks can massively disappoint the expectations of those who expected an easy flow of resources to last forever- a problem which some have called the 'resource curse'. States can be victims of creeping invasion, or the spread of ethnic conflict from neighbouring states, and governmental efficiency may be compromised by imbalances between military and social spending, or by corruption and nepotism. When states decay in this respect, individuals suffer, and their disappointed and despair can drive them into the arms of radical groups. This was what happened in Afghanistan.

## THE AFGHAN CONTEXT

In April 1978, a communist coup overthrew the government of President Muhammad Daoud and replaced it with a revolutionary regime under the Hezb-e Demokratik-e Khalq-e Afghanistan, or 'people's Democratic Party of Afghanistan'. The new regime inherited a rentier state[6], which was unequal to the demands of revolutionary

[5] Ralph Magnus, 'The Military and Politics in Afghanistan: Before and After the Revolution', in Edward A. Olsen and Stephen Jurika, Jnr. (eds), *The Armed Forces in Contemporary Asian Societies* (Boulder: westview Press, 1986) pp.325-344 at p.335.

[6] See Barnett R. Rubin, *The Fragmentation of Afghanistan: State Formation and Collapse in the International System* (New Heaven: Yale University Press, 1995).

transformation, which the new regime imposed on it. The result was an acute sharpening of factional conflict within the regime, the development of popular resistance to its radical policies (particularly in respect of gender and land), and a decline in the ability of the state to obtain revenues to fund its operations. In December 1979, the tottering regime, then under Hafizullah Amin, was overthrown by a Soviet invasion force.

The new Soviet-backed regime- headed until 1986 by Babrak Karmal, and from 1986 by Dr Najibullah- was heavily dependent upon Soviet support. India, imprudently, greeted the invasion in a muted fashion, which facilitated Pakistan's push to present itself as *the* frontline state opposing Soviet aggression. The end of Soviet assistance following the political changes resulting from the failed August 1991 coup attempt in Moscow led directly to the collapse of communist rule in April 1992.[7] At this point, the wreckage fell into the hands of the Afghan resistance. Roughly one million Afghans had perished from a pre-war population of just over 13 million, and a great deal of the country's infrastructure had been destroyed. The school system was in a state of almost total disarray, and much productive land was strewn with anti-personal mines. Millions of Afghan remained as refugees outside their country. In exile, a new generation of Afghans had grown up who had a best a remote and romanticized image to their homeland, and who lacked the skills, which would normally have been learned in the course of

[7] See ibid.; Henry S. Bradsher, *Afghanistan and the Soviet Union* (Durham: Duke University Press, 1985); Oliver Roy, *Islam and Resistance in Afghanistan* (Cambridge: Cambridge University Press, 1990); Amin Saikal and William Maley, *Regime Change in Afghanistan: Foreign Intervention and Politics of Legitimacy* (Boulder: Westview Press, 1991); Assem Akram, *Histoire de la guerre d' Afghanistan* (Paris: Editions Balland, 1996); Henry S. Breasher, *Afghan Communism and Soviet Intervention* (Karachi: Oxford University Press,1999); Gilles Dorronsoro, *La revolution afghane: Des Communistes aux taleban* (Paris: Karthala, 2000); William Maley, *The Afghanistan Wars* (London: Plagrave Macmillan, 2002).

everyday life in a predominantly agricultural economy.[8] The country had no legitimate political institutions. Rarely has a popular resistance movement received so miserable and elusive an inheritance.

At the time the communist regime collapsed, there was no single group or party within the Afghan resistance strong enough rule the whole country. As a result, while the forces of the *Shura-I- Nazar-e Shomali* (supervisory Council of the North) of Ahmed Shah occupied much of Kabul, the authority of the regime which he backed, headed by Burhanuddin Rabbani, was challenged by the Pakistan-backed extremist Hezb-e Islami of Gulbuddin Hekmatyar, which from mid- 1992 rocketed the capital with stockpiled munitions, causing thousands of deaths and reducing the southern suburbs to rubble.[9] However, Hekmatyar's party proved incapable of occupying and holding territory. Therefore, from 1994, Pakistani agencies increasingly threw their weight behind another force, the so-called Taliban movement, which without Pakistan's instrumental support would have remained socially marginal and politically irrelevant. The rise of the Taliban movement reflected the extent to which Afghanistan had become a theatre for the playing out of regional rivalries on territory exposed to creeping invasion by the collapse of the state. For Pakistan, a Taliban-dominated Afghanistan offered a number of ostensible benefits: it would minimize Iranian influence, provide a safe venue for the training of Kashmiri militants, and secure Pakistan's rear flank in the event of renewed

[8] See Nancy Hatch Dupree, 'The Demography of Afghan Refugees in Pakistan', in Hafeez Malik (ed.), *Soviet-American relations with Pakistan, Iran and Afghanistan* (London: Macmillan, 1987) pp.366-395; Nancy Hatch Dupree, 'Demographic Reporting on Afghan Refugees in Pakistan', *Modern Asian Studies,* vol.22, no.4, 1988, pp.845-865; William Maley, 'Afghan Refugees: From Diaspora to Repatriation', in Amin Saikal (ed.), *Refugees in the Modern world* (Canberra: Canberra Studies in World Affairs no.15, Department of International Relations, Research School of Pacific Studies, Australian National University, 1989) pp.17-44.

[9] See William Maley, 'The Future of Islamic Afghanistan', *Security Dialogue,* vol.24, no.4, 1993, pp.383-396; William Maley, 'The dynamics of regime transition in Afghanistan', *Central Asian Survey,* vol.16, no.2, 1997, pp.167-184.

armed conflict with India. With backing from Pakistan and from Osama bin Laden, the Taliban finally succeeded in taking Kabul in September 1996. The Clinton Administration, not greatly concerned with the complexities of Southwest Asia and keen to see a stable Afghanistan in which US energy companies could invest, reacted with fatal calmness to the Taliban take over.[10]

The results, however, proved perverse. The Taliban, overwhelmingly drawn from one ethnic group, the Pustuns, consisted of a curious mixture of extremist Sunni Muslim clerics of Deobandi persuasion, students from madrassas who had been denied anything like a normal family life as a result of two decades of war, and Pushtuns who identified with the Taliban movement out of ethnic solidarity rather than ideological affinity.[11] This led to an increased ethnicisation of the Afghan conflict.[12] From the moment it took Kabul, the movement ran into trouble. On the night the capital fell, the UN's premises were invaded, and the former communist leader Najibullah, located in the premises since 1992, was dragged out and murdered. This attracted the world press, whose attention then fell on the remarkable and bizarre restrictions on women, which the Taliban were seeking to impose.[13] These restrictions, blatantly at odds with the approach to gender in most Western capitals, blocked the

[10] See Ahmed Rashid, *Taliban: Militant Islam, Oil and Fundamentalism in Central Asia* (New Heaven: Yale University Press, 2000); Richard Mackenzie, 'The United States and the Taliban', in William Maley (ed.), *Afghanistan and the Taliban: The rebirth of fundamentalism?* (New Delhi: Penguin, 2001) pp.90-103.

[11] William Maley, 'Introduction: Interpreting the Taliban', in William Maley (ed.), *Afghanistan and the Taliban: The rebirth of fundamentalism?* (New Delhi: Penguin, 2001) pp.1-28.

[12] Amin Saikal, 'Afghanistan's Ethnic Conflict', *Survival,* vol.40, no.2, 1998, pp.114-126.

[13] See Physicians for Human Rights, *The Taliban's War on Women: A Health and Human Rights Crisis in Afghanistan* (Boston: Physicians for Human Rights, 1998); Physicians for Human Rights, *Women's Health and Human Rights in Afghanistan: A Population-Based Assessment* (Boston: Physicians for Human Rights, 2001); Rosemarie Skanie, *The Women of Afghanistan Under the Taliban* (Jefferson: McFarland & Company, Inc., 2002).

movement's attempts to secure international respectability.[14] The Taliban's hospitality to bin Laden, a principal target of US interest following the bombing of US Embassies in Kenya and Tanzania in August 1998, made their regime an international pariah,[15] resulting in mandatory sanctions from November 1999 pursuant of UN Security Council Resolution 1267. The Taliban movement, instead, relied on ongoing Pakistani backing to harass it opponents, and depended for income on revenues from smuggling, and from taxes on opium, of which Afghanistan by 1999 had become the world's largest producer[16] although opium production did fall dramatically in 2001.[17] Those who lauded 'security' brought by the Taliban seemed not to notice that smugglers and drug barons were among the main beneficiaries. And in the north of the country, Massoud and his moderate forces held out in the face of all that the Taliban could hurl at them on the battlefield.

## THE FALL OF THE TALIBAN

On 9 September 2001, two Arab journalists carrying Belgian passports arrived in Khawaja Bahauddin to conduct an interview with Ahmed Shah Massoud. It proved to be anything but a normal interview. They presented Massoud with a list of fifteen questions typed in French. Two questions might have provoked more caution than they did: 'why do you call Osama bin Laden a killer? And 'if you take Kabul, what will you do with him?' But nobody spotted anything out of the ordinary, until the Afghan Ambassador to India, Masood Khalili, happened to notice that the cameraman had a 'nasty

[14] See William Maley, *The Foreign Policy of the Taliban* (New York: Cousncil on Foreign Relations, 2000).

[15] Zalmay Khalilzad and Daniel Byman (2000), 'Afghanistan: The Consolidation of a Rogue State', *The Washington Quarterly,* vol.23., no.1, 2000, pp.65-78.

[16] See Barnett R. Rubin, 'The Political Economy of War and Peace in Afghanistan', *World Development,* vol.28., no.1, 2000, pp.1789-1803.

[17] See the *situation in Afghanistan and its implications for international peace and security: Report of the Secretary-General* (New York: United Nations, A/56/681, S/2001/1157, 6 December 2001).

smile on his face'. It was too late: seconds later, a bomb hidden in the camera exploded.[18] Within a few hours, Massoud was dead, although his death was not officially announced until 15 September. Suspicion immediately fell on Osama Bin Laden[19] and a 'smoking gun' finally surfaced at the end of 2001, when computer files in Kabul belonging to *al-Qaida* were found by Western journalists to contain the list of questions presented to Massoud, typed out in May 2001.[20]

This was one of the most momentous events in recent Afghan history, but it was overshadowed internationally by what happened just two days later. The attack on the World Trade Center and the Pentagon was captured by television cameras, which flashed it to households through out America and screens all around the world. Bin Laden was the instigator,[21] and the closest parallel was the bombing of Pearl Harbour on 7 December 1941, which President Roosevelt described as 'a date that will live in infamy'. That was how the United States saw 11 September 2001, and it spelt the end for the Taliban.

The end came fast. The US military campaign began with massive air strikes on 7 October, combined with support for the anti-Taliban United Front on the ground. Within the space of four days in November, key cities fell to anti-Taliban forces in a cascade. On 9 November, Mazar-e Sharif fell to groups led by Dostam, the Shiite leader Ustad Mohaqqeq, and Commander Atta Muhammad. The following day, United Front forces launched simultaneous attacks

[18] Celia W. Dugger, 'Taliban Foe saw "Blue, Thick Fire" of Assassin Bomb', *The New York Times,* 26 October 2001.

[19] Joseph Fitchett, 'Did Bin Laden Kill Afghan Rebel?', *International Herald Tribune,* 17 September 2001.

[20] AlanCullison and Andrew Higgins, 'Computer in Kabul holds chilling memos, '*The Wall Street Journal,* 1 January 2002.

[21] Karen DeYoung and Walter Pincus, 'In Bin Laden's Own Words,' *The Washington Post,* 14 November 2001; Michael Dobbs, 'A Moment of Candor from a Manipulate, '*The Washington Post,* 14 November 2001.

across northern Afghanistan, in Khwajaghar, Eshkamesh, Baghlan, Pul-e Khumri, Nahrin, Aibak and Bamiyan. All fell, as did Hairatan and Shibarghan to Dostam's forces. Maimama fell on 11 November, and Herat on 12 November. On 13 November, the Taliban fled Kabul, looting the main currency market and the Da Afghanistan Bank as they left.[22] The United Front then occupied Kabul unopposed. There were scenes of ecstatic celebration in Kabul as the new forces arrived. 'Almost all people in Kabul regard the demise of the Taliban as a liberation', reported the BBC's Kate Clark.[23] Huge crowds gathered shouting 'Death to the Taliban' and 'Death to Pakistan'.

On 5 December, a group of Afghan notables, meeting under UN auspices in Bonn, endorsed an 'Agreement on Provisional Arrangements in Afghanistan Pending the Re-establishment of Permanent Government Institutions'. It was endorsed the following day by United Nations Security Council Resolution 1383. It was not a peace agreement, since the participants in the Boom meeting were not war with each other, but rather a road map for the re-establishment of rudimentary state structures. It did not provide for an Interim *Government,* but for an interim *Administration* (with a 'Chairman' and 'Members' rather than 'Prime Minister' and 'Ministers'). The signatories recognized 'the need to ensure broad representation in these interim arrangements of all segments of the Afghan population, including groups that have not been adequately represented at the UN Talks on Afghanistan', and noted that 'these interim arrangements are intended as a first step toward the establishment of a broad-based, gender-sensitive, multi-ethnic an fully representative government, and are not intended to remain in place beyond the specified period of time'.

The text then set out the substance of the agreement, which had been reached. It provided that 'An Interim Authority shall be

[22] Keith B. Richburg, 'In Kabul, a Wide Wake of Destruction: Looting and Vandalism Mark Taliban's Retreat', *The Washington Post,* 15 November 2001.

[23] BBC *Newshour,* 13 November 2001.

established upon the official transfer of power on 22 December 2001', consisting of 'an Interim Administration presided over by a chairman, a Special Independent Commission for the Convening of the Emergency Loya Jirga, and a Supreme Court of Afghanistan, as well as such other courts as may be established by the Interim Administration'. Upon the official transfer of power, it went on, 'the Interim Authority shall be the repository of Afghan sovereignty, with immediate effect. As such, it shall, throughout the interim period, represent Afghanistan in its external relations and shall occupy the seat of Afghanistan at the United Nations and in its specialized agencies, as well as in other international institutions and conferences'.

It then dealt with the processes to be followed thereafter, providing that 'An Emergency Loya Jirga shall be convened within six months of the' establishment of the Interim Authority. The Emergency Loya Jirga will be opened by His Majesty Mohammed Zaher, the former king of Afghanistan. The Emergency Loya Jirga shall decide on a Transitional Authority, including a broad-based transitional administration, to lead Afghanistan until such time as a fully representative government can be elected through free and fair elections to be held no later than two years from the date of the convening of the Emergency Loya Jirga'. With respect to the judicial function, it stated that 'The Interim Administration shall establish, with the assistance of the United Nations, a Judicial Commission to rebuild the domestic justice system in accordance with Islamic principles, international standards, the rule of law and Afghan legal traditions'.

Finally, it made provision for two important Commissions: the Interim Administration was to establish, with the assistance of the United Nations, and 'independent Civil Service Commission to provide the Interim Authority and the future Transitional Authority with shortlists of candidates for key posts in the administrative departments, as well as those of governors and *uluswals*, in order to ensure their competence and integrity'; and an 'independent Human

Rights Commission, whose responsibilities will include human rights monitoring, investigation of violations of human rights, and developments of domestic human rights institutions'.

## CHALLENGE AHEAD

The task of stabilizing a post-intervention situation is not a narrowly technical one: it invariably raises fundamental questions of political philosophy. Should the functions of the state be extensive or limited? Should the institutions of the state the centralized r diversified? How should the institutional of state and civil society relate to each other? Should the constitutional structure be monarchical, presidential or parliamentary? Should voting systems be chosen to foster majoritarianism or proportionality? To these questions there are no simple answers, for there are many different ways in which social coordination can be attempted.[24] Instead, it is useful to briefly highlight six particular challenges which will almost certainly haunt Afghanistan's transition, and to which liberal theory can suggest a response.

The first is the constitution unified elite. In Afghanistan, levels of trust remain low. Where trust is limited, it is important to foster an enviourment in which people can re-experience the benefits of trusting and being trusted, and in which the costs of misplaced trust will not be too high. A neutral security force in one way of minimizing those costs. In Afghanistan, this involves attention to both the disarmament and reintegration of combatants, and the design of new security instruments. A new-armed force will need to be able to secure borders, roads, and cities, and offer aid to the civil authorities in the event of natural disasters. Promoting such a development is one of the responsibilities of the International Security Assistance Force (ISAF). Just as important, however, is the re-establishment of a *policing* capacity. Community policing is a

[24] Russell Hardin, *Liberalism, Constitutional, and Democracy* (Oxford: Oxford University Press, 1999) pp.12-18.

device by which order and justice are guaranteed in local communities, and is designed to give substance to the notion of the rule of law.[25] Once the environment is a safer one, working together for the achievement of some super ordinate goal can rebuild trust between individuals.[26] Social capital does not result from *diktat*: it is a product of iterated engagement between actors who learn that it is beneficial to cooperate.[27] Free markets have a key role to play here.

The second challenge is to deal with the problem of warlords. Warlords who are total spoilers pose a very particular problem, but not one by which Afghanistan is now faced. The greater problem is posed by predatory extraction, which has resurfaced in parts of Afghanistan, not least because the Us armed some warlords in the Kandahar area who offered themselves as opponents of the Taliban.[28] Warlords is a classic problem of the logic of collective action,[29] where those who benefit from a socially destructive activity have a greater direct personal interest in suppressing it. The problem of warlords can be addressed in different ways: by combating them directly, by luring away their supporters, by buying their loyalty, by co-opting them into the state, or, in the long run, by fostering norms of

[25] See John McFarlane and William Maley(2001), 'Civilian Police in UN peace operations: Some lessons from recent Australian experience', in Ramesh Thakur and Albrecht Schnabel (eds), *United Nations Peacekeeping Operations: Ad Hoc Missions, Permanent Engagement* (New York and Tokyo: United Nations University Press, 2001) pp.182-211 at pp.186-188.

[26] See Jolyon Leslie, 'Towards rehabilitation: building trust in Afghanistan', *Disaster Prevention and Management,* vol.4, no.1, 1995, pp.27-31; William Maley, 'Institutional Design and the Rebuilding of Trust', in William Maley, Charles Sampford and Ramesh Thakur (eds), *From civil Strife to Civil Society: Civil and Military Responsibilities in Disrupted States* (New (New York and Tokyo: United Nations University Press, 2002), forthcoming.

[27] See Francis Fukuyama, 'Social capital, civil Society, and development', *Third World Quarterly,* vol.22, no.1, 2001, pp.7-20.

[28] Barnett R. Rubin, 'Putting an End to Warlord Government', *The New York Times,* 15 January 2002.

[29] See Mancur Olson, *The Logic of Collective Action: Public Goods and the Theory of Groups* (Cambridge: Harvard University Press, 1965); Rubin, 'The Political Economy of War and Peace in Afghanistan', p.1794.

behaviour which prohibit predatory extraction. Some state action may be required to deal with the problem, although buying off warlords can bring some short-term relief, albeit with the risk of moral hazard, namely that people will misbehave in order to be paid to stop.

The third challenge relates to the specific shape of new state institutions. *Democratic* institutions have much to commend them, since they provide a mechanism for changing rulers without bloodshed, but there is far more to durable democracy than simply a single election, no matter how well run it may be. The *liberal* dimension of durable democracy must be highlighted. It is vital to have a dense network of institutions and matching norms, which ensure that political power, even if conferred by popular vote, will not be exercised in an arbitrary or capricious fashion.[30] It is also vital to have a democratic political culture, emphasizing a disposition to 'moderation, accommodation, cooperation, and bargaining',[31] and respect for human rights and the rule of law. Afghanistan at the elite level is far from having such a culture, although aspects of these traits are not unfamiliar to observers of local politics in Afghanistan.

Of particular importance is the issue of whether, and if so to what degree, state power should be dispersed through local government, a federal system or regional autonomy.[32] Territorial political autonomy is an arrangement 'aimed at granting to a group that differs from the majority of the population in the state, but that constitutes the majority in a specific region, a means by which it can express its distinct identity'.[33] Some writers are wary of an immediate

[30] See Guillermo O'Donnel, 'Delegative Democracy', *Journal of Democracy,* vol.5, no.1, 1994, pp.55-69; Fareed Zakaria, 'The Rise of Illiberal Democracy', *Foreign Affairs,* vol.76, no.6,1997, pp.22-43.

[31] Larry Diamond, *Developing Democracy: Toward Consolidation* (Baltimore: The Johns Hopkins University Press, 1999) p.165.

[32] See William Maley, 'Institutional Design and Regional Autonomy', in Minako Sakai (ed.), *Beyond Jakarta: Regional Autonomy and Local Societies in Indonesia* (London: Hurst & Co., 2002), forthcoming.

[33] Ruth Lapidoth, *Autonomy: Flexible Solutions to Ethnic Conflicts* (Washington DC: United States Institute of Peace Press, 1997) p.33.

move to deferral organization in Afghanistan, lest it simply formalize the position of predatory warlords and legitimize their practices.[34] This is a legitimate concern, but in the long run, once the existing predators have been marginalized, the case for increasing the scope for localities to compete with each other to optimize the environment for investment in productive economic activity is a powerful one.

The fourth challenge is to determine exactly what powers the state should have. There is evidence that in post-civil war situations, institutions are more effective if they limit concentrations of military power, political authority, and distributive capacity.[35] While faith in the capacity of a powerful state to maintain order seems pervasive in Afghanistan, it is worth noting that where the state has collapsed, the very act of rebuilding a powerful state can fuel conflict, since more than one party may see it as in its interest to monopolise control of such a state. What one does need is a state, which is capable of providing, and enforcing constitutive rules for a civil economy, that is, 'a market economy working within a clear legal framework',[36] and protecting freedom of civil association in the face of uncivil threats, but which otherwise is heavily constrained. It is better for the future Afghan state to do a few key things well, rather than many things badly. Institutions of *justice* deserve priority. A prescient aphorism of the Sasanian period, recorded first by Ibn Balkhi, runs as follows: 'There is no kingdom without an army, no army without wealth, no wealth without material prosperity, and no material prosperity without justice'.[37] The appeal of radical movements, which often foreshadow the advent of a just society, is

[34] Astri Suhrke, Arne Strand, and Kristian Berg Harpviken, *Peace-building Strategies for Afghanistan.* Part 1. Lessons from Past Experience in Afghansitan (Bergen: Chr. Michelson Institute, 14 January 2002).

[35] Caroline A. Hartzell, 'Explaining the Stability of Negotiated settlements to Intrastate Wars'; *Journal of Conflict Resolution,* vol.43, no.1, 1999, pp. 3-22.

[36] Richard Rose, 'Toward a Civil Economy', *Journal of Democracy,* vol.3, no.2, 1992, pp.13-26 at p.14.

[37] Cited In Partricia Springborg, *Western Republicanism and the Oriental prince* (Cambridge: Polity Press, 1992) p.264.

greatly heightened in societies in which justice manifestly cannot be obtained through public instrumentalities. Constitutionalism is at the heart of a just society, because of the emphasis, which it places on the separation of powers and the rule of law. In a situation in which law functions as an instrument of state domination, rather than as a constraint on state power, its legitimacy will be compromised. Where power is in practice divided between the legislature, the executive, and the judiciary, state repression becomes harder to orchestrate, and a truly civil society can more readily function. This opens the scope for a multiplicity of overt social attachments for the individual, and avoids the situation in which the only possible networks of social engagement are familial, state-orchestrated, or uncivil.

The fifth challenge relates to the holding of fee and fair elections within two years of the Bonn Agreement. An election is a very large-scale and complex logistical exercise, with many different elements.[38] Meticulous planning is required, as well as highly trained staff and efficient mechanisms for securing preparation, storage, transportation and counting of ballot papers. It may also be necessary to protect voters against intimidation. Just to meet the deadlines in the Bonn Agreement, it is necessary to undertake a number of quite complex tasks at high speed.[39] The problems are so daunting that Marina Ottaway and Anatol Lieven have argued that the idea of a 'democratic government technocratically administering the country' is an 'impossible fantasy'.[40] It is of course true that racing to the polls

[38] William Maley and Fazel Haq Saikal, *Political Order in Post-communist Afghanistan* (Boulder: Lynne Rienne, 1992), pp.33-48.

[39] Jeff Fischer, *Post-Conflict Peace Operations and Governance in Afghanistan: A Strategy for Peace and Political Intervention* (Washington DC: International Foundation for Election Systems, 2001).

[40] Marina Ottaway and Anatol Lieven, *Rebuilding Afghanistan: Fantasy versus Reality* (Washington DC: Policy Brief no.12, Carnegie Endowment for International Peace, 2002) p. 4.

may contribute to ongoing instability,[41] and that elections are only one element of a democratic order. But a free society must trust its people to choose their rulers.

The sixth challenge is to develop a constructive framework for regional interaction, cooperation, and constructive engagement, based on free trade, freedom of association, and a civil religion of liberty. Many of Afghanistan's problems are problems for its neighbours as well, requiring a collective response, and without an appropriate regional architecture that protects the security of states and human security, progress will be very difficult.[42] The most awkward requirement here is to rebuild a constructive relationship between Afghanistan and Pakistan. On the one hand, Pakistan must understand that the days when it could seek to determine who should rule Afghanistan are over.[43] May Afghans have good reason to feel enrage at Pakistan's meddling in their homeland. However, geography had condemned the two countries to be neighbours, and it cannot simply be wished away. The relationship will develop best if ongoing Us pressure makes it clear to Islamabad that attempts to manipulate Afghan politics will not be tolerate. But that said, there is also a strong case for aid to Pakistan, to support President Musharraf's crackdown on the religious extremists who played such a malign role in destabilizing Afghanistan. The shame brought to Pakistan by the murder of the US journalist Daniel Pearl may serve as a wake-up call to the Musharraf Administration. Many of Pakistan's problems are not the fault of the present generation a

[41] Jack Snyder, *From voting to Violence: Democratization and Nationalist Conflict* (New York: W.W. Norton, 2000).

[42] See Barnett R. Rubin, Ashraf Ghani, William Maley, Ahmed Rashid, and Olivier Roy, *Afghanistan: Reconstruction and Peacebuilding in a Regional Frame-work (*Bern: KOFF Peacebuilding Reports 1/2001, Swiss Peace Foundation, 2001).

[43] William Maley, 'Moving forward in Afghanistan', in Stuart Harris, William Maley, Richard Price, Christian Reus-Smit, and Amin Saikal, *The Day the World Changed? Terrorism and World Order* (Canberra: 'Keynotes' no.1, Department of International Relations, Research School of Pacific and Asian Studies, Australian National University, 2001), pp.18-24 at p.22.

better life may help Pakistanis[44] and measures to offer a new generation a better life may help stabilize the region as a whole. The liberalization of Pakistan will help protect freedom in Afghanistan, and a better relationship with India.

[44] William Maley, 'Talibanisation and Pakistan', in Denise Groves (ed.), *Talibanisation: Extremism and Regional Instability in South and Central Asia* (Berlin: Conflict Prevention Network: Stiftung Wissenschaft und Politik, 2001), pp.53-74.

# IV

# War on Terrorism: The US Role in South Asian Conflicts

*Maj. Gen. (Retd.) Afsir Karim*

*The hunt for al-Qaida in Pakistan and Pakistan-controlled Kashmir and armed insurgencies in Kashmir, Sri Lanka and Nepal has given an opportunity to the US to play a new strategic role in South Asia and its extended neighbourhood.*

*The attacks on the Jammu & Kashmir Assembly in October and the Indian Parliament in December 2001 and an attack on a family complex of the Indian army in May 2002, by Pakistan-sponsored terrorist groups brought India and Pakistan to the brink of another war. Even today more than a million Indian and Pakistani troops face each other across the Line of Control in Kashmir and across the international border in the Punjab, Rajasthan and Gujrat. The navies and the air forces of the two countries also maintain aggressive operational postures.*[1]

*The US, no doubt, has played a significant role in convincing President Musharraf that cross-border terrorism must be stopped if he wants to negotiate on Kashmir with India. He was told that the US would be able to facilitate the process of a meaningful dialogue with India once cross-border terrorism is permanently stopped by Pakistan.*

*The failure of the Kashmir policy based on terrorism and military adventurism was now quite evident in any case, as 13 years of Pakistan-sponsored terrorism had brought no territorial gains or*

[1] Scott Baldauf, *The Christian science Monitor,* 'In Kathmandu, Nepal, The US quietly wades into South Asia's rebel conflicts', <csmonitor.com>, 7 May 2002.

*change of boundaries; it only led to more bloodshed in Kashmir. The precarious economic situation of Pakistan, collapse of its Afghanistan policy, growing violence and lawlessness greatly limits Pakistan's options in Jammu and Kashmir. It is obvious that Pakistan's Kashmir policy is proving to be the second major disaster in the last decade. Disenchantment of the common Kashmiri from the vicious cycles of violence is also now palpable.*

*The spate of visits of American diplomats to India and Pakistan shows the copious efforts America is making to disperse the war clouds and induce India and Pakistan to come to the negotiating table. It seems that Americans are working simultaneously on Pakistan, India and the separatists groups in Kashmir at different levels. America has been, at times, blunt but generally soothingly genial.*

## FOCUS ON MUSHARRAF

After their great escape from Afghanistan, al-Qaida cadres settled down in Pakistan and Pak-occupied Kashmir in great numbers under various guises. The killing of ten Pakistani army regulars in a fire-fight with al-Qaida in Pakistan's North West Frontier Province is a clear indication that al-Qaida has merely changed its address and it remains operational from various remote areas of Pakistan. Reported presence of al-Qaida men in Pakistan-controlled Kashmir and the statement by Donald Rumsfeld on the subject earlier this month confirm the broadening contours of the war against terrorism in South Asia.

Musharraf, who has been frequently praised by the Americans for his bold initiative in joining the war on terrorism, has also been described as a "leathery, hard-bitten commando who personified a swaggering, nuclear-armed rashness".[2] The Bush administration seems to trust him implicitly, but it is difficult for India to trust a

[2] Peter Popham, 'The two faces of Musharraf: Director and Taliban's friend or secular liberal?' <independent.co.uk>, 24 June 2002.

person who rattled his nuclear-tipped short-range missiles during the current stand off and had done this once before during the Kargil operations. He is known to have trained and sustained the Taliban regime till he dropped them like a hot potato in post-11 September scenario.[3]

In the present scenario President Musharraf is a target of Islamic Jehadi groups within his own country, who consider him a rank opportunist who has joined hands with the *Kafirs* to remain in power at all costs. According to reports he has to be surrounded by many layers of security and hundreds of guards when he moves out of his capital, even this did not prevent an attempt made to assassinate him at Karachi recently.

General Musharraf agreed to suspend cross-border terrorism only under sustained American pressure, after "Richard Armitage, the United States' muscle-bound deputy secretary of state made frank threats".[4] General Musharraf, however, gave an impression that the meeting was most congenial and he got an assurance from Richard Armitage that the US administration would help in solving the Kashmir dispute. He is now waiting to see how soon would the US pressure bring India to the negotiating table. Musharraf expects India to take many more conciliatory steps although he has made only vague promises to check cross-border terrorism. He calls the steps taken by India to ease tension as, cosmetic-to ease their own problems.[5] The Kashmir issue needs to be resolved fast, he keeps on harping.

## India-Pakistan Confrontation

The rhetoric and hyperbole about 'the war that never was' has largely abated, but the danger of war between India and Pakistan still exists. Despite massing of troops by India and Pakistan on the borders,

[3] Ibid.
[4] Ibid.
[5] Ibid.

coercive diplomacy from both sides and threats of a nuclear war by Pakistan, cross-border terrorism still continues although at a lower scale. India draws satisfaction from the fact that the international community has eventually accepted that Pakistan has been sponsoring terrorism across the Line of Control in Kashmir. The intense peace efforts led by the US have reduced the chances of an armed conflict but the threat of war has not completely disappeared. Pakistan has carried out a tactical retreat in the face of immense pressure of the western world, but it is likely to persist with its policy of 'bleeding India by a thousand cuts'.

After a temporary suspension of cross-border terrorism Pakistan would expect India to come to the negotiating table and recall its troops from the borders. In the current environment commencement of talks seems unlikely. In any case, what will the two negotiate about unless there is a basic change in their attitudes? As far as India is concerned the status of Indian-controlled Kashmir is not negotiable and Pakistan is not likely to budge from its demand of plebiscite to determine the future status of Jammu and Kashmir. General Musharraf does not accept the sanctity of the Line of Control and has not in essence agreed to stop cross-border terrorism permanently.

The strategy of massing troops on the borders that took the two countries to the brink of another war revealed 'potentially dangerous trends towards application of nuclear power'. Pakistan's nuclear sabre-rattling was evident by its test firing of nuclear-tipped missiles. Casual statements of General Musharraf and his envoy at the UN of nuking India were highly irresponsible. India's strategy of application of military power without waging war was not properly calibrated. At a particular stage India had no option other than going to war in case Pakistan continued terrorist attacks against Indian targets. Total deployment left little room for further coercive manoeuvres short of war.

The ground situation is that the troops of the two countries are still eyeball-to-eyeball and infiltration of terrorists from Pakistan has not stopped. President Musharraf is unlikely to yield any ground because of domestic pressures and his own obsession with Kashmir.

The situation has not changed and is unlikely to change substantially in the foreseeable future. The recent attack in Jammu on 14 July in which at least 28 innocent people, mostly women and children, were killed reinforces this view. The danger of a war in the region persists despite US peace efforts, mainly because of Pakistan's insatiable territorial ambitions over Indian Kashmir.

### THE REBELLION IN NEPAL

Insurgency has killed more than 3,500 people in Nepal; the brutal and dangerous nature of conflict in Nepal brewed unnoticed for long due to turbulence in Afghanistan and Kashmir. It seems the US has lately stepped up its efforts to support Nepal in its war against Maoist rebels. Nepal finalized a $20 million US military aid package in May this year. This deal includes training of the Royal Nepalese Army by US Special Forces in counter-insurgency techniques. Some people believe the Maoists are on the run and need to be given a final push by American assistance.

The Maoists have lately intensified their efforts to overthrow the monarchy and destabilise the Nepali parliamentarian system and establish what they call 'dictatorship of the proletariat'. According to observers they have stepped up violence and "are attacking everything that used to be a success story in Nepal".[6]

The US advisors and Special Forces would be welcome in Nepal because its antiquated "… military apparatus needs to be modernized and reinforced".[7] The Maoists have already created conditions in which tourist traffic, the main industry of Nepal, has declined. People of Nepal and most analysts believe that the Maoists will be controlled once corruption in public life is eradicated and transparency is brought in the governance. There are some indications that al-Qaeda is trying to establish bases in Nepal. In these circumstances American military presence is bound to increase in Nepal.

[6] Baldauf, op cit, n. 1.
[7] Ibid.

## THE SRI LANKA-US DEFENCE AGREEMENT

A defence agreement called 'cross-servicing agreement' between the US and Sri Lanka that would provide access to American forces in the seaports of Sri Lanka is in the offing. The negotiations have been secret, but a brief embassy statement declared that each party will be able "to avail itself of the servicing, repairs, spare parts and equipment of the other in exchange for payment or through the exchange of identical goods or goods of equivalent value".[8]

According to some reports the agreement will also include joint training and supply of spare parts by the US. "The training, which will encompass joint exercises with the United States Armed Forces, will focus on counter-terrorism and related activity..."[9] Unconfirmed reports indicate release of two maritime surveillance aircraft and a patrol boat to Sri Lanka for vigilance over the eastern seas.

Both the US and Colombo have attempted to play down the importance of the deal to avoid provoking any protests by regional powers or political parties. The agreement that provides access of the US military equipment to the Sri Lankan Armed Forces will have far reaching strategic implications for the region. Sri Lanka needs to increase its ability to counter any new LTTE offensive in case of failure of an agreement with the LTTE. The importance and the strategic location of Sri Lanka was highlighted by Ashley Wills, the US ambassador to Sri Lanka, while addressing diplomats, scholars and journalists in Washington in June this year "because of its location and the talent and 'entrepreneurial outlook' of its citizens, the 19-million strong national stands to evolve into the Singapore of South Asia and prosper".[10]

Trincomalee is a key deep-water port with large oil storage facilities, developed by the British during World War II. The US has

[8] Saman Gunadasa, 'Sri Lanka to integrate into US regional military plans', <wsws.org> 11 June 2002.

[9] Ibid.

[10] Ibid.

shown considerable interest in this port in the past; recently an Indian oil company has been provided access to the storage facilities, however, India has agreed to allow use of spare oil tanks to the United States.

Sri Lanka offers an important strategic location in relation to the Indian subcontinent, Indonesia and vast areas of the Indian Ocean from the Middle East to Southeast Asia. The defence agreement with Sri Lanka, presence of US led coalition force in Afghanistan, military bases in Central Asia and Pakistan, possible deals with India integrates with broader US strategic objectives which encompass huge oil and gas resources of Central Asia.

The US is thus gradually increasing its presence in South Asia and the global war on terrorism has provided the US with a tailor-made pretext to expand its influence in this region and its extended neighbourhood.

## THE NEW US STRATEGIC DOCTRINE

The Bush administration is reported to be working on a new strategic doctrine that moves away from the Cold War strategies of 'containment and deterrence'. The new doctrine will advocate pre-emptive attacks against hostile states and terrorist groups who may develop chemical, biological or nuclear weapons. President Bush's address at the June graduation of West Point cadets assumed significance because it described his new strategic doctrine of pre-emption with clarity. The new strategic shift formulated by the White House and Pentagon recommends and justifies the use of military force by the US against any state that is considered as hostile or "makes moves to acquire weapons of mass destruction – nuclear, biological or chemical".[11] This doctrine is being termed as the latest National Security Strategy; it is being called a policy of 'defensive intervention', which may often come into play.[12] The dangerous

[11] Thomas E. Richs and Vernon Loeb, 'Bush Developing Military Policy of Striking First,' *Washington Post,* <washingtonpost.com>, 10 June 2002.

[12] Ibid.

implications of this policy are being brushed aside. The US administration considers this change necessary after the events of 11 September as "...the nature of the enemy has changed, the nature of threat has changed, and so the response has to change".[13]

The first target of this policy is likely to be Iraq. Various reports suggest that contingency planning for invading Iraq and overthrowing its government has already been done. This use of force under the new doctrine whether used against Iraq or some other country, would be a violation of the UN Charter, as pre-emption cannot be validated in peace when there is no crisis situation or hostile action across international borders. At this doctrine ignores the UN Charter and existing international laws its application can have grave consequences. However, the challenge posed by Osama bin Laden and his terrorist allies has created a new situation that requires a reappraisal of the current laws and the effectiveness of the UN charter itself. The current charter does not lay down in precise terms whether aggression by state-supported or other terrorist groups can be termed as an armed attack across international borders.[14]

Andrew Hack notes that the military and political strengths or capabilities determine the ultimate outcome of conflict; terrorist and anti-terrorist campaigns are violent confrontations where military and political capabilities play an important role. The terrorist of the Osama bin Laden variety, however, does not depend on these factors though it requires strong organizational support and safe haven in one area or the other.

It will be difficult to apply the new doctrine against terrorist groups who may have no permanent hosts or bases. Small terrorist groups may operate from the US soil itself or from friendly countries. Some groups may operate without the knowledge of the host country; an attack with chemical or radioactive material based

[13] Ibid.

[14] Richard Falk, 'The New Bush Doctrine', *The Nation,* <thenation.com>, 15 July 2002.

on wrong assumptions or information would endanger the lives of thousands of innocent people.

It is hoped that better councils would prevail and the use of nuclear, chemical or biological weapons will not be actively pursued against countries or organization considered hostile by the US administration. According to some senior officials of the Bush administration, "There is no one anxious to think about the employment of tactical nuclear weapons that is no what we are trying to do".[15]

The Secretary General of NATO, George Robertson, reacted rather cautiously to the US pre-emptive doctrine. He remarked, "NATO remained a defensive alliance- we do not go out looking for problems to solve". The US Defense Secretary, Donald Rumsfeld, however, told NATO that "the alliance could no longer wait for 'absolute proof' before acting against terrorist groups or threatening countries with chemical, biological or nuclear weapons".[16]

According to the well known defence analyst, Harlan Ullman "preemption is attractive on the surface (but) as one gets deeper, it gets more and more complicated and dangerous".[17] A pre-emptive attack may cause be available. For effective application of the new doctrine extensive re-organization of forces, raising of stealth task forces and acquisition of new stealth weapons would be necessary.

The level of armed insurgencies in Sri Lanka, Nepal and Jammu and Kashmir remain dangerously hide and from these areas terrorist organizations like al-Qaida can operate with a degree of anonymity. There are credible reports, which suggest that al-Qaida had already established terrorist cell and nodal points in Pakistan-controlled Kashmir and Nepal and they are poised to infiltrate into Indian-controlled areas of Kashmir. If al-Qaida starts operating from these areas and the process of apprehending and disarming them fails, the

[15] Richs and Loeb, op cit, n. 11.
[16] Ibid.
[17] Ibid.

US troops in Afghanistan, Pakistan and likely induction of the US Special Forces in Sri Lanka and Nepal will create a new situation in South Asia and will certainly test India's resolve not to accept intervention in Kashmir. The US intervention in Indian Kashmir would not really be necessary as India is quite capable of dealing with al-Qaida without foreign assistance, if they intrude into its territory.

## BACKLASH AND BURNOUT

A majority of people in Kashmir now denounce terrorism in all its manifestations and many openly oppose the presence of the foreign terrorist groups. A backlash against terrorism seems to be developing in some terrorist infested regions of the world because terrorism has only resulted in mindless violence without any political gains. A sense of frustration has obviously set in Kashmir where Pakistan-sponsored terrorism has resulted in thousands of civilians casualties and all the promises of liberation and a better quality of life have proved totally false and deceitful. The propaganda that made people proud of the sacrifices made by the Jehadis is now yielding ground to skepticism and bitterness against the people who are sponsoring or supporting terrorism. After 11 September the *Fatwas* of many religious leaders against suicide attacks had dented the legitimacy of *fidayeen* attacks. Common people in terrorist infested areas are now pining for normal life. A similar situation seems to be developing even in the Middle East where years of suicide bombings against Israeli civilians seem to have brought no results. As in Kashmir, here also one can discern the declining support for terrorism, however, the trends are not so definitive because terrorism here is not of the sponsored variety.

In the final analysis, terrorist's political strength depends on their ability to influence people and persuade them to support their cause. Loss of political support, and the consequent use of coercive tactics by the terrorists lead to a backlash against terrorism and its eventual burnout. The backlash provides a framework for attacking terrorism because terrorists seldom if ever achieve their announced political objectives. According to some experts "coercive capabilities, burnout and backlash are general conditions which reduce the political capabilities of groups using terrorism".[18]

In practical terms conditions have to be created by the anti-terrorist forces to start the process of burnout or backlash. It is necessary in most cases to provide alternatives to affected people. A change in leadership may be necessary in some cases as the old mindset of the leadership of the ruling National Conference nor of the separatist Hurriyat group are able to show a way out of violence. The fatigue of the people arising from endless violence and terrorism is not shared by the political leaders who continue to function from their safe cocoons and are not directly affected by terrorist killing. Leaders who are close to grass roots and share the travails of the people will be able to hasten the process of backlash of the people and the eventual burnout of the sponsored terrorist movement. This process can gain momentum through a political process, which is committed to achievable political goals without violence. This process has yet to take a definitive shape but may take a more concrete shape after the elections in Kashmir later this year.

## SIGNIFICANT TERRORIST INCIDENTS

A chronology of major terrorists attacks (excerpts from a list issued buy the Office of the Historian Bureau of Public Affairs, US, dated 31 October 2001) is given below to show that terrorism evolved into a worldwide movement because it remained unchallenged till the events of 9/11[19]:

- "Bloody Friday," July 21, 1972: An Irish Republican Army (IRA) bomb attacks killed 11 people and injured 130 in Belfast, Northern Ireland. Ten days later, three IRA car bomb attacks in the village of Claudy left six dead.

[18] Jeffrey Lan Ross and Ted Robert Gurr, *A Comparative Study of Canada and The United States,* July 1989, pp. 408-409.

[19] US Department of State, <http:// usinfo.state.gov/topical/popl/terror/01103131.htm>, International Information Programs, 31 October 2001.

- Munich Olympic Massacre, September 5, 1972: Eight Palestinian "Black September" terrorists seized 11 Israeli athletes in the Olympic village in Munich, West Germany. In a bungled rescue attempt by West German authorities, nine of the hostages and five terrorists were killed.
- Ambassador to Sudan Assassinated, March 2, 1973: U.S. Ambassador to Sudan Cleo A. Noel and other diplomats were assassinated at the Saudi Arabian Embassy in Khartoum by members of the Black September organization.
- Entebbe Hostage Crisis, June 27, 1976: Members of the Baader-Meinhof Group and the Popular front for the Liberation of Palestine (PLP) seized and Air France airliner and its 258 passengers. They forced the plane to land in Uganda, where on July 3 Israeli commandos successfully rescued the passengers.
- Iran Hostage Crisis, November 4, 1979: After President Carter agreed to admit the Shah of Iran into the U.S. Embassy in Tehran and took 66 American diplomats hostage. Thirteen hostages were soon released, but the remaining 53 were held until their release on January 20, 1981.
- Grand Mosque Seizure, November 20, 1979: 200 Islamic terrorists seized the Grand Mosque in Mecca, Saudi Arabia, taking hundreds of pilgrims hostage. Saudi and French security forces retook the shrine after an intense battle in which some 250 people were killed and 600 wounded.
- U.S. Installation Bombing, August 31, 1981: The Red Army exploded a bomb at the U.S. Air Force Base at Ramstein, West Germany.
- Assassination of Egyptian President, October 6, 1981: Soldiers who were secretly members of the Takfir Wal-Hajira sect attacked and killed Egyptian President Anwar Sadat during a troop review.
- Murder of Missionaries, December 4, 1981: Three American nuns and one lay missionary were found murdered outside San

Salvador, El Salvador. They were believed to have been assassinated by a right-wing death squad.

- Assassination of Lebanese Prime Minister, September 14, 1982: Premier Bashir Gemayel was assassinated by a car bomb parked outside his party's Beirut headquarters.
- Bombing of U.S. Embassy in Beirut, April 18, 1983: Sixty-three people, including the CIA's Middle East director, were killed, and 120 were injured in a 400-pound suicide truck-bomb attack on the U.S. Embassy in Beirut, Lebanon. The Islamic Jihad claimed responsibility.
- Naval Officer Assassinated in El Salvador, May 25, 1983: A U.S. Navy officer was assassinated by the Farabundo Marti National Liberation Front.
- Bombing of Marine Barracks, Beirut, October 23, 1983: Simultaneous suicide truck-bomb attacks were made on American and French compounds in Beirut, Lebanon. A 12,000-pound bomb destroyed the U.S. compound, killing 242 Americans, while 58 French troops were killed when a 400-pound device destroyed a French base. Islamic Jihad claimed responsibility.
- Naval Officer Assassinated in Greece, November 15, 1983: A U.S. Navy Officer was shot by the November 17 terrorists group in Athens, Greece, while his car was stopped at a traffic light.
- Kidnapping of Embassy Official, March 16, 1984: The Islamic Jihad kidnapped and later murdered Political Officer William Buckley in Beirut, Lebanon. Other U.S. citizens not connected to the U.S. Government were seized over a succeeding 2-year period.
- Hizballah Restaurant Bombing, April 12, 1984: Eighteen U.S. servicemen were killed, and 83 people were injured in a bomb attack on a restaurant near a U.S. Air Force Base in Torrejon, Sapin. Responsibilities was claimed by Hizballah.

- Golden Temple Seizure, June 5, 1984: Sikh terrorists seized the Golden Temple in Amritsar, India. One hundred people died when Indian security forces retook the Sikh holy shrine.
- Assassination of Prime Minister Gandhi, October 31, 1984: The Indian premier was shot to death by members of her security force.
- Kidnapping of U.S. Officials in Mexico, February 7, 1985: Under the orders of narcotrafficker Rafael Cero Quintero, Drug Enforcement Administration agent Enrique Camarena Salazar and his pilot were kidnapped, tortured, and executed.
- TWA Hijacking, June 14, 1985: A Trans-World Airlines flight was hijacked en route to Rome from Athens by two Lebanese Hizballah terrorists are forced to fly to Beirut. The eight-crew members and 145 passengers were held for 17 days, during which one American hostage, a U.S. Navy sailor, was murdered. After being flown twice to Algiers, the aircraft was returned to Beirut after Israel released 435 Lebanese and Palestinian prisoners.
- Air India Bombing, June 23, 1985: A bomb destroyed and Air India Boeing 747 over the Atlantic, killing all 329 people abroad. Both Sikh and Kashmiri terrorists were blamed for the attack. Two cargo handlers were killed at Tokyo airport, Japan, when another Sikh bomb exploded in an Air Canada aircraft enroute to India.
- Soviet Diplomats Kidnapped, September 30, 1985: In Beirut, Lebanon, Sunni terrorists kidnapped four Soviet diplomats. One was killed, but three were later released.
- Achille Lauro Hijacking, October 7, 1985: Four Palestinian Liberation front terrorists seized the Italian cruise liner in the eastern Mediterranean Sea, taking more than 700 hostages. One U.S. passenger was murdered before the Egyptian Government offered the terrorists safe heaven in return for the hostage' freedom.

- Egyptian Airliner Hijacking, November 23, 1985: An Egypt Air airplane bound from Athens to Malta and carrying several U.S. citizens was hijacked by the Abu Nidal Group.
- Aircraft Bombing in Greece, March 30, 1986: A Palestinian splinter group detonated a bomb as TWA Flight 840 approached Athens Airport, killing four U.S. citizens.
- Berlin Discoteque Bombing, April 5, 1986: Two U.S. soldiers were killed, and 79 American servicemen were injured in a Libyan bomb attack on a nightclub in West Berlin, West Germany. In retaliation, U.S. military jets bombed targets in and around Tripoli and Benghazi.
- Bus Attack, April 24, 1987: Sixteen U.S. servicemen riding in a Greek Air Force bus near Athens were injured in an apparent bombing attack, carried out by the revolutionary organization known as 17 November.
- Kidnapping of William Higgins, February 17, 1988: U.S. Marine Corps Lt. Col. W. Higgins was kidnapped and murdered by the Iranian-backed Hizballah group while serving with the United Nations Truce Supervisory Organization (UNTSO) in southern Lebanon.
- Naples USO Attack, April 14, 1988: The Organization of Jihad Brigades exploded a car bomb outside a USO Club in Naples, Italy, killing one U.S. sailor.
- Attack on U.S. Diplomat in Greece, June 28, 1988: The Defense Attaché of the U.S. Embassy in Greece was killed when a car bomb was detonated outside his home in Athens.
- PanAm 103 Bombing, December 21, 1988: Pan American Airlines Flight 103 was blown up over Lockerbie, Scotland, by a bomb believed t have been placed on the aircraft in Frankfurt, West Germany, by Libyan terrorists. All 259 people on board were killed.
- Assassination of U.S. Army Officer, April 21, 1989: The New People's Army (NPA) assassinated Col. James Rowe in Manila.

The NPA also assassinated two U.S. government defense contractors in September.

- U.S. Embassy Bombed in Peru, January 15, 1990: The Tupac Amaru Revolutionary Movement bombed the U.S. Embassy in Lima, Peru.
- U.S. Soldiers Assassinated in the Philippines, May 13, 1990: The New People's Army (NPA) killed two U.S. Air Force personnel near Clark Air Force Base in the Philippines.
- Kidnapping of U.S. Businessmen in the Philippines, January 17-212, 1992: A senior official of the corporation Philippine Geothermal was kidnapped in Manila by the red Scorpion Group, and two U.S. businessmen were seized independently by the National Liberation Army and the by Revolutionary Armed Forces of Colombia (FARC).
- World Trade center Bombing, February 26, 1993: The World Trade Center in New York was badly damaged when a car bomb planted by Islamic terrorists explodes in an underground garage. The bomb left six people dead and 1,000 injured. The men carrying out the attack were followers of Umar Abd al-Rehman, an Egyptian cleric who preached in the New York City area.
- Attempted Assassination of President Bush by Iraqi Agents, April 14, 1993: The Iraqi intelligence service attempted to assassinate former U.S. President George Bush during a visit to Kuwait. In retaliation, the U.S. launched a cruise missile attack 2 months later on the Iraqi capital Baghdad.
- Hebron Massacre, February 25, 1994: Jewish right-wing extremists and U.S. citizen Baruch Goldstein machine-gunned Moslem worshippers at a mosque in West Bank town of Hebron, killing 29 and wounding about 150.
- Attack on U.S. Diplomats in Pakistan, March 8, 1995: Two unidentified gunmen killed two U.S. diplomats and wounded a third in Karachi, Pakistan.

- Tokyo Subway Station Attack, March 20, 1995: Twelve persons were killed, and 5,700 were injured in a Sarin nerve gas attack on a crowded subway station in the center of Tokyo, Japan. A similar attack occurred nearly simultaneously in the Yokohama subway system. The Aum Shinri-Kyu cult was blamed for the attacks.
- Bombing of the Federal Building in Oklahoma City, April 19, 1995: Right-wing extremists Timothy McVeigh and Terry Nichols destroyed the Federal Building in Oklahoma City with a massive tuck bomb that killed 166 and injured hundreds more in what was up to then the largest terrorist attack on American soil.
- Kashmiri Hostage-taking, July 4, 1995: In Indian, six foreigners, including two U.S. citizens, were taken hostage by Al-Faran, a Kashmiri separatist group. One non-U.S. hostage was later found beheaded.
- Jerusalem Bus Attack, August 21, 1995: Hamas claimed responsibility for the detonation of a bomb that killed six and injured over 100 persons, including several U.S. citizens.
- Attack on U.S. Embassy in Moscow, September 13, 1995: A rocket-propelled grenade was fired through the window of the U.S. Embassy in Moscow, ostensibly in retaliation for U.S. strikes on Serb positions in Bosnia.
- Saudi Military Installation Attack, November 13, 1995: The Islamic Movement of Change planted a bomb in a Riyadh Military compound that killed one U.S. citizen, several foreign national employees of the U.S. Government, and more than 40 others.
- Egyptian Embassy Attack, November 19, 1995: A suicide bomber drove a vehicle into the Egyptian Embassy compound in Islamabad, Pakistan, killing at least 16 and injuring 60 persons. Three militant Islamic groups claimed responsibility.
- Tamil Tigers Attack, January 31, 1996: Members of the

Liberation Tigers of Tamil Eelam (LTTE) rammed an explosives-laden truck into the Central Bank in the heart of downtown Colombo, Sri Lanka, killing 90 civilians and injuring more than 1,400 others, including two U.S. citizens.

- Athens Embassy Attack, February 15, 1996: Unidentified assailants fired a rocket at the U.S. embassy compound in Athens, causing minor damage to three diplomatic vehicles and some surrounding building. Circumstances of the attack suggested it was an operation carried out by the 17 November group.
- Hamas Bus Attack, February 26, 1996: In Jerusalem, a suicide bomber blew up a bus, killing 26 persons, including three U.S. citizens, and injuring some 80 persons, including three other US citizens.
- Dizengoff Center Bombing, March 4, 1996: Hamas and the Palestine Islamic Jihad (PIJ) both claimed responsibility for a bombing outside of Tel Aviv's largest shopping mall that killed 20 persons and injured 75 others, including two U.S.citizens.
- West Bank Attack, May 13, 1996: Arab gunmen opened fire on a bus and a group of Yeshiva students near the Bet El settlement, killing a dual U.S.- Israeli citizen and wounding three Israelis. No one claimed responsibility for the attack, but Hamas was suspected.
- Khobar Towers Bombing, June 25, 1996: A fuel truck carrying a bomb exploded outside the U.S. military's Khobar Towers housing facility in Dhahran, killing 19 U.S. military personnel and wounding 515 persons, including 240 U.S. personnel. Several groups claimed responsibility for the attack.
- Egyptian Letter Bombs, January 2-13, 1997: A series of letter bombs with Alexandria, Egypt, postmarks were discovered at Al-Hayat newspaper bureaus in Washington, New York City, London, and Riyadh, Saudi Arabia. Three similar devices, also postmarked in Egypt, were found at a prison facility in

Leavenworth, Kansas. Bomb disposal experts defused all the devices, but one detonated at the Al-Hayat office in London, injuring two security guards and causing minor damage.

- Tajik Hostage Abductions, February 4-17, 1997: Near Komsomolabad, Tajikistan, a paramilitary group led by Bakhrom Sodirov abducted four United Nations military observes. The victims included two Swiss, one Austrian, one Ukrainian, and their Tajik interpreter. The kidnappers demanded safe passage for their supporters from Afghanistan to Tajikistan. In four separate incidents occurring between Dushanbe and Garm, Bakhrom Sodirov and his group kidnapped two International Committee for the Red Cross members, four Russian journalists and their Tajik driver, four UNHCR members, and the Tajik Security Minister, Saidamir Zukhurov.
- Empire State Building Sniper Attack, February 23, 1997: A Palestinian gunman opened fire in tourists at an observation deck atop the Empire State Building in New York City, killing a Danish national and wounding visitors from the United States, Argentina, Switzerland, and France before turning the gun on himself. A handwritten note carried by the gunman claimed this was a punishment attack against the "enemies of Palestine."
- Murder of U.S. Businessmen in Pakistan, November 12, 1997: Two unidentified gunmen shot to death four U.S. auditors from Union Texas Petroleum Corporation and their Pakistani driver after they drove away from the Sheraton Hotel in Karachi. The Islami Inqilabi Council, or Islamic Revolutionary Council, claimed responsibility in a call to the U.S. consulate in Karachi. In a letter to Pakistani newspaper, the Aimal Khufia Action Committee also claimed responsibility.
- Tourist Killings in Egypt, November 17, 1997: Al-Gama' at al-Islamiyya (IG) gunmen shot and killed 58 tourists and four Egyptians and wounded 26 others at the Hatshepsut Temple in

the Valley of the Kings near Luxor. Thirty-four Swiss, eight Japanese, five Germans, four Britons, one French, one Colombian, a dual Bulgarian/ British citizen, and four unidentified persons were among the dead. Twelve Swiss, two Japanese, one French, and nine Egyptians were among the wounded.

- Somali Hostage-takings, April 15, 1998: A bomb exploded at the rear entrance of the U.S> embassy in Nairobi, Kenya, killing 12 U.S. citizens, 32 Foreign Service Nationals (FSNs), and 247 Kenyan citizens. About 5,000 Kenyans, six U.S. citizens, and 13 FSNs were injured. The U.S. embassy building sustained extensive structural damage. Almost simultaneously, a bomb detonated outside the U.S. embassy in Dar es Salaam, Tanzania, killing seven FSNs and three Tanzanian citizens, and injuring one U.S> citizen and 76 Tanzanians. The explosion cause major structural damage to the U.S. embassy facility. The U.S. Government held Usama Bin Ladin responsible.
- Colombian Pipeline Bombing, October 18, 1998: A National Liberation Army (ELN) planted bomb exploded on the Ocensa pipeline in Antioquia Department, killing Approximately 71 persons an injuring at least 100 others. The pipeline is jointly owned by the Colombia State Oil Company Ecopetrol and a consortium, including U.S., French, British, and Canadian companies.
- FARC Kidnappings, February 25, 1999: FARC kidnapped three U.S. citizens working for the Hawali-based Pacific Cultural Conservancy International. On March 4, the bodies of the three victims were found in Venezuela.
- Hutu Abductions, March 1, 1999: 150 armed Hutu rebels attacked three tourists camps in Uganda, killed four Ugandans, and abducted three U.S. citizens, six Britons, three New Zealanders, two Danish citizens, one Australian, and one Canadian national. Two of the U.S. citizens and six of the other hostages were subsequently killed by their abductors.

- Indian Airlines Airbus Hijacking, December 24, 1999: Five militants hijacked a flight bound from Katmandu to New Delhi carrying 189 people. The plane and its passengers were released unharmed on December 31.
- Car Bombing in Spain, January 27, 2000: Police officials reported unidentified individuals set fire to a Citroen car dealership in Iturreta, causing extensive damage to the building and destroying 12 vehicles. The attack bore the hallmark of the Basque Fatherland and Liberty (ETA).
- Kidnapping in Kyrgyzstan, August 12, 2000: In the Kara-Su Valley, the Islamic Movement of Uzbekistan took four U.S. citizens hostage. The Americans escaped on August 12.
- Church Bombing in Tajikistan, October 1, 2000: Unidentified militants detonated two bombs in a Christian church in Dushanbe, killing seven persons and injuring 70 others. The church was founded by a Korean-born U.S. citizen, and most of those killed and wounded were Korean. No one claimed responsibility.
- Attack on U.S.S. Cole, October 12, 2000: In Aden, Yemen, a small dingy carrying explosives rammed the destroyed U.S.S. Cole, killing 17 sailors and injuring 39 others. Supporters of Usama Bin Ladin were suspected.
- Manila Bombing, December 30, 2000: A bomb exploded in a plaza across the street from the U.S. embassy in Manila, injuring nine persons. The Moro Islamic Liberation Front was likely responsible.
- Srinagar Airport Attack, January 17, 2001: In India, six members of the Lashkar-e-Tayyba militant group were killed when they attempted to seize a local airport.
- Tel-Aviv Nightclub Bombing, June 1, 2001: Hamas claimed responsibility for the bombing of a popular Israeli nightclub that caused over 140 casualties.
- Hamas Restaurant Bombing, August 9, 2001: A Hamas-planted bomb detonated inn a Jeruselum pizza restaurant, killing 15 people and wounding more than 90.

- Terrorist Attacks on U.S. Homeland, September 11, 2001: Two hijacked airliners crashed into the twin towers of the World Trade Center. Soon thereafter, the Pentagon was struck by a third hijacked plane. A fourth hijacked Plane, suspected to be bound for a high-profile target in Washington, crashed into a field in southern Pennsylvania. More than 5,000 U.S. citizens and other nationals were killed as a result of these acts. President Bush and Cabinet officials indicated that Usama Bin Laden was the prime suspect and that they considered the United States in a state of war with international terrorism. In the aftermath of the attacks, the United State formed the Global Coalition Against Terrorism.

The terrorist attacks have not stopped after the elimination of al-Qaida-Taliban combine from Afghanistan, as the following terrorist attacks show:

- Attack on Legislative Assembly in Srinagar, 01 October 2001: By Lashkar-e-Taiba, killing at least 38 people and wounding many bystanders.
- Attack on Indian Parliament in New Delhi, 13, December 2001: Five terrorists and eight security personnel lost their lives.
- Murder of Daniel Pearl, Wall Street Journal reporter at Karachi in January 2002.
- Attack on a Church in Islamabad, 17 March 2002: Killing five people including two US citizens.
- Car bomb attack in Karachi, 8 May 2002: Outside a hotel, killing 14 people including 11 French technicians.

Most terrorist incidents are related to political, economic, religious issues and the policies of various countries. No act of terrorism can be considered justified, but while waging war on terrorism it is also necessary to look into the underlying causes and policies that foster or encourage terrorism.

V

# War on Terrorism: The State of Flux

*Maj. Gen. (Retd.) Afsir Karim*

*The Pentagon's strategy to launch a major campaign against Taliban and al-Qaeda strongholds in Afghanistan by regular troops is well underway. More than 2000 US troops, Apache helicopter gun ships and Black Hawk Helicopters from 82 Airborne Division are searching remote areas of Afghanistan to find and kill Taliban or al-Qaeda fighters. However, under a new strategy the responsibility of intensifying covert warfare against international terrorists groups is being placed on the US Special Operations Command (SOCOM).*

*The war on terrorism launched in Afghanistan destroyed the infrastructure of the Taliban-al-Qaeda combine but failed to seal their routes of escape. They are now scattered in various countries and are capable of attacking targets around the globe. The situation, therefore, is rather fluid and both the US and al-Qaeda are adopting new strategies to meet the challenges of the developing situations.*

## The New Strategies

### *The US Strategy*

So far SOCOM provided Special Forces to other command for covert operations: under a new arrangement SOCOM would now directly employ specially trained and equipped troops fro operations around the globe. The SOCOM, that has its headquarters in Tampa, has been ordered to prepare detailed plans and enunciate its new operational imperatives.[1]

[1] 'Major US Campaign in Afghanistan', <military.com> 2 October 2002.

SOCOM will focus on high-value targets, leaders and specialized terrorists groups leaving the task of dealing with peripheral al-Qaeda forces to Central Command. Special Forces have been deployed in Pakistan and they training counter-terrorist forces in Yemen and Georgia, while keeping a wary eye on al-Qaeda's terrorist activities in these countries. The US is also reported to have located an unspecified number of special troops in Djibouti, Somalia and Yemen. An amphibious assault ship, which carries attack helicopters and a few Harrier jump jets, has been located off the Horn of Africa.[2]

General Tommy R. Franks, the chief of the US Central Command would continue to oversee operations in Afghanistan, but the command of special operations units in Pakistan now passes on to Air Forces General Charles R. Holland under the new plan. Special Operations Forces of SOCOM will include units that are trained for clandestine operations snatch and kill missions, Navy SEALs, Army's secret Delta Force and some CIA paramilitary units.[3]

The new arrangement would allow Gen. Franks to focus attention on Iraq besides dealing with the on-going military operations in Afghanistan. Special Forces Command will concentrate mainly on Pakistan and Yemen two areas where a large number of al-Qaeda cadres are reported to be in hiding. Incidentally, many important al-Qaeda leaders, such as Ramzi Binalshibh, arrested in Pakistan and other parts of the world are Yemenis.

It seems that both in Pakistan and Yemen al-Qaeda leaders have been given sanctuary by tribal chieftains and fundamentalist groups.

Besides the clandestine operations Special Forces will be wagging a high-tech electronic war against al-Qaeda and the Taliban. Specialized aircraft such as Commando Solo 11 attached to the 193 Special Operations Wing of the Pennsylvania National Guard, will be

[2] Susan Schmidt and Thomas E. Ricks, *The Washington Post,* 'Terror war goes more ocvert', <www.msnbc.com> 18 September 2002.

[3] Ibid.

'shooting' electrons, not bullets. Till recently these missions were highly secret, but journalists have now been permitted on combat mission flights of Commando Solo 11. Solo 11 missions operate from vintage Hercules aircraft (C130) carrying 1000-10,000 watt transmitters. "They lower a conical device, or drogue" that beams greetings in Pushto, Dari and Arabic; folk songs targeting hidden al-Qaeda cadres and their sympathizers are also broadcast over Afghan skies, besides propaganda against bin Laden and Mullah Omar.[4] No one really knows whether these Psywar operations have the desired effect but information warfare proves a big 'force multiplier' in war against terrorism.

The war on terrorism launched by the US-led coalition forces managed to eject al-Qaeda out of its stronghold in Afghanistan, but al-Qaeda cadres who escape continue to remain firmly entrenched underground in Pakistan. Besides Pakistan-Afghanistan the terrorist cells have been established in at least 40 other countries. Al-Qaeda and some other terrorist groups closely associated with it are also well entrenched in Europe, Middle East and North Africa.[5] According to the UN report presented to the Security Council Committee monitoring sanctions, al-Qaeda has gone underground "to reposition its assets and resources, and to seek new recruits…[ it continues] to pose a significant international threat".[6]

Al-Qaeda is still carrying on its training activities in scattered bases, regrouping, changing its tactics and planning fresh attacks against the West. For the first time it is inducting women for soft hobs within the organization. Al-Qaeda cadres based in the Middle East and some other parts of Asia are also trying to hack US computer network in a systematic manner.[7]

[4] Bob Arnot, 'Electronic war in the Afghan skies', <msnbc.com>, 11 March 2002.

[5] Edith M. Lederer, 'UN: al-Qaeda able to strike again', <news.yahoo.com>, 30 August 2002.

[6] Ibid.

[7] Jack Kelley, 'Al-Qaeda fragmented, smaller, but still deadly', <www.usatoday.com>, 9 September 2002.

In Britain, Germany and Spain al-Qeada is looking for disgruntled Americans in mosques and other religious places to recruit them as suicide bombers. In Pakistan al-Qaeda operatives, posing as Saudi socio-religious workers, are propagating 'anti-Americanism' at religious institutions of Karachi, Quetta and Peshawar besides other smaller towns in remote areas.

"We are proving the *Kuffar* in Washington wrong, they said, al-Qaeda would be finished but we are emerging stronger and will hit America's shopping mall, stadium and kindergartens this is our promise", says Jamal Waheeb, a Saudi refugee official in Pakistan.[8]

At least 20,000 Muslim volunteers who were trained in al-Qaeda camps in Afghanistan, Pakistan and Sudan are still at large, dispersed around the world in small groups, and have merged with the local populations. The war against al-Qaeda has certainly not decimated its cadres but merely scattered them around the world.

"For every plot we discover and every terrorist cell we disrupt, there are dozens of others in the works", Donald Rumsfeld, USS Defence Secretary told the Armed Service Committee in July this year.[9]

Bin Laden is still untraced, he was last seen in November last year heading towards Pakistan across Afghanistan's White Mountain; lately, he had been threatening the US through Al-Jazeera channels. The status of bin Laden is a subject of speculation but his power has certainly waned after his defeat in Afghanistan and his capability of mounting a large-scale attack against the US in now doubtful. However, information obtained from Ramzi Binalshibh, indicates that al-Qaeda has definitely decentralized its structure, small terrorist groups have been given more autonomy, making them more dangerous. "The decentralization means the danger from this group is growing" according to US intelligence official-US Attorney General, John Ashcraft, while announcing a higher alert status,

[8] Ibid.
[9] Ibid.

stated, "widely dispersed, unsophisticated strikes by lower level al-Qaeda operatives are a danger."[10]

The new US *Defence Planning Guide for 2004-2009* issuded in May this year, has disclosed Pentagon's plans for introducing high technology fro taking action against the enemies. It has laid a greater emphasis on a high-tech force ready to strike without warning against a perceive threat. 'Cyber-warfare, precision strikes and enhanced anti-terror capabilities, unmanned air vehicles that could destroy a mobile rocket launcher 600 miles away in 15 minutes, will be the new push-button weapons'. Victoria Clark, Rumsfled's chief spokesperson said, "The Secretary has talked repeatedly about the need to be prepare for surprises the unknown unknowns."[11]

The plans published in *Times* reports describe first five-year projections and priorities as under:

- An anti-missile system to guard US territory from missiles, developed by potentially hostile countries such as North Korea.
- The concept of 'asymmetric threats' as in Afghanistan, by foreign elements incapable of doing real harm to the US military on a battlefield, but wiling to attack with unconventional weapons such as terror or crude weapons of mass destruction.
- Domestic security under new conditions in the aftermath of 11 September.

The document emphasizes on better methods of procuring intelligence about a developing crisis that merits military action on the part of the US.[12]

## AL-QAEDA'S OPERATIONAL IMPERATIVES

Al-Qaeda has regrouped with the Taliban, Islamic parties of Pakistan and militant groups operating in Kashmir, and these well-armed

[10] Bill Gertz, 'Terror cells at liberty to strike,' *The Washington Post*, <www.washingtontimes.com>, 19 September 2002.

[11] *The Associated Press*, Military Foresees High-Tech Force', <www.washingtontimes.com>, 13 July 2002.

[12] Ibid.

groups are waiting for an opportune moment to start new operations. Various terrorists incidents in Afghanistan and attacks on the American base areas indicate an al-Qaeda-Taliban tie-up in Afghanistan. Attempts to acquire missiles to shoot down American B-52 bombers show the advent of new tactical doctrines to fight the American forces. "Americans are proud of their control of the air, but they don't take care of the ground, now they [Americans] could lose both,"[13] observes Brigadier Ghulam Haider Chatak, chief of military intelligence in the eastern zone of Afghanistan, bordering Pakistan. This zone includes Kuna Laghman and Nanghar provinces.

According to Brigadier Chatak, these are dangerous times for the top leadership of the Afghan Government. Two Afghan cabinet ministers have already been assassinated and Hamid Karzai himself is under attack, as a recent attempt to assassinate him showed. The main objective of the assassinations of top leaders is to destabilize the transitional Afghan Government. In these game al-Qaeda and rogue (?) elements of Pakistan's ISI seem to be hand in glove.

The capture of two men who had packed their Toyota with 600 pounds of explosives indicated that the car was loaded with explosives in the Pakistani border town of Wana, an area known for al-Qaeda supporters who clashed with the Pakistan Army resulting in the death of 10 Pakistani soldiers. "he car was equipped with two remote control devices along with secondary detonation switches fixed inside the car. It was also packed with nearly a half-ton of C-4 explosives, liquid explosives and shrapnel they had put a lot of thought into it," says Afghan Intelligence Chief, Amrullah Saleh.[14]

About 40 American soldiers have been killed and more than 300 wounded since October 2001 when the US operations started in Afghanistan. Lately an American army helicopter was fired upon in southern Afghanistan. Colonel Roger King the US military

[13] Scott Baldauf, 'Al-Qaeda massing for new fight,' *The Christian Science Monitor',* <www.csmonitor.com>, 9 August 2002.

[14] Scott Badauf, Foiled plot shows al-Qaeda hand, 'The Christian Science Monitor', <www.csmon itor.com>, 2 August 2002.

spokesperson told reporters in Bagram airbase, "one American crewman was wounded in this engagement."[15]

Bin Laden's terrorist network is still intact, al-Qaeda extremists boast, "if America is after US- we are after them, we are nowhere, yet everywhere."

## SINO-US COOPERATION AGAINST TERROR

As a part of the global effort to combat terrorism China had accepted establishment of an FBI legal attaché in Beijing to investigate possible funding of international terrorist groups through Chinese banks. In return Washington gave its implicit support for suppressing of Uighur separatist activities in Xinjiang. China also passed new regulations to assert control over companies exporting missiles and related technology, so that these do not fall into the hands of terrorist groups. The Bush administration has now agreed to equate war on terrorist with global reach with the activities of Muslim separatist groups in Xinjiang. In August 2002 the US finally recognized the East Turkestan Islamic Party (ETIP) as a terrorist organization, which was connected with bin Laden's Islamic International Front for Jehad against the US and Israel. Certain analysts have, however, suggested that the belated recognition by the US of the terrorist groups operating in Zinjiang may be found in obtaining a favourable response from China for an American assault on Iraq.[16]

## US WAR ON IRAQ: AIMS PLUS

War against Iraq is probable. The war aims of the Americans have not yet become clear except for the persistent assertions that Saddam Hussein must be removed from power, dead or alive. Iraq's choices

[15] 'US Helicopter Shot at in Afghanistan, Crewman Hurt', <story.new.yahoo.com>, 5 October 2002.

[16] Chien-peng Chung, 'China's "War on Terror": September 11 and Uighur Separatism', <www.foreignaffairs.org>, 3 October 2002.

are limited and Saddam's aim is to avoid a war and if that is not possible to somehow survive.

In recent years Americans have many success stories to their credit. In Panama, Haiti, Bosnia, Kosovo and Afghanistan, the US has been able to impose its will with minimum losses. Iraq, however, may not prove an easy target for the US to impose its will. Destructions of Iraqi armed forces and eliminations of its leaders may pose tough challenges to the US forces. Replacement of the present leadership with pro-American elements who can ensure Iraq's territorial integrity and prevent chaos may pose great difficulties. If the Iraqi national command authority is eliminated chaos may prevail and WMD (if they are there) may be passed on to the al-Qaeda before their fall. The reactions of the Islamic world may adversely affect US interests in the Middle East in the long run.

To bring the war against Iraq to a successful culmination the US would have to:

- Replace Saddam Hussein and his regime with a pro-US authority.
- Ensure Iraq's territorial integrity so that the new regime can cope with Iranian, al-Qaeda and Kurdish challenges.
- Ensure total destruction of all weapons of mass destruction.
- Prevent high casualties among US troops especially when fighting in key Iraqi towns and other built-up areas.

On the face of it, achieving the long-term political and military aims seems an extremely formidable task for the US-led forces.[17]

In any case a war waged against Iraq at this juncture will certainly draw away attention from the war on terrorism in Afghanistan. It will be a diversion, which may be greatly welcomed by al-Qaeda and its associates operating in the Afghanistan-Pakistan belt.

[17] 'Iraq War plans I: Aims, Perceptions and Issues', <www.stratfor.com>, 9 September 2002.

## SUMMATION

The US ambassador to Afghanistan, Robert Finn told *Reuters* that the war was not over, "military operations are continuing, especially in the eastern part of the country and they will continue our operations against al-Qaeda and the Taliban to ensure that they cannot use Afghanistan as a base of operations again."[18]

Lieutenant General Dan McNeill, the commanding US general in Afghanistan believes that hundreds of al-Qaeda fighters were still active in Afghanistan; they can be dangerous though scattered all over the country. They, however, do not seem to be in a position to launch large-scale operations.[19]

Coalition forces may have to stay on until the Afghan Army is trained and equipped to ensure security. The Foreign Minister of Afghanistan, Abdullah Abdullah, said in a news conference recently that formation of a national army could take three to five years.[20]

The war in Afghanistan has reached a plateau and questions are now being asked about the future course of US-led operations. The US paper on National Security lays down the parameters for was against terrorism in precise terms. Some of these are:

- The United States of America is fighting a war against terrorists of global reach. The enemy is not a single political regime or person or religion or ideology. They enemy is terrorism-premeditated, politically motivated, violence perpetrated against innocents.
- In many regions, legitimate grievances prevent the emergency of a lasting peace. Such grievances deserve to be, and must be addressed within a political process. But no cause justifies terror. The United States will make no concessions to terrorist demands an strike no deals with them. We make no distinction

[18] Ahmed Sear, 'One year on, US says Afghan war not over', <story.news.yahoo.com>, 7 October 2002.

[19] Ibid.

[20] Ibid.

between terrorists and those who knowingly harbor or provide aid to them.

- The struggle against global terrorism is different from any other war in our history. It will be fought on many fronts against a particularly elusive elusive over an extended period of time. Progress will come through the persistent accumulation of success some seen, some unseen.
- Today our enemies have seen the results of what civilized nations can, and will, do against regimes that harbor, support, and use terrorism to achieve their political goals. Afghanistan has been liberated; coalition forces continue to hunt down the Taliban and al-Qaeda. But it is not only this battlefield on which we will engage terrorists. Thousands of trained terrorists remain at large with cells in North America, South America, Europe, Africa, the Middle East, and across Asia.
- Our priority will be first to disrupt and destroy terrorist organizations of global reach and attack their leadership; command, control, and communications; material support; and finances. This will have a disabling effect upon the terrorist' ability to plan and operate.

The bomb blasts at Bali (Indonesia), which killed at least 180 innocent people and wounded hundreds of others; the blowing up of the French tanker off eastern Yemen earlier, are the signs of resumption of al-Qaeda's counter-offensive at the global level.

# VI

# Terrorism in South Asia

*Ramtanu Maitra*

*Terrorism in South Asia began to rear its head with the emergence of independence nations in the region. These newly independent nations were breaking out of centuries-old colonial bondage. The process of achieving independence itself was often wrought with violence.*

*The departing British colonial rulers partitioned the Indian subcontinent in 1947. They created two nations on the basis of religion. Pakistan, with its two wings, West and East, was born amidst bloodshed. Although India declared itself a secular nation with socialistic ideals, the scars of the violent partition did not go away. The mass migration of the people that followed, particularly from Pakistan to India, uprooted them from their ancestral homes and land. And turned them into hapless refugees in what was once their country. This brutal an arbitrary process kept a large section of the population bitter and aggrieved. Neither India's nor Pakistan's weak economies permitted these refugees to get back what they had lost materially. They were not even accommodated adequately.*

*A number of Hindu-Muslim and Sikh-Muslim riots followed the partition throughout the subcontinent. This furthered the cause of violent activities in later days, particularly in northern and western India.*

*Pakistan, on the other hand, opted for ideological cleansing by declaring itself an Islamic state. The declaration automatically lowered the status of non-Muslim citizens. Moreover, this also provided an additional opportunity to criminal elements within*

*Pakistan to force the property-owning Hindus and Sikhs out of Pakistan and to seize their land and properties.*

*In India, particularly in the northeastern part of the country bordering East Pakistan, Nepal, Sikkim (Sikkim was an independent kingdom before it joined the Republic of India in 1975), Bhutan, China and Burma (now Myanmar), a large number of ethnic and tribal groups existed that were never incorporated into British India. During the British period, Christian missionaries actively proselytized among these tribal groups. The impact of the Christian missionaries and indirect support lent from colonial Britain turned these tribal and ethnic groups rabidly anti-India. The entire northeast India went up in flames soon after the Sino-India border clash occurred in 1962, and it soon became evident that these tribal groups were seeking help from the Chinese communists across the border.*

*At the time, China was also driven by its zeal to export communism in the neighbourhood, particularly to India. The Negas, in particular, received formal training in arms from the Chinese in the late 1960s. in the aftermath of the Pakistan-China rapprochement, highlighted by Pakistani Prime Minister Zulfikar Ali Bhutto's brokering on behalf of the United States in the early 1970s, Nagas began to travel from China to Pakistan for further military training and to build an anti-India network. These northeastern tribes and groups, at least some of them, soon turned into hardcore terrorists, battling Indian Army personnel and the Assam Police in a terrain favourable to them and amidst a population supportive of them.*

## COLONIAL POLICIES AND THE COLD WAR

It is evident from the past history of the Indian subcontinent that the colonial powers (in case of South Asia, it was primarily Britain) had instigated violence within the population in order to hold on to power. They used one group against the other with the objective of preventing a political coalition between the majority and the minority groups- ethnic and religious-within the country. Such a political coalition, if formed, London feared, would work towards achieving independence through concerted efforts. The sole objective of a such a combined force would be to drive out the colonial power lock, stock and barrel. It meant that Britain, having ruled the subcontinent for almost two hundreds years, would have to leave its former colonies bereft of its ability to manipulate the newly independent nations in future. As a countermeasure, the British colonial rulers had systematically set up privileged classes wherever they ruled. The privileged groups were usually the ethnic minorities who were instilled with fear by the colonial rulers that the departure of the British from their land would inevitably lead to the majority group gaining absolute power. The consequences of such a transfer of power would mean elimination of the minority groups from all-powerful institutions by the majority group with immediate effect, the minority groups were warned. This fear instilled in some of the minority groups by the British intelligence, created an environment for recruiting terrorists functioning under the umbrella of the British Raj. As a result, a large number of terrorists, some of whom worked as subversive elements on behalf of the ruling colonial power, were inherited by the newly independent nations in the Indian subcontinent. Some of these British intelligence-created terrorists included hardline communist, a gamut of chauvinistic religious and ethnic groups.

## TIME BOMBS LEFT BEHIND

British intelligence did not leave behind only the predisposition to foment separatist and terrorist operations throughout the South Asia region; it also left behind its capabilities. All of the major conflicts in the region are explosions along the fault lines deliberately left as the legacy of direct British colonial rules:

- The Kashmir dispute arose out of the British-instigated 1947 partitioning of the Indian subcontinent to form the Muslim-majority Pakistan. The same manoeuver also created the *mohajirs*- the Indian Muslims who migrated to Pakistan at the time of partition, and thus laid the basis for the ongoing conflicts in Karachi, and the creation of the Mohajir Qaum Movement. Mohajir Qaumi Movement (MQM), which later was re-named, Muttahida Qaumi Movement, was also greatly helped by Pakistan's military ruler President General Zia ul-Haq, who had armed the MQM in the early 1980s to confront their traditional adversary, the Sindhi nationalists, and the Pakistan People's Party, which from its inception in the late 1960s, enjoyed a strong base in Sindh.

- In the southern part, the "Tamil problem" was foisted on Buddhist and Christian Sri Lanka. The British used the Tamil minority group as a privileged class and handpicked Tamils during the Raj days to dominate the colonial bureaucracy. At the time of independence of Sri Lanka, the British revived the Buddhist chauvinists who demanded an enemy, and to the Sinhalas the enemy became the Tamils, and not the British. Thus, the Liberation Tigers of Tamil Eelam (LTTE, or Tamil Tigers) were the product of a conflict, which originated in the British colonial policies.
- In northeast India, the cauldron of contending ethnic entities-all mixed up together in the drugs-for-arms trafficking-stems directly from the British division of Bengal (first in 1905, which got annulled, and then, again, in 1947) which led finally to the creation of Bangladesh, and a strict colonial policy of apartheid between 'tribal' and 'non-tribal'.

The partition, and what had preceded the partition, gave birth to widescale violence, which erupted from time to time throughout the subcontinent, particularly in northern and eastern India and throughout Pakistan. In addition to the scars of partitioning subcontinent on the basis of religion, the British left behind about 550 princely states that they had never formally incorporated into the Raj. These princely states were told to decide their own fate. The options were given to them to either join India, or Pakistan, or to remain independent.

Although most of the princely states opted quickly and joined either India or Pakistan, the state of Jammu and Kashmir did not. Subsequent history shows that Pakistani regulars, dressed as tribesmen, invaded the state in the fall of 1947. The Kashmir ruler, Maharaja Hari Singh, at that point opted pell-mell to join India. However, the Pakistani Army did not move out of the state of Jammu and Kashmir and the state's future remained undecided with India holding almost 65 per cent of the land. Since then, militancy has grown in the state; and in the late 1980s Pakistan threw its wholehearted support behind the Kashmiri militants supplying them with arms and money and moved mercenaries into the state from Afghanistan and Pakistan. As a result, the state of Jammu and Kashmir, the Indian-controlled part in particular, turned into a hotbed of terrorism.

While the fate of the state of Jammu and Kashmir remained undecided, the impact of the Cold War was felt around the subcontinent as early as the 1950s. The most negative impact of this development was the emergence of radical communism in China. Sino-Indian relations, however, remained on an even keel throughout the 1950s. Till then, Beijing was not particularly anti-India and was signaling that it could even join a non-aligned movement, spearheaded by India, Yugoslavia, Indonesia and Egypt. The breakdown of the Sino-Indian relations in the late 1950s, ostensibly over the non-demarcated borders all along the Himalayas, resulted in the border clash between China and India in the northeastern part of India. By 1962, Maoist China emerged as the most dangerous adversary of India. In the decade that followed, China actively pursued aiding and abetting various tribal and ethnic separatist groups that had emerged in northeastern India. What is of interest here is that these separatist movements were spawned by the unwillingness of various ethnic groups' to become a part of the Republic of India and their linkages to colonial Britain. The China factor in northeast India instigated a very high level of violence from time to time.

Finally, the British involvement in various secessionist movements, most of which had taken recourse to violent terrorist means, cannot be underestimated. At the time, within the British establishment there existed a lingering hope that some of the disgruntled groups within the subcontinent could be weaned out through political and covert support. The objective was to break up India.

Max Madden, a Member of Parliament for the Labour Party, perhaps best expressed this hope of London. Speaking on 2 June 1993 at a conference on Kashmir in Denmark, Madden demanded India's self-annihilation: "I've always wondered why in a world where we've seen the British Empire disintegrate, the Russian Empire disintegrate, why is it that alone of the great countries of the world, let's remember, by the end of this century, India will have the greatest population in the world- why it alone should be the Union of India and its present boundaries continue forever? I think there cannot be any immunity to India to the sort of pressures that we see in the rest of the world, and it might well be that the Constitution of India may be amended, there could be a new constitutional settlement in India.... We all hear from Indians that they have the largest democracy in the world; many of us questions that very fundamentally".

Madden suggested that the United Nations should the transition phase for Kashmir's 'independence', a role that could be extended to the entire region, "The United Nations has a legal and moral responsibility and obligation to secure the self-determination for the people of Kashmir. It may require a period of UN administration of Kashmir. So be it. And it may involve the whole region. So be it".

## The Impact of the Cold War on Northeast India

In the late 1960s, the Naxalites, who were identified with a peasant uprising in the late 1960s in a small village called Naxalbari in West Bengal, were openly promoting the leadership of the Chinese chairman Mao Dze Dong and turned themselves into an underground group, whose objective was to annihilate the moneyed landowners. Violence erupted in urban as well as in rural areas in West Bengal and Andhra Pradesh, where these groups were active. The first wave of these Naxalites consisted mostly of educated youth. Following a brutal suppression of these Naxalites by the security forces in West Bengal, the Naxalites movement reappeared in an entirely different form among the landless in Bihar and Andhra Pradesh. These Naxalites are still very active in these two states and indulge in violent acts from time to time.

Although the communist movement in northeast India, particularly amongst the ethnic and tribal groups, never presented a threat to New Delhi, a hostile China nurtured some of these terrorist groups in northeast India. While both the Soviet Union and the West- the United States in particular-had provided finances and arms covertly to some of these groups in the 1960s and 1970s, it was the ideological impact of the Chinese Communists, and the fervour of Beijing to export their form of Communism, which helped terrorism to grow in South Asia. Arms training rendered by Beijing to various northeast Indian ethnic separatist groups and Beijing's open vocal support in favour of the violent Naxatile movement in parts of Indian were instrumental in furthering these groups' terrorist activities. The Soviet Union, although active in India to build up its assets through financial and educational support within the existing democratic framework, on the other hand, was more active in supporting separatist movements in the Pakistani province of Balochistan, bordering Afghanistan. The Soviet Union was interested in weakening Pakistan, which had joined a military alliance with the United States and had allowed setting up of American bases for the surveillance of the Soviet Union and other suspected covert operations against Soviet assets within Pakistan and outside.

Financed by outside powers, some of the domestic movements became violent in the later years. Most notable among such movements were the Naga separatist movement in northeast India, the independence movement in Balochistan and the separatist movement in Jammu and Kashmir. All these three movements drew their support from the expatriates based in Britain, Canada and the United States, and a few other countries in Europe and Asia.

## THE AFGHAN-PAKISTAN CAULDRON

The confrontation of the two Cold War adversaries- the Soviet Union and the West- opposing each other in Afghanistan led to the rise of separatist movements in Balochistan and the North West Frontier Province (NWFP), both bordering Afghanistan. There were clear indications that the Soviets were also actively trying to stoke rebellion by both the Balochis and the Pushtuns in the North West Frontier Province against the Pakistani establishment. The Baloshis picked up arms following Pakistani Prime Minister Zulfikar Ali Bhutto's use of the Pakistani Air Force to bomb Balochistan to quell the secessionist rebellion. However, Balochi terrorism refused to die down and erupted from time to time throughout the 1980s, targeting the Pakistani Army.

The Islamic revolution in Iran in the late 1970s, which stirred up Islamic fervour in most of the Muslim world, and the subsequent identification of Islamic fundamentalism as a bulwark against the Soviet threat by a group of Western ideologues, such as British academic Bernard Lewis and US President Jimmy Carter's National Council chief Zbigniew Brzezinski, set the stage for promotion of terrorism in the Islamic nations, particularly in Afghanistan and Pakistan.

The invasion of Afghanistan by the Soviet Army in 1979 began a new phase in terrorist activities in South Asia. The West came out with all possible help to mobilize the Afghan mujahideen (holy warriors) to wage a Jehad against the Godless Bolsheviks. Islamic zeal was encouraged and the narcotics cartel began to pump in money to help the battling mujahideen. For years, the Western intelligence agencies, MI6 and the CIA in particular, with the help of the Pakistani Inter-Services Intelligence (ISI) and Pakistani

President, General Zia ul-Haq, developed one fighting group after another to hurt the Soviets. It was also the period during which the now-infamous Osama bin Laden was patronized by the United States, and a gamut of Pakistani terrorist groups were allowed to form and operate in and around Afghanistan. Arab jails were evacuated of the hardened criminals, who were brought into Afghanistan to battle in favour of upholding freedom and democracy against the invading Soviet Army.

While the West was keen in getting Pakistan's help to give its chief adversary, the Soviet Union, a bloody nose, Pakistani President, General Zia ul-Haq, saw in this an opportunity to strengthen his army and unleash a terrorist operation in the Indian-controlled part of Kashmir, with the objective of avenging Pakistan's 1971 military debacle in what was earlier East Pakistan and later Bangladesh, India played a crucial role in cutting down Pakistan's size by half by providing military help to the Bangladeshis seeking independence.

## PAKISTAN'S KASHMIR GAMBIT

General Zia ul-Haq, who assumed power through a coup deposing and eventually hanging Pakistani premier Zulfikar Ali Bhutto in 1977, fashioned his revenge against India. In the Indian Punjab, an underground movement for a Sikh homeland, Khalistan, emerged in the late 1970s. The movement got its momentum with funds that came in from outside India, particularly from the Cold Warriors in Britain, Canada and the United States. Pakistan and the Pakistani ISI acted as the host to these terrorists, and Pakistan provided shelter as well as the staging area for the Khalistani terrorists to carry out activities across the border, inside the Indian Punjab and beyond. The movement peaked in the mid-1980s and petered out soon after. Following the demise of the Khalistani movement, Pakistan unleashed an operation to 'liberate' the Kashmir Valley from the Indians.

The withdrawal of the Soviet Army in 1989 from Afghanistan also freed up manpower to carry out operations in Kashmir. Meanwhile, another militant movement began to take shape in the south of the region in Sri Lanka. In 1983, a violent riot broke out in Colombo, Sri Lanka. The rampaging Sinhalas killed Tamils and burnt down their properties and homes. The Sri Lankan government under President Junius Jayewardene did little to protect the Tamil minority. The riot was the fallout of a dispute between the Sinhalas and the Tamil minority that originated in the 1950s.

The passage of the Official Language Act in 1957 precipitated a current of antagonism between the Tamils and the Sinhalas. The Sri Lankan Tamils, represented by the Federal Party, launched a *satyagraha* (non-violent protest) that resulted in a pact between President S.V.R.D. Bandaranaike and the Tamil leader, S.J.V. Chelvanayakam. The agreement provided a wide measure of Tamil autonomy in the northern and eastern provinces. It also provided for the use of the Tamil language in administrative matters. The Bandaranaike-Chelvanayakam Pact also promised 'early consideration' for Indian "plantation" Tamils on the question of Sri Lankan citizenship. But the Buddhist clergy did not carry out the pact because of a peaceful protest. The clergy, backed by the United National Party (UNP), denounced the pact as a 'betrayal of the Sinhala-Buddhist People'. The first Sinhala-Tamil riot took place soon after in 1958 and was the forerunner of the Tamil militancy that spread in the 1980s.

The 1983 riot virtually signaled the end of the Tamil's trust in attaining peace through negotiations with the Sinhala. Tamil militants began to converge under a single flag, demanding a separate state within Sri Lanka, and the moderates were either killed off or condemned to take a back seat. Support also came from the Indian state of Tamil Nadu and, for a while, from Indian intelligence agencies as well. The militants, using a brutal internecine warfare, weeded out the moderates, and assembled others under the banner of the Liberation Tigers of Tamil Eelam (LTTE) seeking a separate nation. The LTTE, better known as the Tamil Tigers, unleashed a wave of terrorist acts inside Sri Lanka and India to press home their demands.

In the late 1980s, when the US and Pakistan-trained terrorists in Afghanistan, known as the *Afghansis,* were spreading all over Pakistan, the Indian-controlled part of Jammu and Kashmir and beyond, the LTTE remained the most well-organized terrorist group in the region. The LTTE had captured the lion's share of the drug trade; and they had established links with the Indian Naxalites operating in Andhra Pradesh and also with the militant tribal and ethnic groups operating in India's northeastern states. LTTE also became the chief arms carrier in the region. They organized the Sea Tigers, LTTE's naval arm that operates in the Andaman Sea and in the Bay of Bengal using fast boats to bring in arms from South East Asia and northeastern India, and drugs from the Golden Triangle area and Pakistan.

## Terrorism in Pakistan

By the mid-1980s, with all recognized Pakistani institutions, expect its military, in tatters; it had become evident that Pakistan had begun its downhill journey. Narcotics addiction, narco-money-related corruption, massive illiteracy and growing disparity between the haves and have-nots gave birth to two different forms of terrorism in Pakistan.

The first kind of terrorism was the one associated with orthodox Islam in the form of the Sunni Deobandi-Wahhabi brand of fundamentalism. President General Zia ul-Haq, an orthodox Muslim himself, began to institutionalize orthodox within the Pakistani polity to help build his own empire and distance Pakistan from the subcontinent. His target was not only the military, which he headed, but also to use orthodox to demolish the political forces, most of whom were unwilling to make religion their political ideology. President General Zia ul-Haq recruited Islamic zealots by the thousands to build his base within the military. Soon, through commissions an promotions, the Pakistan Army became a reservoir of orthodox Islamic zealots trained as military officers. The ISI, active in Afghan affairs in concert with the United States and Britain in particular, also found the Deobandi-Wahhabi variety an effective vehicle to indoctrinate the Pushtun mujahideen. Pakistan opened up madrasas by the scores and the Afghan Taliban was born in the mid-1990s in Pakistan.

Inside Pakistan, the Deobandi-Wahhabi variety of Islamic zealots formed their organization to eliminate those whom they considered heretics. The Shiites and the Qadianis were their targets. The Pakistan Army provided covert support to these Deobandi-Wahhabi groups that soon emerged as powerful terrorist groups operating virtually in the open. The only opposition that these groups encountered came from Iran, an established Shiite Islamic republic. Iran, head of the Shiite Muslims, would not allow the government-aided Sunni terrorists groups in Pakistan to murder Shiites. Tehran, as a retaliatory measure, began to fund the Shiites in Pakistan to band together and form their own militant groups- Tehrik-e-Jaffriya-e-Pakistan, for one-to defend themselves from the marauding Deobandi-Wahhabi Sunni zealots.

The second form of terrorism in Pakistan consisted of those afghan mercenaries, now abandoned by their native countries, and those Pakistani fundamentalist groups who had declared Jehad against India. Their objective was to liberate the Indian-controlled part of Kashmir. They drew support from the Pakistan Army. Their staging ground was inside Azad Kashmir (the Pakistani-held part of Kashmir) and their field of operation was the Indian-controlled part of Kashmir.

The collapse of the Soviet Union and a civil war breaking out in Afghanistan left these *Afghansis* high and dry. They became available for terrorist acts beyond Afghanistan. The *Afghansis* joined the Osama bin Laden-led al-Qaeda, a group that had emerged in Afghanistan, but had spread its tentacles into many Asian and African nations. Their objective was to operate against Russia, the Central Asian nations, India and those Western nations who were backing the Israelis against the Palestinians. The group remained under control of the Pakistani ISI in their terrorists' acts inside the

India-held part of Kashmir. The *Afghansis*, however, had begun to interact with other terrorist organization operating within South Asia, particularly the LTTE.

In essence, then, when one looks at the genesis and growth of terrorism in South Asia, one can see that it grew, metamorphosed and consolidated in phases. The first phase is the effect of colonial policies and the impact of the Cold War. The second phase is the growth of domestic movements. The third and present phase reflects the impact of the Soviet invasion of Afghanistan, collapse of the Soviet Union and the rise of a politically motivated militant Islam.

## THE AFGHANISTAN IMBROGLIO

### *Pakistani Involvement*

Since the beginning of the 1980s, after the Soviet Army had invaded Afghanistan in 1979 and the entire West had come rallying behind Pakistan to drive out the Red Army adopting all possible means, a potent weapon was unleashed in South Asia in the form of narcotics. As the narcotics consumption began to grow in the West and the international narcotics trafficking was taken over by a coalition of state-run international intelligence networks, some of the separatist movements gathered momentum. Over the next decade, the Golden Crescent region, encompassing the mountain valleys of Iran, Afghanistan, and Pakistan, emerged as one of the world's two biggest sources of opium for several years even surpassing the contiguous Golden Triangle. While some of the opium-producing areas of Afghanistan were unquestionably under the control of the Red Army, the majority of poppy fields were in areas like the Helmand Valley in southern Afghanistan that were in the hands of the Mujahideen, especially the Hezb-I-Islami of Gulbudddin Hekmatyar, which also controlled a string of heroin laboratories just across the Pakistani border at Koh-I-Soltan.

In Pakistan, a similar factional struggle over the dope business broke out in 1988, after President, General Zia ul-Haq, along with several top generals and the US ambassador, were killed in a plane crash. When Benezir Bhutto came in as prime minister, she launched a crackdown against the Pakistani Inter-Services Intelligence (ISI). General Fazle Huq, the commander of the North West Frontier Province, was arrested for covering up his own brother's drug trafficking. General Huq's personal pilot, Major Farooq Hamid, was arrested on heroin-trafficting charges. As early as 1983, Norwegian customs officials had arrested a Pakistani smuggling a large quantity of heroin. A follow-on investigation led to the indictment of Hamid Hasnain, the vice president of the Pakistan government's Habib Bank. Hasnain was the personnel account manager for President Zia. The drug crackdown, however, was short-lived. When General Zia's former finance minister, Ghulam Ishaq Khan, became President of Pakistan, many of the indictments were overtuned or never prosecuted. Ghulam Ishaq Khan serving as the president of the Bank of Credit and Commerce International (BCCI) had been General Zia's liaison to the BCCI Foundation; the "charity" through which drug money was laundered, and bribes were paid out.

The key to Afghan terrorism was narcotics and training of the criminals belonging to various Islamic nations with arms and indoctrinating them with militant Islam. While the narcotics were used to pay for the training of these mujahideen and buying their arms, the same was used to bring in more 'volunteers' to fight a Jehad against both the Soviet Union and also India in Kashmir. The Pakistani ISI officers imparted the training at the early stage. Later, in the late 1990s, Pakistani regulars also joined the ISI officers to train the Taliban militia to get control of Afghanistan.

*The Indoctrination*

Indoctrination in orthodox Islam was a key factor in spreading Afghan terrorism. Those who trained these mujahideen, and alter the Taliban in Pakistani madrasas, had created a fusion of two orthodox Islamic tenets – the beliefs of the Deobandi sect in India and the beliefs of the Wahhabi sec from Arabia. The Deobandi sect exists throughout the subcontinent, but Maulana Maududi, a cleric who died in 1972, had influenced Pakistani President, General Zia-ul-Haq, and it is the latter who was the mastermind behind this project. In the view of Maududi, nationalism is a Western idea that rested on non-Islamic concepts. His writings describe how to stem the flood of Western influences, claiming the superiority of Islam over non-Islamic ideas.

In 1941, in undivided India, Maududi created his own fundamentalist group, the Jamaat-e-Islami (the Islamic association). In his view, the best way to transform society was to create a small group of dedicated followers and capture political leadership. After partition in 1947, Maududi went over to Pakistan like scores of other Indian Muslims. There he sent preachers to the villages of the new state. Very soon the number of his supporters swelled and the Jamaat-e-Islami (JI) emerged as a genuine political party, which continued to develop and strengthen. His concept of an Islamic state was used in 1978 by General Zia ul-Haq to justify his coup against the elected government of Zulfikar Ali Bhutto. The General declared that he was a soldier of Islam, dedicated to creating an Islamic state in Pakistan based on Maududi's ideas.

The Wahhabi sect was founded by Muhammad ibn Abdul Wahab Ibn Suleiman al-Najdi (1111-1206 AH.). After obtaining fundamental religious training he developed a special interest in books on false Prophets such as Musailama al-Kathab, Sajah al-Aswad al-An'si and Tulaiha al-Assadi. In 1143 AH. Muhammad ibn Abdul Wahab called upon the people of Najd to follow h is new doctrine. At that time Ibn Abdul Wahab behaved as if he had an absolute monopoly over ijtihad, *i.e.,* the ability to arrive at logical deductions on religious questions.

The Wahhabi sect has two basic tenets, a declared tenet and a hidden one. The declared tenet is commitment to divine unity and opposition to idolatry and paganism. The hidden tenet is sowing the seeds of schism, discord, conflict and war among the Muslims to serve the interest of foreign rulers. This is the real purpose, which the

Wahhabi sect has sought to achieve from its inception to the present day. This means that the declared objective or tenet served only to impress followers and enlist their efforts in achieving the real objective. Experts on the history of the Wahhabia confirm that the movement was originally established on an order by the British colonial administration.

*The Activities of the Original 'Gang of Seven'*

Most of the Islamic fundamentalist parties that were beneficiaries of the aid for the Afghan War against the Soviet Union 's occupation of Afghanistan were actually in existence years before the Red Army marched across the Oxus River. All of them were based in Peshawar in Pakistan.

Following the communist coup-the Saur Revolution-in 1978, the Peshawar-based groups were largely ignored, and they found themselves in total disarray, until the Soviet invasion of Afghanistan in 1979. At this time, Pakistani President, General Zia ul-Haq, handpicked the so-called 'Peshawar Seven ' groups-known by most Afghans as the 'Gang of Seven'-who had served Pakistani interests in the past as the primary beneficiaries of funding and arms to wage the war against the Soviet Union. Nationalist and other anti-communist leaders were deliberately ignored and sometimes even threatened with open hostility, in favour of Hekmatyar, *et al*, A summary of the history and the activities of the original 'Gang of Seven' is given below:

- Hezb-I-Islami (Party of Islam): Led by Gulbuddin Hekmatyar, who was affiliated with the Muslim Brotherhood since the 1970s. As a student of engineering in Kabul University, he led most of the demonstrations in Kabul from 1967 to 1972. He himself was a Pushtun, and most of Hekmatyar's followers belonged to this ethnic group, the largest in Afghanistan. Since he lacked a classical Islamic education and opposed the traditional clergy, the ulema did not trust Hekmatyar. During the war,

Hekmatyar's gang was responsible for the assassination of a new Afghan nationalist figures in Peshawar.

- Hekmatyar was strongly backed by Pakistan and also heavily funded by Saudi Arabia. Some of his income came from the poppy–growing regions in the south of the country, parts of which were under his control. (Heroin was virtually unknown to the region until 1979, when modern western laboratories were introduced to the area and farmers were encouraged to grow the cash crop, instead of wheat.)
- Jamiat-I-Islami (Islamic Society): Led by Burhanuddin Rabbani, a former professor and theologian at Kabul University, whose party consists primarily of ethnic Tajiks from the northern part of the country. Pan-Islamists and members of the Ikhwan also dominate his group. Rabbani, of Sufi Naqshbandi background, is a graduate of Al-Azhar Unviersity. The late Ahmad shah Masood, also of Tajik background, was defense minister. Masood attended the French school in Kabul and French aid agencies, particularly 'Doctors Without Borders', a lmost exclusively helped Masood's group.
- Ittehad Islami (Islami Unity): Islamic Unity is led by fomer university professor Abdul Rasul Sayaf, who received most of his support from radical elements in Saudi Arabia, Iraq and other Muslim countries. Sayaf converted to Saudi Wahhabism at the onset of the war. Sayaf founded the University of *Dawa* and Jehad in 1985, in Pakistan's North West Frontier Province. Sometimes referred to as the 'Islamic Sandhurst', the university provides training for Islamic militants. In spring 1995, the University came under investigation by Pakistan authorities and the US FBI, according to the Pakistan press, reported that it was training Afghani terrorists showing up in Asia and North Africa. Sayaf was funded by Saudi Arabia.
- Hezbi-Islami (Party of Islam): Led by Maulvi Younas Khalis, an Islamic scholar, former teacher, and journalist. Origin ally wih

Hekmatyar, Khalis, being a traditional Islamist, split from the former in 1979. Khalis, being a traditional Islamist, split from the former in 1979. Khalis' group, primarily led by Haji Din Mohammad, led the military actions against the Soviet Army. Its major military commanders were: Abdul Haq (now dead), Qazi Amin Wardak, and Mullah Malang.

- Mahaz-I-Milli Islam (National Islamic Front of Afghanistan): Pir Sayed Ahmad Gilani, leader of the powerful Qadiri Sufi sect, leads the National Islamic Front. The group used to be strong in the Nangarhar province and surrounding areas. Gilani, who prior to the war was the representative in Kabul of the French auto company Peugeot, is a strong royalist. He was also associated with Lord Bethell of the London-based Radio Free Kabul.
- Jabha-I-Nijat-Milli (Afghan National Liberation Front): Sibghatullah Mojadidi, a religious leader from Kabul and royalist, leads the Liberation Front. Although his party had no significant military command, Mojadidi was frequently chosen as a compromise leader, and was the first interim President of Afghanistan following the collapse of the communist regime in 1992.
- Harakat-I-Inqiliab-I-Islami (Islamic Revolutionary Forces): Led by clergyman Mohammad Nabi Mohammadi, whose party's membership was derived from intellectuals.

### *The Terrorist Onslaught*

Soon after the Soviet Army left, Afghanistan plunged into an internecine civil war. For a short while, the United States backed Bulbuddin Hekmatyar to take control of Kabul, but lost interest quickly. With the objective attained, which was to 'defeat' the Soviet Army, the United States left Afghanistan at the mercy of the warlords and the Pakistani ISI.

Initially, the Pakistani ISI did not meet with much success; Kabul remained under a coalition government with Tajik President

Burhanuddin Rabbani and Tajik Defense Minister Ahmed Shah Masood calling the shots. But much of Afghanistan remained ungoverned. The Pakistani ISI quickly moved some of the *Afghansis* of Arab origin into Kashmir and launched a terrorist operation to destabilize the Indian-controlled part of Kashmir. Training camps were set up in the so-called Azad Kashmir and the *Afghansis* were also training the local Kashmiri militants.

To attain this objective, which had the support of the United States and Saudi Arabia in particular, the ISI used marco-money. Funds also came in from Saudi Arabia and the Gulf. With the military success of the Taliban militia in 1996, when they seized almost 95 per cent of Afghanistan, terrorism took a giant leap in the subcontinent, particularly in Pakistan and in the India-held part of Jammu and Kashmir. Pakistani Sunni groups such as Sipah-e-Sahaba Pakistan, and many sub-groups like the Lashkar-e-Tayba, Lashkar-e-Jhangvi, Harakatul Mujahideen and much later, the Jaish-e-Mohammad, received training in Afghanistan with the sole purpose of infiltrating into the India-held part of Jammu and Kashmir to carry on irregular warfare.

A large number of these *Afghansis* were also involved in the Kargil invasion by Pakistan in 1999 when the Indian Army found the Pakistani Army had seized a strategic mountain range in the Kargil sector with the objective of cutting off the road connecting the Kashmir Valley to Ladakh. At that point, it became evident that the *Afghansis* and other Pakistani terrorist groups trained in Afghanistan were working as an irregular army with in Pakistan.

VII

# War on Terrorism

*Maj. Gen. (Retd.) Afsir Karim*

*No weapons of mass destruction have been found in Iraq even with Saddam Hussein in the bag. In these circumstances, the American administration had to find a new justification for prolonging the occupation of Iraq; establishment of a stable democracy in Iraq was trottled out as the new justification. The war in Iraq, however, continues in the absence of viable reconstruction or political plan ; it seems overemphasis on use of heavy guns and air strikes, regardless of collateral damage, is the preferred American response to meet the new challenges posed by the insurgents and to overawe the population into mute submission. The problem is that the people are not likely to submit to the American dictates and the war will continue in one form or the other.*

*In Afghanistan too, US troops are coming increasingly under fire and retaliation by the American forces is becoming harsher. The hunt for the Taliban goes on, but it has so far been undertaken more for protecting the coalition forces and the Afghan regime rather than confronting the Taliban . The form of constitution favoured by the Loya Jirga and the emphasis actually given to Shariat laws will give a clear indication which way the wind is blowing in Afghanistan.*

*Most Islamic countries resent the presence of American troops on Iraqi and Afghan soil and have been busy reshaping their strategies to counter the US designs. Presently the focus of the American administration remains on Iraq and Afghanistan, but it is widely believed that Syria would be the next target.*

*The capture of Saddam Hussein was certainly a cause of jubilation for the Bush administration, but its impact on the war on terrorism has been marginal. The capture of Saddam has given a boost to the Bush administration and raised the morale of the US forces operating in Iraq, but is not likely to change the ground situation radically; establishment of stable democracy and reconstruction of Iraq will still be difficult targets to achieve. The general reaction in the Islamic world in the aftermath of the war in Iraq and the humiliation of Saddam has not been favourable for America or its allies. The pictures of Saddam in which a US army doctor is shown carrying out a medical check up of a drugged Saddam have created a new wave of resentment against the Americans.*

*The confused aftermath of wars both in Iraq and Afghanistan has given al-Qaeda a much-needed breathing space; it is spreading its wings and attacking pro-IUS Islamic regimes from Morocco to Pakistan. A general sense of humiliation prevails in the Arab world and the al-Qaeda is using it to its advantage. While the Americans celebrate the capture of Saddam Hussein, al-Qaeda and its associates prepare for new strikes across the globe. Al-Qaeda has entered the fray in a big way in Iraq, and its cadres remain largely unscathed in sweeps on Iraqi towns or arrest of supporters of Saddam by the American forces. There are reports that al-Qaeda has diverted huge funds and selected cadres from other parts of the world to make Iraq and contiguous areas as the main battle ground against Americans and their allies. The humiliation of Saddam and the events in Iraq have undoubtedly become rallying points for Jihadi forces against the 'Great Satan.'*

## THE CURRENT SITUATION

### *Arab Resentment*

The security situation has deteriorated dangerously after Saddam's capture. The reason is not far to seek—it is the Arab humiliation.

Even those Arabs who do not exactly care for Saddam's capture and downfall consider it a humiliation for the entire Arab world. "A new humiliation to Arabs" was the heading in a column in a London-based Arab daily *Al-Quds al-Arabi*. It was indeed a great shock to millions of Arabs who watched the TV shot of the President being subjected to a humiliating medical check up.[1]

Mohammed Jaber Al-Ansari, a Bahraini columnist wrote, "Saddam is out of the hole, but we have to get him out of the corners of our political psychology, which is draining us with its nightmares;" "This is a test and its one the Americans can 't take for us."[2]

Abdallah Nasser Al-Fawzan wrote in a Saudi Arab daily *Al Watan:* "We all saw pictures… Saddam was miserable, and I, as an Arab felt humiliation. But my other feelings against Saddam were he was a paper knight."[3]

*Collateral Damage*

A major cause of resentment is the 5,000 Iraqi prisoners who are being held in degrading conditions indefinitely with no charges being found against them. They are held in the same dreaded prison in which Saddam detained his opponents. The change of name of this prison to 'Baghdad's Correctional Facility' has neither changed the conditions inside nor outside the prison; relative shave to "trudge a humiliating mud-slog only to be told by the American military police that only 20 visitors are allowed per day. Two days of the week are for lawyers only."[4]

Reliable reports indicate that more than 20,000 Iraqis have been killed in the war and its aftermath till November 2003. American

[1] Nadia Abou El-Magd, Associated Press Writer, 'Saddam's Arrest Brings Humiliation Debate,' <http://news.yahoo.com/news? Tmpl=story2&cid=540&u=/ap/20031219/ap_on_re_mi_ea/s…>, 19 December 2003.

[2] Ibid.

[3] Ibid.

[4] 'Abu Graib Prison, Baghdad Correctional Facility,' http://www/occupationwatch.org, 19 December 2003.

actions against Iraqi insurgents now closely resemble the raids of the Israeli army of Palestinian settlements to ferret out terrorists. Use of heavy weapons and helicopters to bomb out the suspects regardless of the civilian casualties; insulting women and injuring children is the order of the day; doors are broken open and men are huddled together like cattle for personal searches. Degrading treatment meted out to common citizens during interrogation has increased resentment against the Americans to a dangerous level.

The continued involvement of the military in day-to-day administration of Iraq has serious implications for the people of Iraq; poverty conditions have been aggravated by long drawn sweeps, search operations and lack of basic civic facilities. The common Iraqi citizens are desperately looking for jobs, shelter and security, but instead of providing them security the American forces are hounding them in pursuit of militants who melt away in thickly populated areas after attacks. The majority of the population that is not an active participant in guerrilla warfare is being harassed and hounded.

The turmoil will continue because Washington is still far from evolving a strategy for establishing a democratic, secular and stable Iraq that can stand on its own feet. America will need a lot of time and patience to build democratic institutions; presently the danger of emergence of a weak, divided and anti-American Iraq seems more likely. The American problem has been its failure to fully comprehend the scale and the dimension of the task to build a new pro-American Iraq. An invitation to the UN at this point of time may be their best bet to gain support in reconstruction efforts, but hawks in the Bush administration did not wage a war to hand back the spoils to the Iraqis or the United Nations. Handing over to the UN would be an admission that the US policy of unilateral military action has proved a dismal failure. In plain language the occupation of Iraq means control over its immense oil resources and establishment of permanent military bases in Iraq, which as George Friedman noted "will represent the introduction of a new imperial power to the Middle East and of regional geopolitics based on that power."[5]

## REACTION IN THE ARAB WORLD

The capture of Saddam created ripples of various types in Arab countries. Reactions of some countries are summarized below.

Turkey: Regardless of the official policy of supporting the American invasion of Iraq, after capture of Saddam, the Turkish government is concerned that because of the part played by Kurds in capturing Saddam, Americans may accept their demand of establishing an independent or semi-autonomous Kurdish state. The recent ethnic clashes in Kirkuk over this issue have increased apprehensions of a prolonged confrontation between contending factions and Turkish intervention. During the war when Kurdish forces captured Mosul and Kirkuk, Turkey massed troops on the border in readiness to enter northern Iraq.

Syria: Syria is being threatened by the US administration in a language, which was previously reserved for the Baathist regime of Iraq. Syria has been called a 'rogue state' that is testing chemical weapons and providing shelter to Iraqi insurgents. Many observers of the Middle East believe that US policy against Syria is bound to the Israeli agenda and the US will shift its attention to Syria as soon as the situation calms down in Iraq. Syria sand Lebanon are likely to be tackled together if military action is envisaged, but Americans are hated throughout this region after the invasion of Iraq and people are bound to offer stiff resistance to the occupation forces.

Jordan: The people of Jordan strongly opposed the American invasion of Iraq, but the government had maintained a safe posture by declaring 'Jordan First'; during the war they allowed certain

[5] Jim Lobe, Inter Press Service (IPS), "Analysis: Are Iraq's Bases the Main Draq? <http://news.yahoo.com/news? Tmpl=story2&cid=655&u=/oneworld/20031130/wl_onewor...>, 29 November 2003.

facilities to the Americans and assisted Israeli security agencies by maintaining vigilance along Israeli borders. The humiliation of Saddam, however, stunned the Jordanian government.

Saudi Arabia: Saudi Arabia opposed the war and the relations between Saudis and Americans cooled visibly. Gradually American bases were closed down in the country and there was a politico-military shift against Saudi Arabia. Saudi Arabia is now apprehensive about the emergence of a Shiite-dominated regime next door. Saudi pride was hurt because of the treatment given to Saddam in total disregard of the susceptibilities of the Arab world and sentiments of the Arab people.

Iran: Iran welcomed a non-threatening Iraq regime without Saddam and wants an international tribunal to try Saddam for war crimes against it. In the 1980s, Iraq had waged a war against Iran that lasted eight years. .Iran is, however, apprehensive of US ambitions in the Middle East and its propensity to threaten Islamic states after accusing them of harbouring terrorists or developing nuclear weapons.

Israel-Palestine: Israel is happy that a major threat to its existence has been removed; the Palestinians on the other hand are extremely unhappy because of loss of a regime that gave great moral and material support to them. They expect Israel to further harden its stand and its military forays against them.

Egypt: Egyptians opposed the war against Iraq but they are not particularly perturbed by the capture of Saddam. They would perhaps now increase their efforts to improve Israeli – Palestinian relations. There is, however, bitterness against the US for televising pictures of Saddam, which humiliated all Arabs.

## RESISTANCE IN IRAQ

Resistance against continued presence of US troops is growing as the persistent bomb attacks on US establishments, their supporters and soldiers show. The recent attacks on US soldiers and the police indicate good organization and planning behind them. Lately, there have been violent demonstrations in support of Saddam in the so-called Sunni Triangle, and ethnic clashes in the oil-rich northern city of Kirkuk. Demonstrators freely used rocket – propelled grenades and automatic weapons. Improvised Explosive Devices (IEDS), which are frequently used, have a terrifying impact on the US soldiers who have to patrol the streets almost daily. The growing anti-US resistance does not seem to be a passing phenomenon; it is rooted in deep-seated resentment against the American presence and the destruction it has caused. "The growing number, sophistication, and diversity of attacks on US forces suggest that the resistance is growing and becoming more organized – clear evidence that the US may be losing the struggle for the hearts and minds of the Iraqi people."[6]

The Bush administration was greatly elated after the capture of Saddam, but it has not led to the reduction of violence or acceptance of inevitability of the American presence; on the other hand, it seems that a new phase of armed struggle is starting against the Americans. The people have also not accepted the Coalition Provisional Authority (CPA) because they are considered puppets of the US occupation regime. Any future political arrangement without complete withdrawal of American forces from the streets will meet the same fate.

"The failure to realistically assess the anti-American resistance in Iraq means that 'solutions' the US and CPA develop have minimal chance of success because they are derived from an inaccurate identification of the problem."[7]

US troops are likely to remain in Iraq for a long time for combating insurgency while the American administration continues to work with the compliant Iraqi leaders for handing over sovereignty

[6] Scott Ritter, 'Defining the resistance in Iraq – it's not foreign and it's well prepared,' http://www.csmonitor.com/2003/1110/p09s02-coop.htm, 10 November 2003.

[7] Ibid.

to a subservient government. Edward Herman, Professor Emeritus at the University of Pennsylvania is of the view, "The Bush administration plans were to restructure the economy and change the power position in Iraq, so the US would essentially control Iraq; if this new programme is followed through fully, the US could very well lose control almost immediately."[8]

According to Charles Pena, Director of Defence Policy studies at CATO Institute "Keeping US military forces in Iraq muddles stated goals: If we hand the government over to the Iraqi people, our troops will continue to be a target for anyone in Iraq who is disgruntled and dissatisfied for having a military force there or the way a new government is taking place. We become a convenient target and scapegoat."[9]

### AL-QAEDA'S COUNTER-STRATEGY

Al-Qaeda attacks and aggressive propaganda has created turbulence in various parts of the Islamic world. The terrorist network has gained greater support after the invasion of Iraq and it seems that it is mounting attacks to keep Washington off-balance and groping. Faye Bowers of *The Christian Science Monitor* says, "Al-Qaeda foot soldiers seem to be everywhere. They are now claiming responsibility for the bombings in Saudi Arabia. They say they are flocking into Iraq to fight the US 'occupation'. They claim they were behind the massive power failure in the northeast quadrant of the US this past summer. Some may even have penetrated Camp Delta of Guantanamo Bay."[10]

One of the main objectives of al-Qaeda seems to be to create confusion and fear in the American mind. If the graduated threat

[8] Barbara Ferguson, Arab News Correspondent, 'Bremer Retreats from Comprehensive Iraq Plans,' <http://www.arabnews.com/services/print/print.asp?artid=37346&d=30&m=12&y=2003&...>, 30 December 2003.

[9] Ibid.

[10] Faye Bowers, *The Christian Science Monitor,* 'Al-Qaeda's new tactic: deception an denial,' http://www.csmonitor.com/2003/1113/p02s01-wome.htm, 13 November 2003.

perceptions of the US administration are any indication, al-Qaeda has managed to create uncertainty through ominous threats and actual attacks on US allies. The apprehensions and fear created this Christmas were so great that the US administration deployed air patrols and guns to ward off a possible attack, which according to them seemed imminent. In fact nothing happened, but the environment of fear created by al-Qaeda boosted its image in the Islamic world.

American intelligence agencies continue to warn of a new catastrophic attack on the US despite the claim that more than two-thirds of al-Qaeda cadres have been liquidated. The attacks on US allies and moderate Islamic states show that no one is really sure of the real capability and objectives of the al-Qaeda. According to a senior US intelligence officer "Before September 11, we though they were a loosely knit group of decentralized people that cooperated at different times for different reasons, but after 9/11, we decided they had a hierarchical structure organized like the Kremlin. Now we're swinging back the other way to say it is a rather decentralized group." "Nobody knows the exact structure of and substructure of al-Qaeda," says Gunter Mulack, German Commissioner for dialogue with Islamic nations.[11]

Al-Qaeda's strategy seems to be to expand and spread the areas of conflict to dissipate US anti-terrorist efforts and disperse its forces. It would like the US to intrude into more Islamic countries to widen the areas of conflict between the US and the Islamic world. It has started a counter-offensive by mounting attacks in the Islamic countries, which are allied with the US or are enabling US forces to wage war against al-Qaeda and its associate organizations in various parts of the world. Al-Qaeda would like to create a situation where the US either intervenes or just watches the widening circle of anti-Americanism. The initiative remains in the hands of al-Qaeda as the attacks from Philippines to Morocco, from Pakistan to Central Asia

[11] Ibid.

and the Middle East show. The US has to devise a new strategy to meet this threat, because it would not be feasible for the US to disperse its forces all over the globe. The US has to reorient its operational doctrines to deal with guerrilla forces and to defend soft targets considered to defeat the strategy al-Qaeda has embarked upon to exhaust the US administration by keeping it on high alert in its homeland and elsewhere. Constatn threats of terrorist strikes can be psychologically more damaging than a strike itself; the phenomenon witnessed during this Christmas and New Year from Europe to America can be repeated many times in a year.[12] Even if Osama bin Laden and his main field commanders are eventually captured or killed, the terrorist operations will be continued by other combat-hardened veterans. Intelligence sources have identified six emerging leaders as key to running the global military and financial terrorist networks. "The new leaders have been there from the beginning, but were in the shadows; but they have their skills, and in war you need your best commanders."[13]

The new leaders, it is believed, organised recent attacks in Bali, on Turkish and Tunisian synagogues, the British embassy in Turkey and facilities in Saudi Arabia. Al-Qaeda is also involved in attempts to assassinate President Musharraf of Pakistan . Profiles of some of the new leaders based on interviews of US and European intelligence analysts, US law enforcement officials and terrorism experts are reproduced below.[14]

Saif al-Adel: An Egyptian and a member of al-Qaeda's "security committee" for several years, he is viewed as the new military leader for the remnants of al-Qaeda and the Taliban in the Afghanistan-Pakistan border region. He took over as chief of military operations

[12] <http://1w10fd .law10.hotmail.msn.com/cgi-bin/getmsg?msg=MSG1064917276. 1444&start=8…>, 9 December 2003.

[13] Susan Schmidt and Douglas Farah. *The Washington Post, 'New* al-Qaeda leaders emerge,' http://www/msnbc.com/news/8273000asp?0cl=cR, 29 October 2003.

[14] Ibid.

late last year, after US bombs killed Muhammad Atef, al-Qaeda's military commander.

Described by one European expert as "a military man, prepared to take command," he was a Special Forces officer in the Egyptian army before he fled to Saudi Arabia. He then traveled to Pakistan in 1988 to join the mujahidin rebels fighting against Soviet occupation in Afghanistan.

A member of al-Qaeda since its founding in the early 1990s, he was trained by the Lebanes guerrilla group, Hezbollah. Al-Adel is believed to be a key figure in a tactical alliance between al-Qaeda and Hexbollah, cutting across the traditional divide between the Shiite Muslims in Lebanon and the Sunni Muslims that make up al-Qaeda.

He has planned or participated in some of al-Qaeda's most deadly attacks. Al-Adel trained and fought alongside Somalis who ambushed the US Army Rangers in Mogadishu. He helped plan the 1998 attacks on the US embassies in Africa, and he was a key coordinator of the attack on the USS cole.

Al-Adel left Afghanistan in November or December and traveled to Europe, returning to Afghanistan in January to lead some of the fighting against US troops during Operation Anaconda in March, when US forces swept through mountains in eastern Afghanistan. During these battles, which raged for more than a week, al-adel faxed his accounts of the fighting to the Pakistani press.

He was hiding in Iran this summer, but has since moved back to the Afghanistan-Pakistan border area to coordinate strikes against US and allied forces.

Abdullah Ahmed Abdullah : Another Egyptian, he has become al-Qaeda's chief financial officer, at least in Pakistan and Afghanistan. Abdullah, about 40 years old, joined the Egyptian Islamic Jihad and traveled to Afghanistan in the late 1980s. He was among the 480 Arab combatants who joined bin Laden when he moved to Sudan in 1991.

From Sudan, Abdullah traveled to Somalia for a time. In 1998 he moved to Kenya, where he arranged and paid for the travel of the al-Qaeda operative who plane the 7 August bombings of the US embassies in Africa. He left Nairobi on Aug. 6 and went to Karachi, Pakistan.

The following month, Abdullah traveled to Monrovia, Liberia, to buy diamonds on behalf of al-Qaeda. The deal, set up to buy diamonds mined by rebels of the Revolutionary United Front in neighbouring sierra Leone, opened a new way for al-Qaeda to hide its financial assets. The soft-spoken fighter, married with four children, is believed to be in the tribal areas of Pakistan or in Afghanistan.

Abu Musab Zarqawi: A Jordanian, Zarqawi has traveled extensively in the Arab world since the Sept. 11, 2001 attacks, including going to Baghdad for medical treatment after losing a leg.

Zarqawi has also traveled to Iran, Syria and Lebanon during the past year and is trained in the use of poisons and toxins. In early July, he took a poisonous substance disguised as an ointment into Turkey, but the purpose was unclear. "He is their highly mobile top operator and facilitator," a European source said.

Little is known about his path in al-Qaeda. German officials in May identified him as the leader of Al Tawid, a radical Palestinian group that was identified as a branch or subgroup of al-Qaeda. He was sentenced to death in absentia in Jordan for plotting to blow up a luxury hotel in Amman in January 2000, part of a millennium-bombing plot.

Riduan Isamuddin: An Indonesian known as Hambali, he is al-Qaeda's liaison to loose-knit radical Islamic groups in Southeast Asia—and one non-Arab who seems to have been given authority to make independent decisions. "Hambali is a regional leader in southeast Asia," said a US official. "He's a really skilled operator, one of the really capable ones".

A veteran of the wars in Afghanistan, Isamuddin is believed to have plotted the recent, foiled attempts to attack the embassies of the United States, Israel, Britain and Australia in Singapore.

He was a founder of a company called Konsojaya, which police in the Philippines believe served as a financing arm for terror activities, including the failed 1995 airliner plot. [He has been since captured and imprisoned]

Tawfiq bin Atash: Known as Khallad, Atash is either Saudi or Yemeni and is believed to have lost a leg in combat in Afghanistan. He may now be in Pakistan. In recent months he served as a trainer, along with Binalshibh, of the group that plotted suicide attacks in the Strait of Gibraltar.

"This is a major-league killer who orchestrate the Cole attack and possibly the Africa bombings," wrote a CIA officer two months before the Sept. 11 attacks.

In the days after Sept. 11, US official bolstered their charges that the hijackers were linked to bin Laden and al-Qaeda by publicizing the presence of two of the hijackers at a Malaysia meeting with Atash in January 2000.

According to US and Western intelligence sources, al-Qaeda's chattering on web indicates that it is planning a new catastrophic assault on American targets and it is constantly monitoring American security arrangements. It seems al-Qaeda has set up special cells to analyse and collate information to deduce cogent options of attack. A merica is, therefore, under an invisible siege psychologically and physically. The report of the 'Control Risk Group' based in London indicated that medium security risks to Western interests in 2004 will include 71 countries from Thailand to Morocco; the number of countries where risk was considered 'extreme' will increase marginally. The report said that "the al-Qaeda organization that existed on 11 September 2001...really no longer exists, it's been largely dismantled, what we are beginning to see is a much more disparate movement of people who are sometimes coordinating their (work) sometime not, but who are inspired by the example of al-Qaeda and who are carrying out attacks. So we see the threat becoming much more elusive and the danger is that it becomes much harder to track."[15]

### ATTEMPTS TO ASSASSINATE PRESIDENT MUSHARRAF

Two assassination attempts on President Musharraf on the eve of the SAARC conference brought the al-Qaeda presence in Pakistan into the limelight with stunning effect. Assassination is a part of the al-Qaeda strategy of targeting pro-American regimes and leaders. The president of Pakistan was lucky to escape these attempts but the surprising part of these attempts was that they took place areas, which were almost hundred per cent sanitized; this indicates that a part of his security has been penetrated or some elements of the Pakistan army may be involved in a conspiracy to eliminate Musharraf. It is highly improbable that al-Qaeda or any organization outside the security circle would have pinpointed the right car out of two similar ones, which formed part of the presidential motorcade. According to Israeli news sources, during the first attempt the "Pakistani President's armour-plated car was fitted with high-tech jamming devices that stopped the timer for about a minute and also jammed the remote control of the assassins." These devices, supplied by CIA, gave him a chance to cross the bridge unscathed in the first attack.

The second attempt, which was far more ingenious, failed because in addition to jamming gadgets supplie by CIA, the President's car was armed with a second gadget, designed by Israel for prematurely deton ating explosives carried by suicide bombers; these gadgets obviously saved the life of President Musharraf. Those who planned the assassination came to know of the jamming device, which aborted their first attempt; they used two pickup trucks packed with explosives and driven by two suicide bombers with explosives

[15] Beth Gardiner, Asscociated Press Writer, 'Al-Qaeda's Worldwide Threat Evaluated,' <http://news.yahoo.com/news? Tmpl=story2&cid=518&u=/ap/britain_terrorism_risk&print…>, 10 November 2003.

strapped to their bodies to make sure that the plan did not fail. They used two vehicles working in tandem to beat the jamming device, but this time they were beaten by the new Israeli device that detonated the explosive devices prematurely.[16] These devices are still in the experimental stage and have not been mass produce so far.

Shifting loyalties and alliances can prove dangerous for Musharraf. A large number of radical groups and a number of army officers are now disillusioned with Musharraf. The would-be assassins could not have possibly breached his security cordon without inside help. I n case Musharraf is eliminated or ousted, it would make the American position in the Pakistan-Afghanistan region more difficult, if not untenable.

## DEVELOPMENTS IN AFGHANISTAN

The emerging consensus in the Loya Jirga, the 502 member constitutional convention, seemed in favour of Hamid Karzai's proposal of a strong presidential system . However, there have been problems in relation to the role of Islam and Human Rights. The draft constitution does not mention the Islamic term 'Amir', but gives very wide powers to the President; these powers I n the wrong hands can lead back to the brand of dictatorial rule seen during the Taliban regime.

According to Hussein Ramoz, an analyst of the US sponsored National Democratic Institute, "It is a mistake to begin a democracy using the language of an emirate, an Islamic dictatorship – it is a losing game."[17] Karzai's success has been a triumph for the Americans, but ethnic relations between Pushtuns and Tajiks will continue to cause problems of governance. If the radical groups insist

[16] DEBKA file Updates DEBKA-Net-Weekly 139, 'Assassinations Integral to al-Qaeda's Terror Agenca,' http://www.debka.com/article_print.php?aid=752, 28 December 2003.

[17] Dan Morrison, correspondent of *The Christian Science Monitor,* 'Karzai weathers power struggle, but at a price,' http://www.csmonitor,com/2003/1211/p01s04-wosc.htm, 26 December 2003.

on establishing traditional Islamic and tribal laws in consonance with local traditions and interpretations, the situation will worsen. The constitution that has been adopted raises hopes of establishment of democracy and peace if followed in letter and spirit.

The Taliban have not gone away; they still enjoy grass-roots support in several tribal areas and find safe havens in Pakistan. Pakistan's western frontiers have always been a second home to the Taliban. A Pakistan-based diplomat says, "Balochistan has always been, and still is, a second home to the Taliban. It has served as a second headquarters after Kandahar during the Taliban's rule and it is providing a new lease on life to its guerrilla warfare against the Us and its western allies."[18] He adds, "The more they gain ground in Balochistan, the more their movement will get strengthened; they can easily channel their financial support and regain their ideological support."[19]

In the refugee camps in Balochistan, it is impossible to distinguish a Taliban fighter from other ordinary refugees. Taliban flags still flutter from rooftops in several camps and donations amounting to millions of rupees are collected from the surrounding villages. Local villagers say, "People support the Taliban not only because they are Muslims, but when they were in power people here could travel across the border easily, as there was peace and security."[20]

Zalmay Khalilzad, the US ambassador in Afghanistan, feels Pakistan is not doing enough to stop attacks on US soldiers by militants who are operating along its borders.[21] The situation in Afghanistan is fluid, and it will be difficult to bring stability to the

[18] Scott Baldaug and Owais Tohid, "Where Taliban go to find warm beds and recruits,' *The Christian Science Monitor*, http://www.csmonitor.com/2003/1211/p01s04-wosc.htm, 11 December 2003.

[19] Ibid.

[20] Ibid.

[21] Mike Allen, the Washington Post, 'US envoy faults Pakistan as ally: Grim assessment of Afghan security by new ambassador,' <http://www.sfgate.com/cgi-bin/article.cgi?file=/chronicle/archieve/2003/11/19/MNGJ635...>, 19 November 2003.

region as long as the Taliban continue to find shelter in Pakistan. A delegation of former US ambassadors to Pakistan recently called upon the US administration to curtail aid to Pakistan because of "Pakistan's failure to do a better job in preventing the use of its territory by terrorists." The report by former ambassadors FranK Wisner and Nicholas Platt concluded, "US and Pakistani policies only partially coincide.[22]

US military action within Afghanistan has been highly erratic. For the second time within a week dozens of Pakistani children and many adults were killed in air strikes; in the first attack six and in the second d nine children died. This kind of erratic air action has been a major US failing; however, the powers that be show no regret. They seem to justify their action instead. In these conditions, Pushtuns are bound to become more alienated and resentful towards the US and may again incline towards the Taliban. Manoel de Almeida e Silva, a UN spokesman says, "As well as contributing to a sense of fear and insecurity, these incidents make it easier for those who wish to spoil this process to rally support."[23]

[22] Scott Baldaug and Owais Tohid, "Pakistani unrest is Taliban boon,' *The Christian Science Monitor*, http://www.csmonitor.com/2003/1224/p06s03-wosc.htm, 24 December 2003.

[23] Stephen Graham in Kabul, 'US military admits it killed Afghan children in attacks,' http://news.independent.co.uk/world/asia/story.jsp? Story=472095, 11 December 2003.

VIII

# International Laws to Control Terrorism: A Comparative Study

*Dr. S. Sanyala*

*Terrorism has become a worldwide phenomenon, yet the world has failed to reach a legal definition of terrorism. Even today there is no single universal definition. The UN member states still have no agreed definition. This has become a major obstacle to meaningful international community is hard pressd to combat a problem, which it cannot with an assurance identify. Cynics have often commented that one state's "terrorist" is another state's "freedom fighter". In this way, the fight against terrorism will always suffer from "cultural relativism". (Ganor, 2001). The free world must understand that cultural relativism applied to terrorism irrespective of their goals will lead only to more terrorism.*

*Limitations in the international laws are many in number. It has been accepted by legal experts that the international law is not effective when it comes to dealing with terrorists and international terrorism. Some terrorists are killed and others are captured who are at times not even brought to trial, instead quietly dispersed to some safe haven . Even the state's response towards the definition, or the basic legal concepts of terrorism remains confused. Worse still, how might a definition impact seeming terrorist acts by a state's armed forces? It is a million dollar question, said Subrahmanyam (2002), to know how far special laws would be of use in containing the menace of cross-border terrorism. Terrorism has to be fought according to the rule of law, and combating terrorism must be legal. The United Nation has made a concerted effort to arrive at a consensus definition of terrorism and it has been revealed by surveys that all states desire that the UN should play a more significant role in controlling terrorism.*

*The present paper has taken up two salient issues for discussion: (1) the definition of terrorism as given in various acts (2) the activities identified as terrorism. To obtain an in depth knowledge, the anti-terrorist acts of certain countries are studied and the communal ties and the non-commonalties between the different acts are identified. The aim is to make a diagnostic analysis of the laws of different countries with the help of content analysis. Countries like United Kingdom, USA, Canada, Israel, India, Pakistan and Sri Lanka are studied. They are selected on the basis of their vulnerability to terrorism in the last few decades.*

*The paper concludes that, firstly, all countries discussed mentioned that the use of threat or action meant to disturb the national integrity and sovereignty falls in the category of 'terrorism'; secondly, any organizations involved in promoting these activities were considered as terrorist organizations. Thirdly there is a growing appreciation that acts of terrorism and political violence are distinct genres and should be dealt with separately.*

International law cannot be effective until and unless there is a clear and universally agreed upon definition of the term 'terrorism'. There is also a need for all countries to identify the acts, which define terrorism so as to facilitate in the arrest and deportation of the criminals involved in cross-border terrorism. Almost all municipal laws are unclear on thee points and fail to evolve common strategies to fight terrorism as an international phenomenon.

National and international laws suggest common practices to control or prevent terrorism. Individual states respond to terrorism by amending their domestic laws to achieve a certain level of control or prevention. The domestic response, therefore, is part of the international community's collective or regional response, but at the same time each country's legal response is determine by certain factors such as the form of terrorism operating within its jurisdiction, the particular political conflicts that engender the terrorism and the extent of public support given by a particular state to the terrorist.

As early as the 1930s the issue of terrorism had been discussed in a series of conferences where emphasis was laid on the unification of penal law. It was recommended that acts, which fell within the scope of the definition, should be excluded from the protection of political offences. The Chief Justice of India, Justice Barucha,[1] expressing serious concern over the menace of terrorism believed that it had survived mainly because the definition or basic legal concepts on the basis of which the state responded to terrorism remained confused. He who strikes terror in one country would be given refuge by another country. In his opinion, the law should be uniform in making the terrorist in one country a criminal in every other country who should accordingly be subjected to arrest and extradition for trial in the country in which the heinous crime was committed.

## LIMITATIONS IN THE INTERNATIONAL LAWS

It has been accepted by legal experts and academicians that the universal law was not effective in dealing with international terrorism. Some terrorists are killed and others are captured. Few of the latter are not even brought to trial and are instead quietly dispatched abroad to a safe haven. The diversity and the complexity of terrorist activities complicate the task and despite a number of existing classifications there is still no generally accepted definition of terrorism. It is observed that terrorism, in essence, is a criminal activity in many countries. In applying laws domestically, the

[1] Barucha, S.P., "Laws on Terrorism must be uniform", *The Hindustan Times*, 2 April 2001.

governments have failed to punish and deter those who use terrorism to advance their political goals.

There is a deep controversy concerning which crimes are to be defined as international offences, especially as regards their definition by reference to the nature of the injured person. Nations have argued for generations about a legal definition for terrorism. Without a clear definition, the international community is hard pressed to combat the problem of terrorism. Differences, therefore, continue to prevail among the states regarding the types of crimes, which could be considered as international offences and could be countered through international measures. As reported,[2] the International Conventions are often ambiguous and inconsistent in the use of the term 'international offence'. The United Nations needs to draft a comprehensive convention for which it is necessary to arrive at a consensus regarding the definition of terrorism. Consequently, even today there is no standard procedure for extradition and deportation of terrorists involved a trans-border terrorism.

## REVIEW OF LITERATURE

Studies have 'from time to time' reflected on the issue of the definition of terrorism and have also expressed concern over the fact that countries are still to reach a common agreement and help the United Nations to formulate an effective universal law to combat cross-border terrorism. Morris & Hoe[3] and Gill[4] were of the opinion that a number of conventions duly signed by the members had battled through the General Assembly of the United Nations, but eventually slipped into oblivion. They strongly averred that the justice system in its entirety would have to devise procedures and

[2] A report – United Nations General Assembly; "Measures to Eliminate International Terrorism", <Littp!//www.meadev.nil.in/ind-terjunga-res.Ltm>.

[3] 1987 Terrorism: *Threat & Response*, Moris and Hoe: Macmillan Press, pp. 8, 119-125.

[4] "Systematic overhaul headed to fight terror", *Pioneer*, December 2001.

processes that might remain in conformity with democratic norms, but at the same time, they should be effective enough to neutralize the strength of the terrorists and deter those who intended to join the organization. Soafer[5] was very critical about the law and felt that it legitimized international terrorism instead of punishing the criminals. He believed that this was not the product of negligence or mistake. It was intentional. He was supported by Cassese[6] who said that there was not a complete consensus on what constitutes terrorism. Noemi[7] and Verma[8] accepted the fact that the lack of a universally recognized definition of terrorism and the failure in global condemnation of terrorism made the law ineffective and unsuccessful. Noemi stated that the word 'terrorism made the law ineffective and unsuccessful. Noemi stated that the word 'terrorism' was required to be redefined separately because he perceived terrorism as a flexible concept dependent upon the evolution of law.

Most researchers tend to believe that it is difficult to have an internationally accepted definition of terrorism because "one man's terrorist is another man's freedom fighter". The reason for saying so is the belief that the definition depends entirely on the subjective outlook of the definer. Ganor[9] described terrorism as the deliberate use of violence against civilians in order to attain political. Ideological and religious aims. He hoped that after arriving at an international agreement on the definition of terrorism the nations would feel responsible to withhold giving support to terrorist organizations. He

[5] Soafer, A "International communities legal response to terrorism", Antonio Cassesse, *Terrorism, Politics and Law* 108 Cowley Road, Oxford, UK: Basil Blackwell Ltd, 1989.

[6] Cassese, n.5.

[7] Noemi, *International Cooperation to Support Terrorism,* London & Sydney: Croom Helm, 1985, pp. 127-128.

[8] Verma, M.N. "Havens for Terrorism: Strike against Global Terrorism", *Times of India,* 10 January 2002.

[9] Ganor, Boaz "Terrorism: No Prohibition Without Definition", 7 October 2001 <http://www.ict.org.il/articles/articledet.cfm?articleid=393>.

is supported by Teichman[10] who believed that the obstacle, which made the task difficult, was the disagreement about the activities, which could be justified as terrorism. Certain states had even tried to persuade the international community to define terrorism in a manner that the particular terror groups they sponsored would be outside the definition.

Terrorism today has become a profession and a way of life. When the terrorists of one country operate on the soil of another country in utter disregard of the international borders, it is received as international terrorism. Two writers Subrahmanyam[11] and Laos,[12] attributed the failure of the conventions to the two prominent weaknesses inherent in them: firstly they did not provide a space for common definition of terrorism and secondly, there seemed to be no clear difference between terrorist crimes and political offences.

What could be more substantial to support the aforesaid view than a well-known report of the FBI[13] which said that the United States-led war against terrorism had been stymied by the failure of federal agencies to agree on what exactly terrorism meant. It was observed by a sub-committee that every agency of the United States Government with a counter-terrorism mission used a different definition of terrorism, terrorist crimes and political offences.

More studies with similar findings make the issue a matter of serious concern. It is no secret that the terrorists of today form tightly cohesive and functionally effective groups, which are so much better organized than the responses from the government. Certain concrete measures are required to be adopted to counter the

[10] Teichman, "How to define terrorism: Philosophy", in Con or Greaty's *Terrorism the International Library of Criminology, Criminal Justice and Penology* London: Dartmouth Publishing Co Ltd, 1989, pp. 50-517.

[11] Subrahmanyam, K. "Terrorism & the Law" *The Hindu* 24 January 2002-04.

[12] Laos, K Nicolas, "Fighting terrorism: What can international law do"? File:/ /C:/WINDOW/Desktop/Internet,cod/laos.htm.

[13] FBI report, "US agencies can't agree on a definition for terrorism", file://C:/ WINDOWS/Desktop/Terrorism/ss terrorism, 07 21htm.

growing evil. A political climate of cooperation and goodwill is needed between the signatory states so as to enable the police forces and counter-terrorist organisations to work together and coordinate their activities in their fight against terrorism. Kofi Annan, UN Secretary General,[14] had said on 18 November 1999 that the force used to fight terrorism should always be proportional and focused on actual terrorists and not inflicting indiscriminate violence and terror on innocent civilians and children. In his address to the United Nations General Assembly, he further insisted on developing a framework of shared values and understanding within which countries could freely and voluntarily interact with and support each other instead of getting in each other's way.

No doubt that terrorist attacks constitute a clear violation of recognized norms of international law. The main purpose of many of these organizations is to undermine the international stability and, thereby, create a vicious circle of violene between the countries or even disturb the inter-ethnic relationship. A deep concern was also expressed by Valerie Kuchinsky,[15] Ambassador and Permanent Representative of Ukraine to the United Nations on 1 October 2001 that intensive study was necessary of the causes of terrorism, its socio-economic roots and conditions for an international effort to combat terrorism.

What emerges from the foresaid studies and literature is the feeling that certain conditions are required to make the law effective. The primary approach should be to obtain an agreed to definition of what an act of terrorism is; the internationalization of terrorism would, therefore, result in a more efficacious global response by means of greater legal assistance among the states.

[14] Kofi Anan, UN Secretary General Address to the UN General Assembly, 24 September 2001, quoted in *international Terrorism: World Viewpoint* ed. KR Gupta: Atlantic Publishers and Distributors, 2002.

[15] Valerie Kuchinsky, Ambassador and Permanent Representative of Ukraine, in October 2001 quoted in n. 14.

Moreover, terrorist acts should be criminalized in every state. The criminal procedure must be revised accordingly and courts' territorial jurisdictions should be more readily recognized even when attacks are carried out by nationals outside their home territory.

## STATEMENT OF THE STUDY

It is by now clear that there are consistent problems, which are creating hurdles in the formation of a universal law to combat terrorism. What could these problems be? The author here agrees with Laos[16] who indicated that the mass media in many instances had confused the meaning of terrorism by using the term in a superfluous manner. In addition, the notion of terrorism became complicated by being discussed in different guises and terrorist acts were often treated as part of insurgency and subversion. Certain states went to the extent of using the term arbitrarily in order to be in agreement with their national propaganda and foreign policy goals.

Accordingly, in this paper two salient subjects are selected for discussion: firstly, the definition of terrorism; secondly, the section which denotes the acts as terrorism. It is believed that an objective definition is indispensable to any serious attempt to combat terrorism. Without it no coordinated fight against international terrorism can achieve a goal.

## UNIVERSE OF THE STUDY

Countries which have witnessed terrorism in the past few decades are selected and their anti-terrorism acts are studied closely. These countries are divided in to two groups such as United Kingdom, United States of America, Canada, Israel on one hand and India, Pakistan, Ceylon and other Arab countries on the other hand. So we have developed and developing nations included in our study.

[16] Op cit n.12.

## ANALYSIS

No statistical measures could be applied in the study, as it is not data-based. However, content analysis has been done of all the given acts and the salient features are assessed. Besides, the definitions as mentioned in the SAARC Conventions and also that of EU including the NATO countries are also projected here.

A close examination will reveal the inadequacies of the definitions, which have stalled full consensus.

The League of Nations convention in the year 1937 defined terrorism as "all criminal acts directed against a state and intended or calculated to create a state of terror in the minds of a particular person or a group of persons or the general public". The UN resolution later in 1999 strongly condemned such acts and termed them "unjustifiable whatever the considerations of a political, philosophical, ideological, racial ethnic, religious or other nature that might be invoked to justify them".

Schmid[17] proposed a short legal definition to the UN crime branch (1992) "Act of terrorism = Peacetime Equivalent of War Crime". An academic consensus definition was propagated in 1988 that "terrorism is an anxiety-inspiring method of repeated violent action employed by clandestine individual, group or state actors for idiosyncratic, criminal or political reasons whereby in contrast to assassination the direct targets of attacks are not the main targets". In this context, we must also study the definition given by the US department of defense, which says that terrorism is "the calculated use of violence or the threat of violence to inculcate fear; intended to coerce or to intimidate governments or societies in the pursuit of goals that are generally political, religious or ideological".

To have a comprehensive view of the definitions as given by various countries, the views of the Islamic conventions are also included to know their mind as to what they think about terrorism.

[17] Schmid, A , "Definition of Terrorism", 28 August 2002, file://c:windows/Desktop/terrorism/terrorism_definition.htm.

The convention of the Organization of the Islamic Conference on combating international terrorism believes that "terrorism constitutes a gross violation of human rights, in particular the right to freedom and security, as well as an obstacle to the free functioning of institutions and socio-economic development, as it aims at destabilizing states. It is, therefore, defined as an act of violence or threat thereof notwithstanding its motives or intention s perpetrated to carry out an individual or collective criminal plan with the aim of terrorizing people or threatening to harm them or imperiling their lives, honour, freedoms, security or rights or exposing the environment or any facility or public or private property to hazards or occupying or seizing them, or endangering a national resource, or international facilities, or threatening the stability, territorial integrity, political unity or sovereignty of independent states". Accordingly, the 'terrorist crime' is any crime executed, started, participated in to realize a terrorist objective in any of the Contracting States or against its nationals, assets or interests or foreign facilities and so on. It means that the Islamic convention takes cognizance of any crime, which is committed against innocent people with the intention to terrorize them. However, it appears that terrorism today has become a profession and a way of life for some fanatics whose object is to destroy the political and social system and get money and publicity.

The European countries also took a stride to give their opinion about the concept of terrorism. Bunyan[18] said that the war on terrorism had turned into an ongoing war on freedom and democracy. The EU considered those acts as terrorist acts, which 'given their nature and context may seriously damage a country or an international organization, as defined as offences under national law. They are committed with the aim to intimidate a population to destabilize the social structure of a country or compel a government or an international organization from committing any act.'

[18] Bunyan, Tony "The war on freedom and democracy: an a nalysis of the effect and democratic culture in the EU", http://www/statewatch.org/news/2002/sep/analysis/3,htm.

The views regarding the definition of terrorism and the identified terrorist activities mentioned in the anti-prevention acts of the countries selected for study are discussed with the help of a chart.

Chart I indicating the definition of terrorism and the activities considered as terrorism by the respective countries. (As given in the acts)

| States/ Countries | Name and the year of the act | Definition of terrorism/ terrorist organizations | Acts defined as terrorist activities |
|---|---|---|---|
| United Kingdom | Terrorism Act 2000 | Terrorism means the use of threat of (a) action (b) threat designed to influence the govern-ment or to intimidate the public or a section of the public (c) threat is made for the purpose of advancing a political, religious or ideological cause. | Serious violence against a person. Serious damage to property Endangers a person's life other than that committing the action creates a serious threat to the health or safety of a person seriously interferes with or disrupts an electronic system. |
| United States of America | United States Code Section 2656f(d) | Terrorism means premeditated, politically motivated violence perpetrated against noncombant targets by sub-national groups or clandestine agents intended to influence an audience. | Terrorist groups are groups practicing or have significant subgroups that practice international terrorism. |
| Canada | Anti-terrorism Plan 2001 | Targeting people and activities that pose a threat to the security and the well being of the Canadians. | Knowingly participate in, contribute to or facilitate the activities of a terrorist group or to instruct anyone to carry out a terrorist activity. |
| Israel | Prevention of Terrorism Ordinance (Amendments) Law 1980 | "Terrorist organization" means a body of persons resorting in its activities to acts of violence calculated to cause death or injury to a person or to threats of such acts of violence. | A person performing a function in the management, instruction, participating in the deliberation and acting as a member of the tribunal of the organization. |

The General Assembly of the United Nation in its Declaration on Measures to Eliminate International Terrorism, adopted on 9 December 1994, encouraged States to review urgently the scope of the existing international legal provisions on the prevention, repression and elimination of terrorism in all its forms and manifestations, with the aim of ensuring that there was a comprehensive legal framework covering all aspects of the matter. At the Legal Committee's 29th Meeting in November 2000, several countries responded to the call to define terrorism.[19] Israel was concerned that some states believed acts of bombing were not terrorism if done for national liberation. Without a standard definition and without unified political will terrorism thrives. On the contrary, Syria noted that state terrorism by Israel had resulted in the deaths of Palestinian women and children. It also criticized Israel for selective choice of targets, which were often symbolic, placing their actions under the umbrella of terrorism.

In assessing Canada's capacity to contribute to the war on terrorism, two broad categories need to be examined: (1) Canada's strategic capabilities and (2) domestic political and economic constraints. The first category refers to Canada's ability to bring relevant military and diplomatic assets to bear in the war on terrorism and the second concerning the domestic political and economic constraints refers to the level of political support in Canada for the war on terrorism and the level of financial support Canada is able to allocate. However, while Canada lacks the capacity for broad and sustained combat, it is able to fulfil "niche" military roles.[20] In its anti-terrorist plan, Canada identifies terrorist activities as those involved in participating, contributing, facilitating the activities of a terrorist group or instructing one to carry out terrorist activities.

[19] "Legal definition of terrorism", GA: Legal Committee http://www.unamich.org/MUN/SEMMUNA/legal.htm.

[20] Jay Makarenko "The war on global terrorism: Canada's role" , 1 October 2001 http://www.Mapleleafweb.com.

The subcommittee of the United States has found that practically every agency uses a different definition of terrorism. The report says, "Without a standard definition, terrorism might be treated no differently than other crime". The report presented the subcommittee's definition of terrorism "Terrorism is the illegitimate premeditated use of politically motivated violence or the threat of violence by a sub-national group against persons and property".[21] We find that USA according to the details mentioned in the chart has defined terrorism and terrorist groups basically focusing on violence done in a premeditated and motivated manner. The terrorist groups are, therefore, those, which indulge in activities, meant for destabilizing a government or killing innocent people.

The United Kingdom has been very specific in its view regarding the concept of terrorism. The government believes that any use of threat made for the purpose of advancing a political, religious or ideological cause can well be labeled as "terrorism" and activities accordingly meant for causing serious damage to person or property are, therefore, included in the sections of "terrorist acts". The government believes that new counter-terrorism measures are needed to take into account changes in the nature of terrorism and the methods deployed in it. It proposes to introduce permanent legislation applicable throughout the UK to meet the general threat faced from terrorism.[22]

USA has introduced 'new tools' to fight terrorism.[23] President Bush signed a new anti-terror law that will expand the government's power in the surveillance and gathering of intelligence regarding the working of terrorist organizations. The bill also strengthens penalties for those who help terrorists and lengthens the statute of limitations

[21] "Definition of terrorism" {Source: Patterns if terrorism. Washington: Dept. of State, 2001:vi} file://C:WINDOWS\Desktop\Terrorism\ss_terrorism_07_21.htm.

[22] "Legislation against terrorism", file://C:WINDOWS\Desctop\Internet.doc\chap-02.htm>.

[23] "War against Terror. Bush signs antiterrorist bill into law". < http://asia.cnn.com/2001/US/10/26/rec.bush.antiterror.bill/>.

for terrorist acts. Bush asked the Congress to implement the two treaties, one being the 'International Convention for the Suppression of Terrorist Bombing' and the other treaty called the 'International Convention for the Suppression of the Financing of Terrorism'. Such measures would help the law enforcement agents prevent future terrorist attacks rather than simply respond with prosecutions after the occurrence of the incident.

The SAARC Convention at the Dhaka Summit on 7-8 December 1985 and then the Bangalore Summit Declaration of 17 November 1986 resolved to take effective measures to ensure that the perpetrators of terrorist acts did not escape punishment by providing for them extradition and immediate prosecution. The conventions condemned all acts, methods and practices of terrorism as criminal and deplored their impact on life and property, socio-economic development, political stability, regional and international peace and cooperation and recognized the principles laid down in the UN resolution 2625. In Article 1 of the convention, subject to the overall requirements of the law of extradition of the Contracting State it had been mentioned that those acts would be regarded as terrorist and for the purpose of extradition said article not be regarded as political offence or as an offence connected with a political offence or even inspired by political motives. It also includes beside others in Article 8 that the contracting states should cooperate among themselves to the extent permitted by their national laws, with a view to prevent terrorist activities through precautionary measures (Hameed).[24]

Chart II Table indicating the definition of terrorism/terrorist activities by the four countries mentioned below.

[24] Hameed, Shahul, A.C. minister of foreign affaires Democratic Socialist Republic of Sri Lanka.

| Countries | Name and year of the act | Definition of terrorism/ terrorist organization | Acts defined as terrorist activities |
|---|---|---|---|
| India | Prevention of Terrorist Act 2001 | Terrorism means intentions to threaten the unity, integrity, and security of India or to strike terror in the people or any section of the people by using bombs, explosive substances, firearms or other legal weapons. | Terrorist acts are such acts, which resulted in the death of any person be punishable with imprisonment for a term not less than five years and, which may extend to imprisonment to life and liability of fine. |
| Pakistan | Pakistan Anti-Terrorism (Amendment) Ordinance, 1999 | Terrorism means to strike terror or create disturbances by using bombs. Explosives firearms or inflammable substances. It also includes an act of gang rape, child molestation, or robbery coupled with rape. | Commits a scheduled offence the effect of which will be to strike terror or fear and insecurity in the people or to adversely affect different sections of the people, or commits a gang rape, child molestation or robbery, commits an act of civil commotion. |
| Sri Lanka | Prevention of Terrorism (Temporary Provisions) Act No 48 of 1979 | Terrorism means causing the death of any specified person, committing any other attack upon such person, which would be punishable with death or imprisonment for seven years. | Offences mentioned are causing the death of any person, commits criminal intimidation of any special person, commits the offence of robbery of the property of the government, etc. |
| Nepal | Terrorist and Destructive Activities (Control and Punishment Ordinance) 26 November 2001 | Any act or plan of using any kinds of arms, grenades, or explosives with the objective of hurting the sovereignty or the security and law and kingdom of Nepal. | Acts are production, distribution, accumulation, peddling, import and export or installation of any kind of arms, ammunition, bombs or explosives, acts aimed at creating and spreading fear and terror in public life. |

A close look at the statements given in the acts mentioned above indicate that the respective countries once again consider any threat to the integrity, security and sovereignty of the nation or to strike terror in the people or any section of the people as terrorism. In India, the Prevention of Terrorism Act extends to the whole of India, subject to the acceptance of the state government concerned. The provisions of the act also apply to the citizens of India outside India.

The punishment for the terrorist act resulting in the death of a person is death or imprisonment not less than five years extending to imprisonment for life with fine.[25] We find that Pakistan's Anti-terrorism (Amendment Ordinance 1999) promulgated to amend the Anti-terrorism Act of 1997 makes similar provisions for punishment for the acts of terrorism as given in POTA of India, except that there has been an insertion of 7A and 7B, which deal with the creation of civil commotion meaning creating of internal disturbances in violation of the law. The punishment for such an act is rigorous imprisonment for a term not less than seven years or with a fine or with both.[26]

The other two countries, Sri Lanka and Nepal have also severely condemned terrorism in their countries. Sri Lanka[27] had specified that any act causing the death of any particular person or kidnapping or abduction of a specified person or causing death to such a person would be punished with death or imprisonment for seven years. The Government of Nepal resorted to the measure of introducing their Anti-Terrorist Act on November 2001 after the Maoist insurgency brought to an end and the cease-fire that was being observed by them and the government since July 2001.[28]

A correct and objective definition of terrorism can be based upon accepted international laws and principles regarding what behaviours are permitted in conventional wars between the nations. These principles are clearly laid out in the Geneva and Hague conventions. They differentiate between soldiers who attack a military adversary and war criminals who attack innocent civilians. Some believe that terrorism defies clear definition because of its emotive and non-

[25] Prevention of Terrorism Act 2001 http://mha.nic.in/poto.htm.

[26] Pakistan Anti-Terrorism (Amendment) Ordinance 1999 http://www.satp.org/satporgtp/countries/Pakistan/document/act anordinen——/antiteworrorismht.

[27] Prevention of Terrorism (Temporary Provisions) Act No 48 of 1979 http://www/Humsatporgtp/countries/Sri Lanka/documents/act-/prevention of terrorism.ht.

[28] Terrorist and Destructive Activities (Control and Punishment) Ordinance 2001, file://C:/window/desktop/Terrorism/Terrorism Ordinance.htm.

specific nature. Globalization itself is allowing terrorist organizations broader and more efficient means of communication and access to technology. Besides, many countries still continue to offer a 'safe haven' for terrorist groups either by choice or through their inability to root them out.

There are some genuine technical problems obstructing the formulation of a universal definition of terrorism. The latter pertains to questions concerning the perpetrators of terrorist acts, the targets, range of acts, motive and the international component. The states are divided on the issue whether the definition shculd involve a wide or a narrow frame of reference to terrorist acts, and the same relates to the motive, which has been a source of controversy in UN debate and among legal scholars.

Only on the basis of an international agreement on the definition will it be possible to demand that all nations withhold all support from terrorist organizations. What is important in these definitions, according to Ganor,[29] is the differentiation between the goals and the means used by the terrorist. The aim of terrorism and guerrilla warfare may well be identical, but they are distinguished from each other by the means used or by the targets of their operation. While the guerilla fighters' targets are military ones, the terrorists deliberately target civilians. If all the world's civilians are not to become pawns in one struggle or another, terrorism– the deliberate targeting of civilians–must absolutely be forbidden regardless of the legitimacy of its goals. The ends do not justify the means. By carrying out terrorist attacks, the perpetrators make themselves the enemies of mankind.

While the issue behind terrorism are usually national or regional, the impact of terrorist campaigns is often international. Their form of psychological warfare is "propaganda by deed}; it is thus not possible to look at international terrorism in isolation from

[29] Ganor Boaz "Terrorism: No Prohibition without Definition" 7 October 2001, http://www.ict.org.il/articles/articledet.cfm?articleid=393.

domestic terrorism. It is seen that domestic terrorism has its effect in other countries and linkages with foreign terrorist groups are not uncommon. Some analysts had claimed that there had been a shift from low to high casualty terrorism, but this cannot really be established in the absence of a consensus as to what constitutes terrorism.[30]

A general criterion is that a terrorist act is carried within the scope of International Terrorism if it has clear international consequences. Alongside, it is suggested that a conduct contains an international element when the perpetrator and the victim are citizens of different states and the act is performed in more than one state. Such was the case in 1960 when the concept of terrorism became an international one, with a series of hijackings hitting the headlines and later the then Secretary General Kurt Waldheim asked that the issue should be placed in the General Assembly's agenda under the heading 'Measures to prevent terrorism and other forms of violence which endanger or take innocent lives or jeopardize fundamental freedom.'

Most national governments have responded to international terrorism at a tactical level and not at a strategic level. As a result, the traditional response has neither mitigated nor deterred terrorism. Gunaratna[31] believes that the terrorist organizations, by employing technical and human expertise, have managed to enter the domestic groups operating oversees or foreign groups operating on their soil. They are well aware of the technical means of gathering intelligence.

International laws should protect states from the terrorist activity of insurgents and other criminals by putting emphasis on the condemnation of the means used by terrorists to achieve their goals. A quick look at the work of Laos and many others would reveal their suggestion that international organizations, for instance the UN and

[30] "Terrorism" http://www.undep.org/odeep/terrorism.htm.

[31] Gunaratna, R. *Transnational Terrorism. Support Networks and Trends in Faultlines; Writings on Conflict and Resolution*, vol 7. Printed and published by Bulwark Books for the Institute for Conflict Management, November 2000.

NATO, could actively contribute to the fight against terrorism and judge the means used to achieve any political, social or economic goals with the help of international regulations. The pursuit of any goal by violence directed against non-combatant people or by creating a public danger or a state of terror must be clearly condemned by international law.

## CONCLUSION

The states of the world should comply with the principle of free and fair justice so that terrorists would have no opportunity to remain unpunished for their crimes and moreover, certain crimes would not be vindicated as a means to any political end. The establishment of a permanent International Criminal Court of Justice could play a very important role in the anti-terrorist struggle. Besides, states would be able to use it instead of their national court. It would help them to avoid political tension between the states. However, law alone will not eradicate terrorism from its very roots. Systematic and intensive investigations are needed to study the causes promoting terrorism and thereby attempts should be made to mitigate the grievances through political, legal and administrative processes. Sometimes extreme economic deprivation, organized exploitation and police brutalities also lead to an outburst of violence and organized resistance through terrorist methods. The government must take care that these incidences are handled with care and do not precipitate into terror.[32] What is needed to the utmost is the remodeling of old laws and enactment of new laws, which would give law enforcement personnel and judges adequate statutory and legal authority to respond to the terrorists' criminal acts in an expeditious manner. The terrorists should not be considered as political leaders or soldiers of war. They must be dealt with as the

[32] Menon, Madhava, "Anti-Terrorism Law-1" *The Statesman* editorial column, 10 December 2001.

criminals they are (Greeenstone).[33] However, we must be prepared to answer jurisdictional questions and be able to cut off the terrorists' ability to gain the media recognition and coverage, which they readily achieve.

International approval of a common definition of terrorism could substantially facilitate the anti-terrorist struggle. Terrorism should be differentiated from war crimes or crimes against humanity and from common murder. Terrorist activities differ from common murder in their psychological impact. Terrorists aim to create a climate of fear in which they expect to realize their goals. I, therefore, repeat that without a change in the approach of all the nations and their determination to fight terrorism, it will not be possible to wage war against terrorism, and without this, any significant attack by the terrorists, be it the 11 September or 13 December incidents, would become insignificant compared to the attacks yet to come.

[33] Greenstone, James. L. "The Laws on Terrorism" http://www.emotionalfirst aid.com/volume.3/n umber4/30.htm l.

# IX

# Global Terrorism

*Maj. Gen. (Retd.) Afsir Karim*

*The war that the Islamic terrorist organizations began on 11 September 2001 has now entered a more dangerous phase, but the war against terrorism waged by the US is yet to be reoriented to meet new challenges. The primary focus of terrorist attacks has been on American allies during the past few months; both the coalition forces in Iraq and US allies elsewhere in the world have been targeted with renewed vehemence.*

*Once terrorist groups had divergent objectives and these mostly concerned their own countries or governments. Egyptian Islamic Jehad, Islamic Movement of Uzbekistan, Gamaa-al-Islamiya, Jamaat-ul-Ulema-e-Islam, Lashkar-e-Taiba, Jemaah-e-Islamic and all other such groups gradually shifted their objectives to target America and its allies after Bin Laden created International Islamic Front for Jehad against the Jews and Crusaders (IIF) in February 1998. The IIF has now forged ties with Islamic terrorist groups and organized Crime Syndicates all over the world. A new group active in US prisons is Jamaat-ul-Fugra, the group that murdered Daniel Pearl, Richard Reid who had hidden explosives in his shoes to blow up an international flight also had links with Sheikh Gilani, the Fugra Chief.*

*Al-Qaeda's ideology is still obscure; besides its destructive vision, it has no eventual goals. The main purpose of lethal attacks is to hurt, horrify and frighten the adversaries. The objective of al-Qaeda has shifted from forcing US troops out of Saudi Arabia to lethal attacks on America, a rather dubious aim that would serve no purpose. The Bush administration rather than using the 9/11 tragedy to settle scores with Iraq should start working on creating conditions that would bring stability to the Middle East.*

*The terrorist strategy has been to keep US attention focused on Iraq and Afghanistan so that they are free to spread their tentacles in various other parts of the world. An escalation of terrorist violence must be expected both in Iraq and Afghanistan. Moreover, terrorist groups based in Pakistan are likely to increase the scale of their activities in Kashmir to focus international attention on this area. If the terrorists are able to acquire and use WMD against selected targets, the security situation may deteriorate irreversibly in the entire region.*

*NATO has simply become an instrument for increasing and widening the US global influence. The advent of NATO in the Indian subcontinent could have a far-reaching effect on the security environment of South Asia, as this would change the strategic equations in this region. Uzbekistan is taking advantage of the US backing to extend its influence in Central Asia; however, militant Islamic groups have already launched a counter offensive. A similar situation may develop in South Asia.*

*The Hunt for al-Qaeda and the Taliban continues in Afghanistan and the Northwest Frontier Areas of Pakistan. Strangely enough, a country that gave shelter and help to these fundamentalist groups so far has now been made in charge of hunting them down.*

*Despite the new status of Pakistan as the major non-NATO ally and the combined US-Pakistan operations in and around Pakistani Northwest Frontier province, Osama bin Laden and his top associates are yet to be found. One wonders if it is possible that the top al-Qaeda leaders would continue to hide in a belt which is under siege both by the US and Pakistani forces, unless important elements within the Pakistani establishment continue to secretly support the global Jehadi groups.*

*The most serious threat, however, arises from the nuclear devices that seem to be in the possession of the stateless terrorist groups. A new nuclear era has already dawned since the extensive nuclear-smuggling operations from Pakistan have come to light. Pakistan has, however, been rewarded for creating the worst menace for America and its allies. There are reports that the terrorist groups are now in a position to use toxic chemicals such as osmium tetroxide to boost explosions. Some reports suggest that this chemical was used to boost the blasts during bomb attacks on the British embassy in Istanbul and British compounds in Saudi Arabia.*

*Crises are also brewing elsewhere because global terrorism largely remains unchecked due to the focus of US attention on Iraq, although the Caucasus, Saudi Arabia, Uzbekistan, Pakistan, Thailand and Indonesia have been subjected to terrorist attacks. The US policy makers remain unconcerned with the terrorist activities in Chechnya despite the fact that Islamic terrorists have lately stepped up attacks on Russia.*

*The global image of the US has taken a severe beating in the recent past because of the double standards it maintains, and according to a New York Times report – a state department official, Margaret Tutwiler, in charge of public diplomacy acknowledged that "it will take us many years of hard, focused work" to restore and repair the image.*[1]

*The change of the government in Spain must have come as a shock to the US policy makers and they would have realized that democracies can adopt policies, which may not serve US interests. The Spanish turnabout may be the beginning of the process; now some other US allies who face the danger of terrorist*

[1] Tom Regan, 'US image abroad will "take years" to repair,' *The Christian Science Monitor,* http://www.csmonitor.com/specials/sept11/dailyUpdate.html , 9 February 2004.

*attacks may also revise their policies.*

## FACES OF GLOBAL TERRORISM

### *Turmoil in Iraq*

Terrorists thrive on local support to survive, and the current American policies are largely responsible for increasing alienation of the local population in Iraq that translates in to support for the terrorists. The situation in Iraq has visibly deteriorated in the past month. The bomb that exploded on 31 March in Anbar province, not far from Fallujah killed five US soldiers. In another lethal incident, two civilian cars carrying some foreign nationals, reported to be contractors, were burnt and all the occupants killed. The worst part was that "angry crowds dragged the bodies through the streets, dismembered them and hanged some of the mutilated corpses."[2] The kind of crowd behaviour witnessed in Fallujah is a new phenomenon that shows the growing anger and impatience of the Iraqi people with the present situation.

In another car bomb attack in the town of Baquba north of Baghdad, at least 12 people were wounded. Three British soldiers were injured in Basra when an explosive device was activated close to their vehicle. A violent confrontation between Spanish troops and Shiite mobs supporting Muqtaba Al-Sadr, a leading Shhite cleric, opposed to future American plans for Iraq, left at least 60 dead including four Salvadorean soldiers. Since then the situation has worsened and American troops have suffered their haviest post-war casualties in April. The recent upsurge in violence would obviously invite reprisals and tough measures from coalition forces and the cycle of violence will continue to grow. At least two leading US senators have warned the administration of the danger of civil war in Iraq.

Virulent anti-American propaganda is now emanating both from

[2] Howard LaFranchi, 'Killings in Iraq challenge US will,' *The Christian Science Monitor*, http://www.csmonitor.com/2004/0402/p01s03-woiq.htm, 2 April 2004.

Shiite sources and Sunni mosques. It seems that the US must make up its mind about the exit strategy soon, even if some kind of a government is put in place; but if US forces continue to be deployed, the situation will not change. To limit the duration and scope of confrontation between the US forces and the people is important as prolonged confrontation between the two can only help the forces of destabilization.

A few months back, car-bombings were the greatest threat to American forces, but in recent weeks, the focus has shifted to well planned attacks and mob violence, besides attacks on foreigners and the US soldiers. It is evident that use of military force, no matter how strong, cannot end civil resistance permanently, specially when latent anger against foreign presence is boiling over. Patriotic fervour and bitter anti-Americanism have created an explosive situation in Iraq.

The US military remains occupied at several levels of insurgency in Iraq. A US report describes terrorist cells, which comprise Yemenis, Saudis and Moroccans; it seems several terrorist forces are now in the fray. The local population supports and nurtures these elements despite strong US pressure. Suicide attacks certainly point at the involvement of the al-Qaeda trained groups whose main aim is to create maximum chaos besides targeting the US forces and other coalition troops.

Both Sunnis and Shiites are against the continued US presence; elements from both the factions are now lending support to anti-coalition forces. Since armed Shiites have joined with Guerrilla forces, US military forces are facing serious confrontation. The effort and the attitude required to earn cooperation is still lacking as the US civil and military leaders do not seem to understand the internal dynamics of the present impasse. The US can no longer depend on creating a rift between Sunnis and Shiites as both the factions are equally critical of the continued US presence in Iraq.

The coalition forces in Iraq are passing through one of the most difficult periods in post-war Iraq; a wave of violent protests, lethal car bombs, explosions, targeted assassination of police officers, and sabotage of oil pipelines have become a common occurrence. Violent resistance has intensified in Sadr City and Najaf where armed Shiites and the US forces confront each other. Moqtada Al Sadr who inspires the Shiite uprising in the southern cities of Iraq continues to be defiant. In the last few weeks, Shiite groups in Baghdad and the southern cities of Iraq have gone on the rampage. One year after the combat phase of the Iraq war, the US-led coalition forces find themselves fighting on several fronts, and the promised stability is nowhere in sight.

On 5 April, US forces opened a new offensive called 'Vigilant Resolve' against guerrilla strongholds of Fallujah and Ramadi. They also blocked two highways to Baghdad from the Jordanian frontier to bottle up the guerrillas. According to Washington Post, an attack by Iraqi militia on the US government's headquarters in Najaf was repulsed by eight commandos from a private security firm, the Blackwater Security Consulting. The role of private armies like the Blackwater's commandos in fighting in Najaf throws light on the role of private armies in Iraq.[3]

The American military opened a second front in Shiite populated areas in southern Iraq, besides surrounding Fallujah where fighting has erupted. In Karbala, Sadr's militia attacked a police station and a television station. In Basra, Iraq's second largest city, they occupied the governor's office and were involved in an exchange of fire with British troops. In Amarah, Sadr's militiamen, the Mahdi Army, repeatedly clashed with British soldiers near the governor's office.

The US soldiers face bullets every night; long ambushes begin with sneak attacks; rocket propelled grenades fired from winding alleys. Americans inside Humvees retaliate fiercely and the confrontation then quickly escalates into nightlong firefights. The

[3] Blackwater Security Consulting, www.globalsecurity.org, and *Washington Post*, http://conspiracyplanet.com/channel. Cfm?channelid=80&contentid=1137, 6 April 2004.

battleground in the vast warren of narrow streets called Sadr City, reminds 1st Lt. Dave Swanson of Mogadishu. "As soon as we came into the city, it's like the whole place came alive with fire," Swanson said of his arrival, in a 1st Cavalry Division Bradley Fighting Vehicle, in the district he used to regard with arm's length affection of a cop on the beat. "In our minds, it totally changes our opinion about how we think about this area," said Swanson, from Owensville, Ohio. "In a day, we went from a humanitarian mission to combat. It's just amazing that the kids I talked with two, three days ago are the same ones that are throwing the rocks at us as hard as they can"[4]

Despite strong US military presence, fighting continues in several fronts in Iraq, insurgents are attacking military supply convoys, setting fire to armored personnel carriers and looting supplies and equipment. Kidnapping of civil and military personnel to use them as bargaining chips is another new development. These actions suggest a well-planned strategy under a centralized control to intimidate the coalition countries.

### *Terrorism in Uzbekistan*

Terrorist violence in Uzbekistan has caused more than 40 fatal casualties in Tashkent. The presence of suicide bombers who blew themselves up at a police checkpoint suggests involvement of al-Qaeda trained terrorists. This checkpoint leads to the US embassy in Tashkent. In two separate incidents, two women blew themselves up in a busy Tashkent market and at a bus stop. The Russian paper Vremia said, "The black widows have arrived in Uzbekistan," referring to Muslim women seeking revenge for the death of their husbands in earlier incidents.[5]

Uzbekistan serves as one of the important bases for the US-led

[4] Farl Vick and Swell Chan, 'Violence in Sadr City Embitter s Both Sides,' *Washington Post*, Baghdad, 5 April 2004.

[5] Ronald Flamini, Chief International Correspondent, 'Analysis: Terrorism in Tashkent worries US, " http://www.upi.com/print.cfm?StoryID=20040330-022006-4548r, 30 April 2004.

coalition forces operating in Afghanistan. The US has a large-size supply base and an important airbase in Tashkent. A US official in Washington is reported to have said that unrest in Uzbekistan could seriously undermine Operation Enduring Freedom because "Tashkent is its lifeline." The Islamic Movement of Uzbekistan (IMU) maintains close links with al-Qaeda and most of the fighters who have received training from al-Qaeda are still active in this area.[6]

*Terrorism in Russia*

Among the mountain people of the Caucasus, Chechens are the fiercest. Two rounds of warfare — 1994 to 1996 and 1999 to the present have their roots in history and the martial traditions of the Chechens. Chechens want freedom and Russia cannot allow it because it may lead to the disintegration of Russia. The advent of Wahabi Islam and al-Qaeda trained terrorists has added a new dimension to the conflict in Chechnya. In this theatre of terrorist operations, Russians continue to pay a heavy price in men and material. Despite various terrorist attacks in the Russian heartland, the US and its allies do not view it with any great concern; violence in Chechnya and terrorist in its wake is viewed quite differently from the usual condemnation of terrorist.

The Moscow metro blast is the latest act of terrorism that killed at least 30 people; earlier, an explosion aboard a train in Stavropol region had resulted in six fatal casualties. The series of terrorist attacks since 1999 should be considered a grave threat of global terrorism and not ignored by the Western nations.

Recently, there has been a major upsurge in violence; the most significant strikes since 1999 have been listed here:

31 August 1999 – A bomb explodes in an underground shopping center near the Kremlin, injuring 20 people.

September 1999 – Bombs destroy apartment blocks in Moscow, Buynaksk and Volgodonsk, killing 200. The government blames

[6] Ibid.

Chechen rebels, who in turn accuse Russia's secret services. Prime Minister Vladimir Putin then responds by sending troops into Chechnya for the first time since 1997.

7 June 2000 – In the first attack of its kind in the breakaway republic of Chechnya, two Russian special police are killed in a suicide car-bombing near the regional capital Grozny.

2-3 July 2000 – Chechen guerrillas launch five suicide bomb attacks on bases of Russian forces within 24 hours. In the deadliest, at least 54 people are killed at a police base near Grozny.

8 August 2000 – A bomb in a busy Moscow underpass kills eight people.

23 October 2002 – About 50 Chechen rebels seize a Moscow theater and take about 800 hostages. After a three-day siege, Russian forces storm the building using gas, killing most of the rebels and 120 hostages.

27 December 2002 – Chechen suicide bombers ram vehicles into the local government headquarters in Grozny, bringing down the roof and floors of the four-storey building. Chechen officials say about 80 people were killed.

12 May 2003 – Two suicide bombers drive a truck full of explosives into a government administration and security complex in Znamenskoye, in northern Chechnya. Fifty-nine people are killed and scores hurt.

14 May 2003 – At least 16 people are killed in a suicide bomb attack during a religious festival in the town of Iliskhan-Yurt, east of Grozny, and 145 are wounded.

5 June 2003 – A woman bomber ambushes a bus carrying Russian air force pilots near Chechnya, blowing it up and killing herself and 18 other people.

5 July 2003 – Two women suicide bombers kill 15 other people when they blow themselves apart at an open-air rock festival at Moscow's Tushino airfield. Sixty are injured.

1 August 2003 – A suicide bomber kills at least 50 people at a military hospital in the town of Mozdok in North Ossetia

bordering Chechnya.

3 September 2003 – Six people are killed in an explosion on board a commuter train near the northern Caucasus spa town of Pyatigorsk, but police say it is not the work of Chechen rebels.

5 December 2003 – An explosion on a commuter train in the Stavropol region north of Chechnya kills at least 36 people and injures more than 150.

9 December 2003 – A suicide bomber in central Moscow kills at least five people.

6 February 2004 – A rush-hour blast kills at least 30 people and injures 70 on a metro train in Moscow.[7]

*Terrorism in Thailand*

Recent terrorist attacks in Indonesia, the Philippines, Afghanistan and the Middle East have drawn significant attention of the West to the looming terrorist threats, but little notice has been taken of the terrorist incidents in southern Thailand. It would be a grave mistake to take these highly organized attacks lightly, as they indicate, "in the fight against terrorism, Thailand may be turning into 'Southeast Asia's soft underbelly'." In January, Islamic separatist insurgents had set fire to 21 government schools and raided the 4th Army Engineers Battalion camp, killing four soldiers.[8]

There is a long history of resentment toward the government in the southern Muslim region, five million Thai Muslims have suffered from decades of government neglect, the region is backward compared to the rest of Thailand. Thailand's Muslims want the state to recognize their language and distinct Malay ethnicity. The recent killing of Buddhist monks and two students indicated that radical Islamist groups are making an attempt to polarize the society and

[7] Excerpted from World Timeline: 'Terrorism in Russia,' <cnn.com>, http://edition.cnn.com/2004/WORLD/europe/02/06/russia.timeline/, 6 February 2004.

[8] John Brandon, 'In Thailand south, fertile ground for terrorism,' *Herald Tribune*, http://www.iht.com/cgi-bin/generic.cgi?template=articleprint.tmplh&Articleld= 128942>, 11 February 2004.

create distrust between the Muslim and Buddhist communities. Osama bin Laden's appeal has increased among the Muslims in southern Thailand since the invasion of Iraq by the US.

The Thai government declared martial law in the Muslim – dominated provinces of Pattani, Yala and Narathiwat after violence in January in which more than 60 people lost their lives. Re-establishing peace in southern Thailand is necessary, draconian laws and oppressive measures would only serve to widen the gap between people and the authorities. Such policies would alienate Muslims and push them into the arms of Islamic militant groups. The Thai Jamaat Islamiah (JI) is known to maintain close links with al-Qaeda; Islamic militants and terrorists have been using Thailand as a transit area for years. Hambali, the mastermind of the Bali bombings is believed to have planned the blasts while he was in southern Thailand. Hambali was arrested in a suburb of Bangkok in August 2003 with close cooperation between US intelligence agencies and the Thai police. The Thai government's decision to support US policy on Iraq has given impetus to fundamentalism and anti-government sentiments, which could lead to more violence. The focus of attacks may shift to soft targets such as night clubs, tourist centers and market places.[9]

*Terrorism and Pakistan*

Pakistan, once an ally of Bin Laden and the Taliban, is now in charge of hunting them down. Its scientists obviously with the permission of its regime were until recently selling nuclear secrets and technology to the countries, which were listed as the 'Axis of Evil' by the American administration. In view of these facts, Pakistan should have been named as a prominent member of the 'Axis of Evil', but instead it has been rewarded economically and named as major non-NATO ally by the US. In the meanwhile, Bin Laden and Mullah Omar continue to enjoy the hospitality of tribal Pakistan. Whether it is with or without the connivance of the Pakistani regime, only

[9] Ibid.

time will tell.

By designating Pakistan as major 'non-NATO ally', the US has given it a military and economic insurance policy and neutralized India's conventional advantages to a great extent. This limits India's options to act against Pakistan-based terrorists, but allows Pakistan to continue support of Islamic terrorist groups operating in Kashmir. Two recent statements of General Musharraf warn India to settle the Kashmir problem within a short time frame or things will return to square one. This bodes ill for the peace process in the subcontinent. Musharraf as a staunch ally of the US is now assured of receiving new technology and weapons required to neutralize India's conventional superiority in the region.

Recently, Pakistan was warned by US Ambassador to Afghanistan, Zalmay Khalilzad, "Pakistan must eliminate terrorist sanctuaries or the United States will step in and do its part in obliterating them." Unless the issue of sanctuaries is solved, it will be difficult to fully settle security problems in the southern and eastern part of Afghanistan. He further added, "We cannot allow this problem to fester indefinitely." Khalilzad told about 100 people at the Center for Strategic and International Studies, a Washington think tank. "We have told the Pakistani leadership that either they must solve this problem or we will have to do it ourselves."[10]

### *Terrorist in Europe*

It seems that Europe has become the future target of Islamist terrorists in the Western world. Al-Qaeda's European branch recently promised to turn Spain into "an inferno." The French Special Forces recently rounded up more than a dozen suspected members of a group with ties with the network. Terrorist organisations are specially active in UK, France, Turkey, Germany and Italy, besides

[10] 'US May move vs. Pakistan Terror Areas,' *New York Times*, Washington, 6 April 2004.

other European countries.

"Europe is now clearly in the spotlight of terrorist," said Daniel Keihane, a security and defence expert at the Center for European Reform in London. He says it is highly probably that al-Qaeda was behind the Madrid bombings. "It is the greatest terrorist threat the continent has ever faced."[11]

In Spain, a powerful bomb was found on the tracks of a high-speed train soon after the Madrid outrage. During a raid, four suspected terrorists blew themselves up with explosives rather than surrender. One of the dead was identified as the leader of the 11 March train bombings, which had killed 191 people. According to the police, the explosive planted on the tracks of the Madrid-Seville railway line was similar to the one used in the 11 March attacks. Near Dortmund, Germany, a disaster was averted when the engineer of a high-speed train discovered that sheet metal had been bolted to the track to derail the train.

People and terrorists move freely across borders in Europe, whereas police and other officials cannot do that. What is required is to 'tear down that last frontier in Europe' and unify information and intelligence efforts.

A document written in Arabic and considered genuine by some government experts threatened further attacks in Spain unless the country ceased to support the United States and pulled its soldiers out of Iraq and Afghanistan by 4 April. It was signed by Abu Dujana al-Afghani, who called himself a member of "al-Qaeda in Europe."

Experts believe European governments must coordinate their efforts, as that is the only way of effectively combating global terrorist networks. It is necessary to infiltrate Islamic militant organisations and to join forces on intelligence across Europe.[12]

### *Terrorist Activities in India*

The known 'East Turkistan' terrorist organisations are: the World

[11] Europe: http://ww/cns.com, IHT.com. *Washington Post*, 6 April 2004.

[12] Ibid.

Uygur Youth Congress (WUYC), the East Turkistan Information Centre (ETIC), East Turkistan Islamic Movement (ETIM) and the East Turkistan Liberation Organization (ETLO). Since its founding, the World Uygur Youth Congress has all along been actively pursuing subversive activities, conspiring to split the country by various means, inciting, organizing, abetting and supporting violent terrorist activities and financing terrorists and terrorist organisations.

An official list of the identified 'East Turkistan' terrorist organisations and terrorists was issued on 15 December 2003. It was stated that from February 2001 to September 2002, the president of the East Turkistan Information Centre (ETIC) Abudujelili Kalakash trained on eAbudumijit Enas, in Hotan of Xinjiang, to carry out terrorist activities. Abudumijit Enas confessed that he had received equipment, more than 30,000 yuan (US$3,625) and the mandate to gather information, plot and carry out violent terrorist activities in China.

In July 2002, Dolqun Isa tried many ways to prevent the repatriation to China of Rahmutulla Islayil and Arken Yakuf, who murdered Wang Jianping, a diplomat of the Chinese Embassy in Kyrgyzstan . In October 2000, WUYC leader of Dolqun Isa directed Yulwas Tulak, Eli Mutalif and other runaway terrorists were captured by Nepalese police on the charge of illegal possession of guns. Dolqun Isa then sent Abudueni Rehmen to Nepal carrying a huge sum of money, which bailed out the terrorists and sent them to a terrorist camp in South Asia to receive training.

In March 2003, ETIC President Abudujelili Kalakash directed a dreaded terrorist named Silam Eshan to do a field survey along the railway between Lanzhou of Gansu province and Hami of Xinjiang in China in preparation for blowing up the railway. Silam Eshan confessed that during his trips to China's Hebei, Anhui and Shaanxi provinces and the national capital of Beijing, he frequently received orders from Abudujelili Kalakash to spread leaflets that preached "Jihad," and to take delivery of formulas for making explosives and poison sent by a foreign terrorist Yasen Turid, and to conduct a field survey of the Lanzhou-Hami Railway together with terrorists Adi, Muhtar Memet, Abudurexit Yisak and Kdir Mamut, located in China to map out explosion schemes.

He said that since May 2003, Dolqun Isa and another die-hard member of this organisation, Abuduxukur, have successively provided financial support for more than ten backbone members of a terrorist group including Tayir Nasir, Ruz Memet, and Rusuf Memet that made explosives illegally.

From May to August in 2003, Dolqun Isa and current WUYC chairman Memet Tuhut actively provided financial aid for Miryumili Memet, an "Eastern Turkistan" terrorist who had fled to Thailand, and later sought legal channels for him to flee Thailand.[13]

### *Terrorism in Africa*

Although the US has established a military base in Djibouti, in the vicinity of Somalia, Ethiopia, Eritrea and Sudan, which are area threatened by terrorist violent, many analysts believe that it will take more than mere military presence to uncover the terrorist plots and their support organisations operating in this area because there are indications that al-Qaeda has chosen these remote and troubled areas of Africa to establish new cells. The Salafist Group for Preaching and Combat (GSPC), one of the two major Islamic groups in Algeria, is making inroads in Mali, Chad, Niger and Mauritania. It appears to be a new thrust of Al-Qaeda into this region.

The other countries in the danger zones are Sudan and Algeria. Sudan is a safe haven for terrorist groups operating in Algeria, Tunisia. Morocco; it is on the US list of states sponsoring terrorism. Eight people suspected of planning terrorist attacks on US sites in New York City have Sudanese passports. State patronage of terrorism by Sudan must be addressed, if the US has to curb the

[13] Information excerpted from Chinadaily.com and http://www.uygur.org/wunn21/2001_12_01.htm.

rising tide of terrorism in this region.

A former US Ambassador, David Shinn, who served in a number of African countries, says, "Factors such as poverty and social injustice porous borders and competition for scare resources contribute directly to terrorism...the United States' approach fails to address these key issues."[14] There is little doubt terrorists are finding safe havens in various regions of Africa and comprehensive long-term planning is required to counter terrorism affectively. According to Douglas Farah, of the National Strategy Information Centre, "Osama bin Laden's network used weak law enforcement systems in West Africa to build up its defenses and hide in financial assets with illegal trading in weapons and jewels."[15]

"Chad's information minister, Moukhtar Wawa Dahad, said in N'Djamena for 12 March that the fighting erupted when a Chadian patrol on the country's northwestern border stumbled across five trucks packed with GSPC fighters after they had infiltrated from Niger near the remote desert town of Zouar. It was not clear how many militants were involved in the fighting, but they launched rocket-propelled grenades and mortars at the patrol. Dahab said that among those killed were nine Algerians, with the rest from Niger, Mali and Nigeria."[16]

The activities of various terrorist organisations, with known links to Al-Qaeda, indicate that it has established its presence in various countries of Africa to recruit and train a sizeable number of militants in regions that are still safe from the US war on terrorism.

[14] Marissa Melton, *Washington,* 'More focus Needed on Africa in Fight Against Terrorism,' say experts, http://www.janes.com/regional news/ Africa middle east/news/jiaa/jiaa040323 1 n.shtml, 14 April 2004.

[15] Ibid.

[16] Ed Blanche, 'Northeast Africa: Al-Qaeda's new battleground,' http://jiaa 040323_1_n.sht,l, 23 March 2004.

X

# War on Terrorism: Failure of Policies

*Maj. Gen. (Retd.) Afsir Karim*

*According to the US 'September 11 commission', Pakistan and Saudi Arabia were instrumental in facilitating the September 11 attacks on US targets. It was well known in South Asia that Pakistan recruited and trained personnel for al-Qaeda and the Taliban, while Saudi Arabia provided financial aid to them. It was also widely believed in this region that Osama bin Laden could not have possibly carried out the September 11 aattacks without sophisticated technology assistance, and such technology and advice could only be rendered by Pakistan. The September 11 commission has clearly stipulated that Saudi Arabia provided funds and equipment to al-Qaeda; Pakistan's military and intelligence agencies coordinated efforts with al-Qaeda and the Taliban. By directly aiding bin Laden, both Pakistan and Saudi Arabia promoted global terrorism. After 9/11, al-Qaeda networks found shelter in Pakistan and that enabled al-Qaeda to reorganize though the US attacks had destroyed its entire infrastructure in Afghanistan.*

*American policy makers could not have been so naïve or grossly incompetent not to notice the collaboration between Pakistan and the al-Qaeda. The obvious failure of the US policy was later compounded by the US-led invasion of Iraq that increased the threat to Europe and America. Osama bin Laden and associated groups could not have hoped for a more favourable environment to enlarge their network because of the diversion of effort towards Iraq from war against global terrorism.*

*Persistent reports deliberating about Saudi Arabia and Pakistan being in collusion with al-Qaeda were dismissed by the US administration as mere rumours until a lawsuit against Saudi Arabia by September 11 victims claimed that both Saudi Arabia and Pakistan intentionally ignored the preparations of attacks by al-Qaeda on US targets and even collaborated with Osama in various ways. After the definitive conclusions arrived at by the September 11 commission, there is little doubt that Saudi Arabia and Pakistan were the main supporters of al-Qaeda and the Taliban. The recently released report of the September 11 commission says, there was no convincing evidence that the Saudi government had directly supported the September 11 attacks but "Riyadh had engaged in very limited oversight of the religious charitable entities that have long been accused of being key financial backers of al-Qaeda". According to the report, Pakistan "significantly facilitated the Taliban's ability to provide bin Laden a haven despite international sanctions against al-Qaeda, including the freezing of its assets and prohibitions on travel".*[1]

*The amazing part was that US officials did very little to break the nexus, even when it was established beyond reasonable doubt that Saudi Arabia and Pakistan while deriving great benefits from the US played significant roles in the growth of al-Qaeda. This raises serious questions about the United State's counter-terrorist policies, the recent alliances with Pakistan and continued support of the Saudi regime.*

*"Bin Laden moved to Afghanistan in 1996 with assistance of ISI. He would not go back there without Pakistani approval and support, and had to comply with their rules and regulations; Pakistan opened its air space to Bin Laden and flying flotilla of operatives", said a senior commission member; Pakistan was in*

[1] Josh Meyer, "2 Allies Aided Bin Laden, Say Panel Members", *LOS ANGELES TIMES*, <http://by18fdbay18.hotmail.msn.com/cgi-bin/getmsg?curmbox=F000000001&a=8100ec4…>, 20 June 2004.

*with the Taliban to its eyeballs, Pakistan helped bin Laden and the Taliban forge an alliance that enabled al-Qaeda to establish camps for training guerrilla forces and terrorists.*[2]

One wonders why the US administration continues helping the same forces that have been instrumental in spreading the menace of international terrorism across the globe. The danger is far greater now since Pakistan and its scientists, many of whom have connections with al-Qaeda, leaked nuclear secrets to external agencies. Gen Musharraf's efforts to show commitment to the American war against terrorist has increased political polarization in Pakistan; whether the Pakistani Army is earnestly tracking down al-Qaeda leaders, who have been under Pakistan's protection so far is a moot point.

The strategy of the US government in its war against terrorist is in shambles because of the strategic and tactical failure of its policies in Iraq. It is not certain if the US can recover from this massive tactical failure in Iraq and regain strategic initiative against global terrorist soon. If past mistakes are glossed over and justified under any pretext, it may lead to a strategic collapse. To defeat terrorist at the strategic level, the US must adopt innovative strategies.

The strategic framework of war against al-Qaeda has suffered a serious setback since the US involvement in Iraq; this diversion allowed al-Qaeda time to reorganize and disperse in various parts of the globe. To offset the advantage gained by al-Qaeda, US policy makers should reset their goals carefully and take care not to dilute the war against terrorist by invading other Islamic countries that may not seem helpful in combating international terrorism.

## Iraq after the Handover

The low profile handover in Iraq two days before the scheduled date showed that things were not really under control; perhaps it was the

[2] Ibid.

right thing to do considering the adverse security environment in the whole country. The secret ceremony showed the dangers, which lurk in Iraq. Despite this Bremer said, "I will leave Iraq confident in its future…". This was a typical example of unrealistic public statements which have now been commonly heard from Washington and Baghdad. The very nature of a quiet, secret ceremony acknowledged the dangers the insurgents posed to the Iraqi regime. The nature of the insurgent movement in Iraq is such that the US with all its might has not been able to control it. The spiraling violence forced the US to abandon the original plan under which Iraq would have remained under US control till the elections in January 2005. This was a clear message that insurgents enjoy widespread support and have the capacity to hurt the election prospects of President Bush.

The popular sentiment in Iraq is that they are now facing a power vacuum in which no one can feel safe. "We are in the middle of a cultural and moral revolution", said Munir who had spent three years in Abu Ghraib for dissident activities against Saddam. A schoolteacher, Mohsen Hamid, who runs a store in a busy Baghdad street says, "I am just tired of being afraid for my family".[3]

The situation is dangerously fluid in Iraq, but even a token handing over rather than a continued stalemate is a step forward. A lower American visibility and low profile deployment of US troops can help in creating an atmosphere in which the people may be able to prevail upon the insurgents to stop attacks against common people. The greatest advantage of the handover is that it opens doors for help from the international community. Bringing back normal conditions will not be easy as the administrative and economic infrastructure was mindlessly devastated by the Americans during occupation. Seeds of an internecine conflict and struggle for power between Sunnis, Shiites and Kurds have been sown by the policies

[3] Dan Murphy, "Quite handover, secret ceremony", *The Christian Science Monitor*, http://www.csmonitor.com/2004/0629/p01s02-woiq.htm, 28 June 2004.

of the US authorities in Iraq, which can prove disastrous for peace in the condition in which the American occupation has left Iraq.

The damaging impact of the actions of the occupation forces on the common people was never taken into account and the strategy of Iraqi insurgents was never carefully assessed by the US. The political uncertainty in Iraq and the rising tide of organised insurgency in a multidimensional mode gives little hope of peace in the near future. Most analysts believe that violence will increase in the coming months. Bruce Hoffman, acting director of the Rand Cooperation Center for Middle East Public Policy observes, "I have never seen an insurgency that has been successfully defeated in months... Insurgents don't have to win, they just have to avoid losing, and that means they can prolong any conflict they're involved in".[4]

In the recent past, militants have mounted several attacks to undermine the power and the authority of the new governing body. The attacks have taken varied forms ranging from mortar or rocket bombardment to roadside bombs set off by remote control devices. Attacks on oil pipelines, frequent suicide car bomb attacks and shooting of transport aircraft have contributed to an atmosphere of violence and uncertainty. The increasing intensity of attacks has driven the multinational forces in Iraq to ensure their own safety first. The US forces obviously failed to foresee the expanding dimensions of the insurgency and did not adopt appropriate responses to deal with it. According to Bruce Hoffman, "The insurgents have the initiative and are a constantly dynamic force whereas the coalition forces have been cast very much in a responsive mode".[5]

The frequency of attacks on coalition forces still ranges from 30 to 60 a day. Gen Abizaid the commander of the US Central

[4] Nicholas Blanford, "The Strategy of Iraq's Insurgents", *Thew Christian Science Monitor*, http://www.csmonitor.com/2004/0629/p25s02-woiq.com.htm, 29 June 2004.

[5] Ibid.

Command has described the insurgency as a "classical guerrilla-type campaign". Many attacks have been attributed to Abu Musab al-Zarqawi, a Jordanian militant who leads the Al-Tawid and Al-Jihad groups. He is supposed to be operating from a secret hide-out in Fallujah. Coalition forces seemed at a loss to crush urban insurgency; they had, therefore, to accept a compromise solution, which meant withdrawal from Fallujah. The rebellions in Najaf, Karbala and Kufa along with the strong resistance at Fallujah showed the shared determination of the people to fight the forces of occupation. "The Fallujah resistance sparked the emotions and touched the hearts of the people throughout the Arab world because it was one of the few recent instances of Arabs making a stand on their home ground and fighting to defend their community in the face of almost certain death", observes Rami Khouri, executive editor of Beirut's *Daily Star* newspaper.[6]

Professor Nizar Hamzeh of the American University of Beirut notes that "The Sunni Islamic resistance are not accepting what has been handed over to Iraq by the Americans… whatever means you use here is not going to work and the only outcome is a clash". Lt Gen David Petraeus, who is supervising the creation of the new Iraq Army, however, believes that the insurgency is diminishing because "motivation has to lose its appeal over time".[7] One hopes Gen David is right, but experience has shown that the US officials and generals often make statements without valid reasons to support them.

Indications are that the insurgency will intensify during the seven-month mandate of the interim Iraqi government. The regime lacks legitimacy in the eyes of the Iraqi people and it has little political or moral support to crush the insurgency. If, however, the new government is able to bring in some semblance of peace, it may receive greater support of the people. If the interim government uses

[6] Ibid.

[7] Ibid.

strong-arm tactics with the help of the coalition forces as it intends to, people will turn against it and violence may spread in more areas resulting in greater chaos and turmoil. It may be better if the Iraqis are left to fight their own battles without high visibility of the American-led coalition forces.

Ehud Barak, the Israeli Prime Minister, though he supported the war on Iraq later, quietly told US Vice President Dick Cheney that America had lost the war in Iraq. Barak told Cheney that Israel "had learned that there is no way to win an occupation, the only issue was choosing the size of your humiliation".[8]

The proposal of a new amnesty law that would offer a pardon to insurgents, including those who have participated in attacks against US troops, provided they were not involved in 'murder and rape of Iraqis', may be a step in the right direction.[9]

## COUNTERING INSURGENT-TERRORISM

The Iraqi interim government announced a new security law recently that gives it sweeping powers to tackle insurgency. Prime Minister Iyad Allawi may declare martial law in most disturbed areas. According to a draft copy of the law, "Iraq's interim prime minister will be able to close off entire towns and cities, impose curfews, restrict communications, and limit travel in and out."[10]

Once signed by Iraqi leaders, the emergency law would give Allawi power to declare martial law for a set period of time, either in specific areas or nationwide. To impose martial law in a specific area, Allawi would have to get approval from his 32-member cabinet. To declare it nationwide, he would also need approval from the Iraqi president and two vice presidents.

[8] Seymour M. Hersh, <http://65.54.187.250/cgi-bin/getmsg?curbox=F000000001&a=a2117e4252b81f0149b056...>, "As June 30th Approaches, Israel Looks to the Kurds", 28 June 2004.

[9] Haidar Salahuddin, http://www.reuters.com/printerFriendlyPopup.jhtm?type=topNews&storyID=5607084, "Iraq Unveils Security Law Amid Clashes in Baghdad", 7 July 2004.

[10] The Associated Press, "Iraq Announces Emergency Powers Laws", 7 July 2004.

There is no mention of the cabinet or the president having the ability to rescind the law. If martial law were to be declared, according to this draft, Allawi would have the power to:

- Take command over all police, intelligence, army, and other security forces in that area.
- Create special civilian courts for people accused of major crimes – anything from murder, rape, and kidnapping to destroying government property – if the criminal courts are swamped.
- Appoint civilian or military administrators in areas under martial rule.
- Release any defendant from custody, if Allawi deems it necessary for reasons of security.
- Monitor and restrict mail, telegrams, and wireless communications in affected areas.
- Freeze the assets of anybody accused of crimes that undermine national security, as well as those who are accused of providing shelter, funding, and assistance to suspected insurgents.[11]

"If there is martial law, there will be arbitrary searches and arrests," says Abu Ghayed al-Kubaisi, a chicken farmer. "They will use the excuse of fighting terrorism or national security. If someone has an enemy, he will use that as a pretext for getting this person arrested".[12]

Kubaisi, who is a resident of Ramadi, said he had to spend three hours at a checkpoint on the outskirts of Baghdad where Iraqi troops held him 'in the 120-degree sun'. "I think they took them to Egypt and Israel to teach them Israeli methods," he said with disgust.[13]

"Emergency rule is often the Achilles heel of Arab constitutional systems," says Nathan Brown, an expert on Arab legal systems at George Washington University in Washington. "In many countries,

[11] Annia Ceizadlo, "Iraq's PM poised for martial law", *The Christian Science Monitor*, http://www.christiansciencemonitor.com/2004/0707/p01s04-woiq.htm, 7 July 2004.

[12] Ibid.

[13] Ibid.

emergency rule becomes a permanent state that allows rulers to bypass the constitutional order completely."[14]

The interim government can wield power without restraint as the country's national assembly has yet to be convened; without a legislative body to act as a moderator, there is no check on it. "There is no parliament yet, so there is virtually no possibility of oversight of the use of emergency powers," says Professor Brown, "Even where oversight exists in theory, the weakness of constitutional institutions generally means oversight in practice is quite weak. In Iraq, it seems to be totally absent."[15] Most Iraqis will consider the present regime a continuation of the harsh US occupation.

## INSURGENT NETWORK IN IRAQ

Insurgents in Iraq have formed several alliances to fight the war against the occupation forces and their Iraqi collaborators. The intensified insurgency by this 'Netwar' took US counter-insurgency agencies by surprise and they were found to be remarkably inefficient in dealing with the situation. The Iraqi insurgents have been able to move from random violence to well coordinated and sophisticated attacks resulting in larger number of fatalities among the coalition forces and their Iraqi collaborators. The American counter-insurgency operations are perhaps proving ineffective because political factors have not been meshed with operational doctrines and strategic planning. The US policy makers also failed to read the obvious signs of incipient insurgency and the capability of the insurgents to entrench themselves in thickly populated areas. The insurgents seem to learn from their mistakes quickly and alter their plans and change their tactics. According to the latest American estimates, the number of hardcore insurgents are between 3000 and 5000, out of which there are about 300 foreigners. This indicates that a much larger number of indigenous elements are now involved in insurgency operations.

[14] Ibid.

[15] Ibid.

According to the Bathist generals, who disappeared from the scene during the war, "transfer of power will not change anything, the present puppet government will not last and liberation of Baghdad is not far away".[16] They believe that as long as the insurgents continue to disrupt normal life and force the interim authorities to take harsh measures against the civil population they are winning the war.

Two Iraqis generals, who met Alix de la Grange and some other journalists, said, "We would like to rectify some information now circulating in the western media; that is why we took the initiative of meeting you". The main points which emerged in this three hours long meeting can be summarized as under:

- We knew we had no chance in the face of American technology and military power in conventional war; we, therefore, prepared for post-war resistance well in advance.
- As expected, strategic zones came under the control of the American forces quickly and while they consolidated their position, opposition to the occupation was finalized. This plan (called B) seemed to have totally eluded the Americans.
- The plan to liberate Iraq and expel the coalition forces was founded much before 20 March 2003 when the war against Iraq commenced.
- The American offensive in Fallujah proved a turning point because of the ruthless and indiscriminate pillage by American forces during search operations and the sexual humiliation of prisoners. A Shiite lady, who was former undercover opposition militant against Saddam, felt that "The biggest mistake of the occupation forces was to despise our traditions and our culture. They are not satisfied with having bombed our infrastructure; they tried to destroy our social system and our dignity. And this we cannot allow. The wounds are deep and the healing will take

[16] Alix de la Grange, "The liberation of Baghdad is not far away", http://www.atimes.com/atimes/printN.html, 7 April 2004.

long. We prefer to live under the terror of one of our own than under the humiliation of a foreign occupation".[17]

- Presently both Sunnis and Shiites form the resistance groups. They have a united front from Fallujah to Ramadi, Najaf to Karbala. All combatants regardless of ethnic political distinctions speak in one language.
- The attacks are meticulously planned and are mounted preferably at night; insurgents do not possess weapons of mass destruction or heavy artillery, but only mortars and rocket-propelled grenade launchers. They have to depend on the 50 million small arms they possess for most of their operations. Their most devastating weapon remains the use of vehicles loaded with high explosives; a 5000-strong special unit composed of 90 per cent Iraqis and 10 percent foreigners has been trained to carry out these operations.
- Resolution 1546 adopted on 8 June is not accepted by the Iraqis because it officially ends the occupation by foreign troops while authorizing the presence of multinational forces under American command without stipulating a date for their withdrawal.[18]

## CONTROLLING STRATEGIC SPACE

There are many weak and failing states where the US has major strategic stakes, but where fundamentalism is gaining ground. After a certain stage, it may not be possible to control fundamentalism and terrorism in these states. The failed or failing states, which extend from Middle East to Central Asia to South and Southeast Asia, can become strongholds of fundamentalist groups who would assist and facilitate global terrorist operations. Many African states and Caribbean have shown tendencies of encouraging terrorism, ethnic violence and unrest. In these conditions, global terrorist groups may

[17] Ibid.
[18] Ibid.

find safe havens in many of these countries. Even in countries like Afghanistan, Somalia, Liberia and Pakistan, pro-US elements may eventually lose control and the US may have to mount a fresh offensive against anti-American elements and global terrorism.

The Israelis want a permanent foothold in Kurdistan to get the benefit of its extensive oil resources. Israel is trying to find ways and means to minimise the damage that prolongation of war in Iraq is causing to it and to its future prospects in the Middle East. It is currently expanding its clandestine relationship with Iraqi Kurds with the aim of assisting Kurds in establishing a semi-autonomous Kurdish state. Reports suggest that Israeli military personnel are quietly training Kurdish commandos for this purpose.

A semi-autonomous Kurdish state in alliance with Israel will create serious problems for the security official, "It would be a new Israel – a pariah state in the middle of hostile nations".[19] However, some analysts suggest that neo-cons in the Bush administration are not averse to this idea regardless of the fact that it will increase instability and conflicts in the region.

It appears that the US policy makers have yet to formulate any strategy other than military intervention or economic sanctions to combat global terrorist – both these measures have not been able to curb terrorism in the past. America simply does not have the capability to intervene militarily in all parts of the globe; its military assets are already over-extended. Military intervention has generally caused immense suffering, human tragedies and loss of America's credibility as an upholder of democratic freedom.

Members of the US commission on weak states and National Security believe that national security demands restructuring and managing US policy towards weak and failed states. They consider pre-emptive action is necessary, otherwise these states will pose a major global challenge to US security. They believe that the US

[19] Op cit, n.9.

should 'develop a unified intelligence strategy to rectify failures in gathering and disseminating information to identify states which are on brink of failure'.[20]

Al-Qaeda is no longer based in one country nor is it a centralised network dependent on any one leader. Al-Qaeda cells now operate independently connected by an overall policy with complex interconnections. Since there is no one enemy that can be defeated, the American war on terrorism has got lost in a maze of rhetoric and unachievable aims. The war against terrorist has transformed itself into America versus the Muslim world; after the invasion of Iraq, it has deviated from its main objective and lost direction. However, by calling it a 'war', it makes it incumbent on America to win this war.

## 9/11: THE PAKISTAN CONNECTION

Reliable reports indicate that the Bush administration had been in close contact with Lt Gen Mahmoud Ahmad of the ISI, while he was hobnobbing in the US with Mohamed Atta – the ringleader of the World Trade Centre (WTC) attacks. Perhaps by the time the US administration discovered this connection it was too late and they could now only prevail upon Islamabad to sack him. It is now known that 9/11 attacks were in all probability assisted and facilitated by the ISI of Pakistan. The existence of ISI-al-Qaeda-Taliban links have been a matter of public knowledge in South Asia for many years; after the assassination of Ahmad Shah Masood, the Northern Alliance had officially declared that ISI – Osama bin Laden were responsible for the assassination. The US administration could not possibly have been unaware of General Mahmoud Ahmad's close association with Osama bin Laden during the pre-assassination stage.[21]

[20] Stuart E. Eizenstat and John Edward Poster, "Weak states are a US security threat", *The Christian Science Monitor*, <http:/www/csmonitor.com/2004/0629/p09s02-coop.htm>, 29 June 2004.

[21] Michel Chossudovsky, "The Role of Pakistan's Military Intelligence (ISI) in the September 11 Attacks", http://globalresearch.ca/articles/CHO111A.html>.

Pakistan's Inter Services Public Relations wing claimed that former ISI director-general Lt Gen Mahmoud Ahmad had sought retirement after being superseded; reliable sources indicated that the general was sacked because the evidence made available by India confirmed his links to one of the suicide bombers involved in the attack on the WTC. The US authorities ensured his removal after confirming the fact that $1,00,000 was sent from Pakistan to WTC hijacker Mohamed Atta by Ahmad Umar Sheikh at the instance of Gen Mahmoud Ahmad. While few details have been revealed, it seems that inputs from Indian sources including Sheikh's mobile phone number enabled the FBI in clinching crucial evidence that established the link.[22]

A direct link between the ISI and the WTC attack should have had grave repercussions for US-Pakistan relations because it indicated that some other senior Pakistani army officers could also have been involved. This possibility, however, did not shake US confidence in Pakistan's credentials as a reliable partner in the anti-terrorism coalition. The revelation has several far-reaching implications because it suggests that the September 11 attacks were not an act of 'individual terrorism' organised by al-Qaeda, but a military operation in which the ISI and al-Qaeda were partners.[23]

[22] Ibid.
[23] Ibid.

# XI

# Changing Contours of Terrorism

*Maj. Gen. (Retd.) Afsir Karim*

*Bin Laden and Abu Musad al-Zarqawi have been able to convince a large majority of Muslims that after the Iraq war the offensive against Islam by the US can no longer be dismissed as a figment of the imagination. The American military action in Iraq provides undeniable proof of what bin Laden has described as "an ocean of oppression, injustice, slaughter and plunder." He justifies Jihad in any form and considers American attacks on Iraqi civilians as terrorism of the worst kind. He has succeeded in convincing almost the entire Muslim Ummah that it is necessary resist the 'crusaders' and their supporters. This has led to a situation where every Muslim is expected to contribute to this Jihad by any means within his capability and status. Jihad can take the form of passive resistance, financing, passing of information about the enemy, bombings, assassinations, and mass murders.*[1]

*Norms for waging war have been changing throughout history, but terrorising the enemy into submission has remained an essential element of all forms of war. Attacking innocent civilians whether by non-state actors or nations during a war is being equated by certain leading scholars of the Islamic world to justify acts of terror by Islamic terrorist groups.*

*The hopes of peace and democracy seem to have receded in Iraq as the lethality and frequency of attacks against the US and its allies have gradually increased alarmingly. The US forces, according to various analysts are now dispersed and frustrated;*

[1] Anonymous, *Imperial Hubris,* Brassey's INC, Washington, D.C. 2004, pp. 129-132.

*Islamic groups on the other hand, have regrouped and are on the offensive. The situation has deteriorated in Iraq and the opinion of various strategic experts seems to be that the US policy makers have entered a quagmire from where it may be difficult to retreat unscathed. There is a limit to what the American and British troops can achieve in Iraq. Pumping in more soldiers is not the answer. Sunnis must be brought on board, they require reassurance not bullets.*

*The opinion in South Asia is sharply divided about American military operations in Afghanistan and Iraq. Many in India seem to be of the view that the destruction of al-Qaeda's infrastructure in Afghanistan and the consequent U-turn by Pakistan has greatly reduced the threat of global terrorism against India, at least for the time being. The people of Pakistan despite Musharraf's support to America stand at the crossroads and can take a turn in any direction depending upon the flow of events in Pakistan, Iraq, and Afghanistan. The Islamists are still a force to reckon with in Pakistan and building a moderate Islamic society may not be easy.*

*The inability of the American forces to curb or stop global terrorism has led a large number of scholars to surmise that the theory of pre-emptive strikes to thwart perceived terrorist threats is proving to be a disaster. Al-Qaeda has changed the concept of asymmetrical warfare against America by giving a new shape to its war objectives and changing the worldview of the Muslim Ummah. Many Muslim scholars now equate bin Laden to leaders and heroes of Islamic history. In this environment, the war against terrorism is not likely to be won in the foreseeable future and terrorism in its present form is not likely to abate soon. A new criterion for combating terrorism is required because military action against non-cooperative Muslim states has not stopped expansion of terrorism; on the other hand, it has allowed terrorist organisations to spread their influence and infrastructure across*

> *the globe. According to Yusri Fouda of Al Jazeera, "United States should declare war on illiteracy, hunger and disease instead of terrorism. ... the US should stop supporting undemocratic Muslim governments in the Muslim Youth, and when bin Laden criticizes these corrupt governments, angry young Muslims view him as their hero."*[2]

## NEW BASES OF TERROR

After the destruction of the infrastructure of al-Qaeda in Afghanistan and lack of official support for al-Qaeda in Pakistan, terrorism had to find new areas of operation and new avenues of support sources and income. New safe bases in South Asia and Africa were explored first and later in South America; a disturbing development of this kind was reflected in an article by Thomas Muirhead. He asserts that away from the known hot spots of the world, infiltration of known terrorist cells is taking place in a region known as the Triple Border in South America. This is a remote and secluded area in the Patagonian desert region. It is easy to conceal the operations of the organisations that provide funds to terrorists by narcotics trafficking, which goes on across the borders of Argentina, Brazil, and Paraguay.[3]

Due to increased pressure from the US after 9/11, flow of funds to terrorist groups has slowed significantly. This factor forced al-Qaeda and its allied organisations to find new based and sources of finance in remote areas where US intervention is not easy or likely. African countries, Bangladesh and South America are the favoured destinations. Here al-Qaeda has been able to continue its activities undisturbed; they operate here in different garbs and miniscule cells. At the meeting point of borders-the cities of Ciudad del Este

[2] Hamid Mir, 'Al-Qaeda 2.0: Wehre will it strike next?', http://in.rediff.com/cms/print.jsp?docpath=//news/2004/dec/23guest.htm, 22 December 2004.

[3] Thomas Muirhead, 'Terrorism's Triple-Border Sanctuary: Islamists Organise World Teror from Bases in Argentina, Brazil and Paraguay,' http://globalpolitician.com/articles.asp?ID=236 &print=true, 13 December 2004.

(Paraguay), Puerto Iguazu (Argentina), and Foz de Iguazu (Brazil)– terrorists have found suitable environments to raise funds because growth of contraband economy is supported by various governments. Illegal trafficking of arms, drugs, and laundered money has official acceptance in this region. "It's not really contraband – it is commerce of all types, if the buyers sneak their purchase into another nation without paying taxes, that's the problem of the buyer not the seller here," says Interior Minister Jorge Garcete stating the official position in these matters.[4]

Terrorists have chosen to tap this area, as it is one of the largest black markets in the world. It has a mixed population, from the Middle East, Lebanon, Syria, Gaza, and West Bank, and there are two Arab language TV channels here to cater for this Arabic-speaking population. The police in this area are notorious for corrupt practices and law enforcement is in any case difficult because of the Brazilian reinforest and inhospitable terrain. Lately, some strong measures have been taken by the 'Tripartite Command' set up by the three countries, which have common borders because of the terrorist threat in the area. The FBI is also operating here along with some US troops to assist and train the military of all the three countries. Intelligence agencies report the presence of Hizbullah, al-Qaeda, Hamas, Islamic Jihad, at Gamaat, and al-Islamiyya operatives in this area. If these reports are accurate, it is a very serious development with far-reaching implications for the security of the US. Prominent Hizbullah activists reported in the area are Ali Khalil Mehri, a Lebanese and Assad Ahmad Barakat, the ringleader of a financial network. Al-Qaeda cells are also active here and according to Brazilian intelligence sources Osama bin Laden and Khalid Sheikh Mohammed once visited the Triple Border region. The ambassador of Lebanon to Argentina and Paraguay recently stated that Assad Ahmad Barakat has been sending funds to Hizbullah

[4] Ibid.

intended for "humanitarian aid for orphans of Muslims killed in action."[5]

It is believed that a week before the 9/11 attacks, a Moroccan, Abdel Fatta, who was a former al-Qaeda operative in Triple Border, passed on a letter to his lawyer to be handed to the US embassy, which contained a warning regarding 11 September attacks. If this report is true Abdel Fatta, who is in a jail in Brazil, must have been a high-ranking operator of al-Qaeda in this region. It is not known if the US embassy actually received this letter.[6]

It seems the aggressive war after 9/11 against terrorist organisations launched across the globe by the US has forced al-Qaeda to change tactics, and the shape and infrastructure of al-Qaeda and all its associate groups. They have since undergone a complete transformation and this has translated into a well-organised international coalition of terrorists being positioned in various parts of the world. Sunni and Shiite groups are cooperating to form the new infrastructure for mounting terrorist attacks against American targets and those Muslim countries that are supporting the US war against terror.

## Al-Qaeda in Bangladesh

A drift towards religious extremism is apparent in Bangladesh and it is one of the major reasons for escalation of political sectarian violence in the country. Bangladesh Muslims are generally followers of moderate Islamic norms and the fundamentalist trends noticeable lately are not a part of natural process, but a deliberate attempt by the al-Qaeda led Islamic Jihadi groups to change cultural values. Al-Qaeda is in the process of creating bases and opening a new area of operations here with the aim of extending influence over certain parts of South and Southeast Asia. This process started after the crackdown on al-Qaeda in Pakistan in the post-9/11 scenario when

[5] Ibid.
[6] Ibid.

Gen. Musharraf started cooperating with the US in destroying al-Qaeda bases in Pakistan. This forced al-Qaeda to relocate important leaders and cells in Bangladesh where they could operate in comparative safety. Fundamentalist forces have been active for quite some time now and the earliest signs of the changes in cultural norms were:

- Changes in history books at secondary school level emphasising the Islamic identity of Bangladesh.
- Undermining and denigration of Bengali cultural values by fundamentalist groups.
- Increase in number of incidents of violence against minority communities.
- Collaboration between radical Muslim groups with separatist groups of northeast India and Rohingya Muslims of Myanmar.
- Pressure on the government to enact 'Sharia' laws in the country.[7]

The rise of Jamaat-e-Islami had affected a significant segment of the population and given rise to sectarian and religious violence. Yet another kind of communal violence pertains to Chakmas of Chittagong Hill Tracts (CHT). In the absence of any attempt of the government to curb ethnic violence against Chakmas and the threats to their identify, the Chakmas formed Shanti Bahini, a militant organisation that created an armed confrontation between government forces and Chakma militants.

After the victory of Bangladesh National Party (BNP) and its radical Islamists' allies in October 2001, communal violence erupted in several parts of Bangladesh, mainly because Hindus were considered pro-Awami League, a secular party led by Sheikh Hasina. Influx of Hindu refugees into India started soon after; large segments of the Hindu population were hounded out of their homes and this

[7] Sreeradha Datta, *Bangladesh: A Gragile Democracy*, Delhi: Shipra Publishers, 2004, pp. 22-23.

became a major irritant in Indo-Bangladesh relations. According to Sachetan Nagorik Samaj, a Public Awareness Society "Repression of minority people which started in different parts of the country after the elections (in Oct 2001) is not a local problem, rather it is a national crisis."[8]

Another sign of communalisation was visible in anti-India policies and the fact that a large number of India's armed separatist groups were provided safe houses in Bangladesh. The government of Bangladesh remained a mute spectator to the operations of United Liberation Front of Asom (ULFA) and National Democratic Front of Bodoland (NDFB) from its soil. Rohingya Muslims of Myanmar who are fighting against the military Junta also found safe haven in Bangladesh. There are reports that indicate Rohingyas are being recruited and trained in large numbers by al-Qaeda operatives in Bangladesh. Presently al-Qaeda is keeping a low profile here, but the process of indoctrination that is usually the first phase of al-Qaeda operations is going apace. Growing incidence of communal, ethnic, and political violence against moderate parties is one manifestation of this process.

The army has been frequently requisitioned to quell political-communal violence. Internal security operations such as 'Clean Heart' and 'Spider Web' undertaken by the army and paramilitary forces to quell intenal violence resulted in communalisation of a segment of the armed forces.

Lately, violence against the moderate Awami League has escalated. In August 2004, the leader Sheikh Hasina was attacked by hand grenades in an attack in which at least six people were killed. Most political observers of Bangladesh believe that the attack had the tacit sanction of the BNP, the ruling party which has formed the government in coalition with Jamaat-e-Islami (JEI) and Islami Oikya Jote (IOJ) which are Islamic fundamentalist parties. The

[8] B. Raman, 'Bangladesh-Myanmar-Thailand— The Jihad Corridor,' http://www.saag.org/ papaers9/paper887.html,

precision and professional efficiency and the choice of weapons, 20 to 30 hand grenades and automatics, indicated complicity of some elements of the army or paramilitary in the attack. It is rare to find grenades, which are in use by the Bangladesh army with political activists. This points to the involvement and links of Islamic militants with the Army or paramilitary forces. Although a little known group called 'Hikmatul Jihad' took the responsibility for this attack, the complicity of Harkat-ul-Jihad al Islami (HUJI-B) a member of bin Laden's International Islamic Front (IIF) was apparent from the pattern of attack.

Various reports have also been appearing in the western media on the possibility of al-Qaeda operations from Bangladesh; there is little doubt that al-Qaeda elements are at work in collaboration with organisations such as 'International Khatme-Nabuwot' and [Jaish-e-Mustafa'. These organisations like their counterparts in Pakistan have demanded that 'Ahmadiyas' (a Shiite Muslim sect) be declared as non-Muslims, as has been done in Pakistan.[9]

It is a well known fact that the HUJI-B has been training Rohingya Muslims for the past few years; reports now suggest it has started training small groups of Muslims in Thailand, Cambodia, Indonesia, and Brunei in the madrassas controlled by it. The aim seems to be to train militants for assisting the IIF and step up their movement of establishing the 'Sharia' laws in Muslim majority pockets in these countries. At least 150-200 cells of al-Qaeda and the IIF are reported to be active in Bangladesh. The JEI, IOJ and HUJI-B have lately been joined by Hizbul-Tehrir for training militants groups and working on the junior officers of the armed forces.[10]

It is clear that al-Qaeda is spreading its roots in Bangladesh with a view to influence large segments of the Muslim population in South and Southeast Asia and to draw attention away from the hot spots of Pakistan and Afghanistan by opening a new front in South Asia.

[9] Ibid.

[10] Ibid.

Anti -American sentiment after the invasion of Iraq and continued struggle between Iraqi rebels and the American forces has increased greatly in Bangladesh. In the present environment, it is necessary for the US to take timely action to curb the growth of Islamic fundamentalism in this moderate Islamic country, and prevent al-Qaeda and its associate groups from finding a new home and concealed bases for operations in the sensitive Malacca straits and increase their collaboration with the fundamentalist groups of Thailand, Indonesia, and Myanmar, besides the Indian subcontinent. The process of Islamisation can prove a disaster for Bangladesh since it will transform a peaceful society into an area of violence, turmoil, and terrorism.

## PERCEPTIONS OF TERROR

Most Asian analysts who spoke at the Asia-Pacific Roundtable organized by Malaysia's Institute of Strategic and International Studies (ISIS) were sharply critical of the US invasion of Iraq and expressed the view that American use of inordinate m ilitary force against Muslim radical groups is alienating Muslims and is strategically flawed. ISIS director General Mohamed Jawhar Hassan said, " he US-led international battle is losing while al-Qaeda-led international net work I winning"[11]

The director of Singapore's Institute of Defence and Strategic Studies, Barry Desker was of the view that, "The response cannot be a military one. This is fundamentally a US error." He added that the US-led war on Iraq and subsequent occupation had driven Islamic militants to wage Jihad against Washington.[12]

Noordin Sopiee, Chairman ISIS, said that the world was losing the war on terror because "We have expanded the sea of hatred and expanded the reservoir of deep-seated rage in the Muslim."[13]

[11] Middle East Online, 'Al-Qaeda winning the war against terro, analysts say,' 31 May 2004, Kuala Lumpur.

[12] Ibid.

[13] Ibid.

The basic questions that arise from various analyses about the present status of al-Qaeda despite the global war on terrorism led by the US are:

- Is al-Qaeda still capable of attacking the US mainland in the manner it did in September 2001?
- Has al-Qaeda regained its strength and potential to strike at America and its allies or has its basic infrastructure been so damaged and scattered that it cannot reorganize in the near future?
- Has al-Qaeda turned itself into a political organisation and spread its tentacles in most parts of the Muslim-populated world to emerge as a new danger to the western world?
- Has the American invasion of Iraq given a new lease of life to al-Qaeda after its destruction and defeat in Afghanistan?
- Will al-Qaeda successfully subvert the governments in Saudi Arabia, Pakistan, and Afghanistan and create new areas of chaos involving the US?

Bin Laden's popularity and appeal depend on theological credibility for a defensive Jihad against anti-Islamic forces broadly identified as US-led crusaders, Christians, and Jews. His credibility in convincing the Muslims about the aim of crusaders to destroy Islam has increased because of US policies in the Muslim world which bin Laden describes as "an ocean of oppression, injustice, slaughter and plunder carried out by you against our Islamic Ummah. It is therefore commanded by our religion that we must fight back. We are defending ourselves against the United States. This is a 'defensive Jihad' as we want to protect our land and people."

Bin Laden cites various conflicts waged by the 'crusaders'—US against muslims – in the recent past that have converted most muslims around the world to his point of view. Some of these are:

- Massacre of Palestinian people for the last five decades.
- Blockade against the people of Iraq and their killing in a brutal manner without a shred of evidence, which is unprecedented in history.

- Unleashing Serbs against the Muslims of Bosnia-Herzegovina under UN cover.
- Invasion and killing of people of Chechnya, Afghanistan, and the Central Asian Republics.
- Crimes against the people of Kashmir.

Bin Laden's indictment may be coloured by his abiding hatred towards Christians and Jew, but the conflicts are real and it seems plausible to Muslims that the wars are indeed being waged by the 'crusaders' to annihilate the Islamic world. The ultimo ate appeal of all Muslims to unite and fight is having the desired effect; al Zawahiri says all Muslims are ready to fight: "The vanguard of a Muslim nation that decides to fight you to the last breath and not to surrender to your crimes and vices."[14]

Eminent terrorism experts and high ranking US officials accept the fact that al-Qaeda is still active and at least 15 al-Qaeda associate groups are operating even in Europe and Canada. It is also generally believed that al-Qaeda is planning new attacks in Saudi Arabia and Pakistan.[15]

The threat is not only posed by the strong Islamic countries, but also by weak and failing states that have large Muslim populations. The US needs to evolve an adequate and effective new policy to restore and rebuild such states before some of them replicate the events of Afghanistan, Pakistan and Iraq.

The US has been found woefully lacking in watching the developments in moderate Muslim states. Urgent attention is required to be paid to this aspect; multiple think tanks may be utilized for this purpose. The US policy maker's focus misses an important point that the weak governance of poor states and the emergence of the fundamentalist groups there are co-related. The kind o economy that breeds skyrocketing production of opium and other drugs that translate into small arms and explosives in the long

[14] Op cit, n.1.
[15] Op cit, n. 2.

run can prove extremely dangerous.[16] At present the US government is far too involved in ongoing military operations to focus on the rising instability and spreading terrorism and fundamentalism in various countries of the developing world. The US should craft a comprehensive strategy to avert the tide of terrorism that ay rise from these areas. Unrest and turmoil is already brewing in many unstable regions of Asia, Africa and South America.

[16] Ibid.

# XII

# War on Terror: Shift in Strategy

*Maj. Gen. (Retd.) Afsir Karim*

*The US has eventually accepted that war on terrorism requires allies of various shades, and this is good news because it comes from a country that had proclaimed that it is capable of dealing with global terrorism alone. At least one of the Pentagon's important figures who was a strong proponent of unilateral action in Iraq now accepts that it will not be possible for the US to defeat enemies without the help of allies. Ryan Henry, principle under secretary of defence for policy, who had proposed a go-it alone strategy for the Quadrennial Defence Review (QDR) for the global war on terrorism, now says "A fundamental realization is to win the global war on terrorism; this is not something the United States can do in isolation, we are making an effort to be more inclusive than we have been in the past."*[1]

*Ryan's views are now supported by many military and civilian officials, who sy that any notion the United States would reject help in the future is unfounded, and that the Pentagon was working hard to formulate strategies that would bring allies in. "It should be pretty obvious that the global war on terrorism doesn't give us much choice or room for debate," said Maj. Gen. Charles Simpson, chief of requirements and technology integration for US Joint Forces Command. "The key to victory will rest on our ability to work together and to do so on the battlefield shoulder-to-shoulder with our partners." Now the QDR will propose a*

[1] Christian Lowe, Pantagon Official, 'US Needs Allies to Defeat Terrorism,' <http://www.defensenews.com/story.php?F=741176&C-america&P=true?, 24 March 2005.

*strategy that 'helps countries maintain their path towards peace and keeps them firmly in the anti-terrorism camp.*[2] *Apprehensions persist, however, that plans for invasion of Iran made earlier are being dusted of the shelf and Syria has been added to the list. A plan to sideline Hezbullah is now being given a new look; a Lebanon minus Syrian troops and a weakened Hezbullah is now a US project. This operative push for these plans indicates that a go-alone policy will persist regardless of professions to the contrary.*

## AL QAEDA'S CAPABILITY

Al-Qaeda and its associated organisations have lately been active in Kuwait, Qatar, the Philippines, Thailand, Saudi Arabia, Yemen, and Egypt although at a diminishing scale. Senior officials of the American administration seem to be of the view that al-Qaeda is regrouping and may mount another massive attack as it is desperately seeking nuclear, chemical, and biological weapons. Pakistan, on the other hand, paints a different picture, claiming that its military operation s and arrest and interrogation of top al-Qaeda operatives in Pakistan indicate that al-Qaeda has been effectively neutralized. However, one has to take this assertion of the Pakistani intelligence and army sources with a pinch of salt. A statement like "We have broken the back of al-Qaeda" by the Interior Minister of Pakistan, Aftab Khan Sherpao and a statement of Gen. Musharraf that his government has "eliminated the terrorist centers in the Waziristan tribal region" may be attempts to highlight the success of their counter-terrorist operations for the benefit of the American administration an the international community . there have been fears on the other hand, substantiated by latest reports, that Pakistan's rogue nuclear scientists with some help from the establishment may have provided Bin Laden with requisite

[2] Ibid.

information to assemble 'dirty bombs' or some other crude nuclear devices.[3]

"It may be only a matter of time before al-Qaeda or other groups attempt to use biological, radiological or nuclear weapons," CIA director Porter Goss warned recently. This is a danger that cannot be ignored as this posses a threat to the entire international community.[4]

Maj. Gen. Eric Olson, the American second-in-command in Afghanistan, however says, "I think the pressure on them [al-Qaeda] here, the pressure on them in Pakistan , pressure on them in Iraq, is pretty great and it makes very difficult for them to operate."[5] Recent attacks in Saudi Arabia where security forces fought a four-day gun duel before they could eliminate 14 armed al-Qaeda men in a battle in a compound where they had entrenched themselves shows that al-Qaeda is undefeated even in Saudi Arabia.

Al-Qaeda's wing in Iraq claimed responsibility for the recent set piece attack on Abu Ghraib prison in which at least 44 US soldiers were wounded. According to the Internet reports, more attacks may follow. On balance, it would seem that though al-Qaeda has suffered a severe setback in the recent past, yet it is recovering rapidly and may be able to mount larger operations and target US troops in Iraq to prove their resurgence. In any case, an alliance between al-Qaeda and the Zarqawi group is now a reality and this poses a greater danger to the US forces in Iraq. A brief survey f the conflict situations in some countries where Islamic radical groups are active, carried out below, shows a dangerously volatile global security environment.

[3] Associated Press, 'al-Qaeda Ability Diminishing,' <http://www.military.com/Content/Printer_Friendly_Version/1,11491,00 .htm?str_filename...>, 14 March 2005.

[4] Ibid.

[5] Ibid.

## POST-ELECTION IRAQ AND THE MIDDLE EAST

The post-election scenario in Iraq shows a poisoned ambiance. The insurgents and terrorists who are generally targeting Iraqis are basically haring their own country, even if they do manage to kill a few American or coalition soldiers. In fact, it is no longer clear as to what is the aim of violence against the Iraqi army or police personnel since the day-to-day administration has by and large been passed on to Iraqis themselves. Attacks on civilian targets in the post-election scenario can no longer be viewed as being against American occupation; continued attacks against civilians will provide a justification for Americans for prolonging their stay and consolidating their position further.

There is little doubt that violence and insecurity will continue to prevail in Iraq, and the American forces will be targeted by the Jehadis who cross over porous borders to join hands with the Sunni warriors of Iraq. These attacks may cause disruption for short periods and prove an irritant for the Iraqi administration, but they can neither delay the elections due at the end of the year nor force the American army to leave Iraq. The leaders of insurgent groups share the sentiment with all others in Iraq for early pulling out of American troops, but they should realize that this can be more effectively managed by an elected government rather than by the insurgents. American troops without doubt remain the most hated entity in Iraq and other parts of West Asia because of their brutal treatment of civilians and callous disregard for Iraqi lives, but internal disturbance would not force American troops to change their attitude or speed up their departure. If the Sunni majority does not decide to join the mainstream, an internecine conflict will be on the cards, and American troops will be directly involved in it.

According to Iraq Body Count database set up by some British academics, at least 16,000 Iraqis have died since the start of the war. Iraqi soldiers and policemen have been the worst sufferers in the post-war period – at least 13,000 soldiers/policemen have been killed. According to American sources, despite deadly insurgent attacks on Iraqi forces, around 142,000 soldiers and policemen are ready for service and their strength is growing steadily.

Over 1546 American soldiers have already been killed since the start of the war, at an average of about 60 soldiers a month. Larger American losses have only been during set piece attacks on populated areas. During the first assault on Fallujah last year in April, 135 Americans soldiers lost their lives and about 107 were killed in the second assault this January. The US forces suffered the lowest monthly casualties in a year this summer, but insurgents have persisted with lethal attacks that show greater sophistication in planning and tactics; the killing of several Americans during a well-organised attack on Abu Ghraib predicts a new bloodier phase to come.[6]

The reconstruction of Iraq is on hold because a large number of encounters continue between the US troops and the insurgents; this is an ominous development an d points to greater determination on the part of the insurgents to cause maximum disruption to normal life and inflict larger number of casualties. According to a British Parliamentary committee, US forces in Iraq are provoking civilians and hindering reconstruction efforts by using extensive force. The US forces have yet to understand that use of force to deal with urban insurgency has to be finely calibrated; air strikes and use of armoured vehicles in populated areas can prove highly counter-productive.

According to 'icasualties.org,' which keeps tabs on casualties announced by the government, attacks on US forces have dropped to about 40 a day, since the 30 January election, 22 percent below the average rate last year. But lately more soldiers and Marines have been killed – besides the well-organised attack on Abu Ghraib prison, in which 44 US troops and 12 prisoners were injured. The

[6] Agence France Presse (AFP), 'Iraq insecurity rife two years after invasion,' http://www.dailystar.comlb/printable.asp?art_ID=i3553*cat_ID=2 , 19 March 2005

pattern suggests that insurgents may be shifting to fewer but larger operations that would directly engage US forces.[7]

A government that is not dependent on the American forces for its survival will have a greater dampening effect on the course of insurgency than any military operation. The effort to get a representative government is well under way. The national assembly recently voted Kurdish leader Jalal Talabani as President, who in turn announced the name of Ibrahim Jaafari as the prime minister. These steps will speed up the process for the formation of the rest of the government, but this could take several weeks and face obstruction. The entire cabinet is expected to be named shortly; hopefully it will make a tangible difference in the daily life of the citizens and help control the insurgency.

"Counterinsurgency is about governance," says Col. Thomas X. Hammes, an insurgency expert at the National Defence University in Washington. "You have to prove to the people you can govern them fairly and effectively – then they will tell you who the bad guys are." The course of insurgency indicates that even at the best pace, the tough internal warfare is likely to continue for many years. "Don't expect solutions now. We're two years into this," Hammes says. "We're at the top of the third inning and this is a nine-inning game."[8]

American forces have been responding to insurgency in Iraq in a typical conventional manner; there is an urgent need of recognizing the nature of insurgency, gradually bringing in appropriate equipment that can deal with it effectively.

Propaganda against the insurgents and counter-propaganda by them goes on; lately, interviews with captured insurgents have been televised on state television and these have become quite common. 'Prisoners, often with visible bruises and cuts, sit behind a table and

[7] Ibid.

[8] Jill Carroll, *The Christian Science Monitor,* Evolution in Iraq's insurgency, 7 April 2005.

confess the gruesome details of their crimes.' An off-the-screen military or police officer harangues them and tells them what Jehad should really mean."[9]

The insurgents counter this propaganda by describing their campaign of large, spectacular attacks. 'They project that insurgency cannot expect to defeat a larger, better-equipped force, but rather make it so politically costly that they are forced to withdraw. A massive attack like the one in Abu Ghraib or the car bomb that killed more than 100 people in Hilla in February are effective in spreading fear in Iraq and a sense abroad that things are out of control.'[10]

A method of testing the strength of the insurgency is 'how safe a Westerner feels on the street.' Foreign women generally disguise themselves in Islamic headscarves, and foreign men grow Muslim-style beards. "No foreigner is safe unless he blends with the surrounding and of course no foreigners travel outside Baghdad without protection."[11]

There is presently a stalemate in the war against terrorism to the advantage of fundamentalists. The appeal of al-Qaeda and its associates still motivates despite many in the Muslim world now disowning their activities. The most obvious step to wean away people from al-Qaeda would be quickly settle the problem between the Palestinians and Israel and complete the reconstruction of Iraq at a rapid rate.

## TOWARDS DEMOCRACY

The temptation to rush towards democratic changes in the Middle East should be resisted. It is necessary to gently heal the wounds of the Iraqis and the Arab world, by improving the daily life of the people and providing an atmosphere that is free from fear and

[9] Ibid

[10] Ibid.

[11] Ibid.

oppressive presence of the American forces. No regime in the Arab world will adopt democratic norms under the shadow of fear and American threats. The American hope of bringing democracy by overthrowing a dictator while devastating the countryside has proved an unmitigated disaster; a policy that showers death will bring neither peace nor democracy to the Arab world.[12] Presently the US options are rather limited as resentment and suspicion of America remain high, 'the belief that America has a hidden agenda and it seeks to manipulate events will not disappear easily.'[13]

## WRITING ON THE WALL

Various reports published after the recent anti-American/Saddam demonstrations in Baghdad predict danger of internal conflicts unless American troops are withdrawn easily from Iraq's new president, Jalal Talabani's, view that 'US forces must remain in his country for at least two more years, the time it will take to rebuild security forces and defeat the insurgency,' has not helped dispel doubts about American intentions of remaining in Iraq indefinitely. Excerpts from two such reports are reproduced below:

> "Tens of thousands of Shiites marked the anniversary of the fall of Baghdad with a protest against the American military presence at the square where Iraqis and US troops toppled a statue of Saddam Hussein two years ago."

The protesters back Muqtada al-Sadr, a radical Shiite cleric whose militia led uprisings against US troops last year, and their large numbers reflected frustration both with the US government and anger toward the Sunni Arab-led insurgency.

"This huge gathering shows that the Iraqi people have the strength and faith to protect their country and liberate it from the occupiers," said Ahmed Abed, a 26-year-old who sells spare car parts.

[12] Ibid.

[13] David D. Newsom, 'Premature euphoria over US-style Mideast democracy?'

US officials, who are slowly handing over security to Iraqi forces, have refused to set a timetable for withdrawal, saying that the troops will stay until Iraqi forces are able to secure the country.

The protesters filled Firdos Square and spilled on to nearby avenues, waving Iraqi flags. Mimicking the famous images of US soldiers and Iraqis pulling down a statue of Saddam as Baghdad fell, protesters toppled effigies of President Bush, British Prime Minister Tony Blair, and Saddam—all dressed like Iraqi prisoners in red jumpsuits. Other effigies of Bush and Saddam were burned.

'Force the occupation to leave from our country,' one banner read in English. The Shiite protesters also called for the now-jailed Saddam to face justice, and they help up framed photos of al-Sadr's father, a prominent cleric executed by Saddam. Mahdi Army militiamen searched people entering the demonstration area as Iraqi policemen stood to the side."[14]

Another report by Reuters says: chanting "No, no to the occupiers, " men loyal to clerk Muqtada al-Sadr streamed from the poor Shiite district of Sadr City to Firdos Square in central Baghdad where Saddam's statue was torn down two year s ago, in a peaceful show of strength.

The square and side street were quickly packed with crowds waving Iraqi flags and brandishing effigies of Saddam, British Prime Minister Tony Blair, and President Bush.

No America! No Saddam! Yes to Islam! Many chanted. One group of demonstrators burned an American flag.

"We want a stable Iraq and this will only happen through independence," said a statement from Sadr's office read out at the rally. "There will be no security and stability unless the occupiers leave … The occupiers must leave my country."[15]

[14] Ibid.

[15] Antonio Castaneda, 'Shiites Mark Anniversary of Baghdad's Fall,' <http://news.yahoo.com/news?tmpl=story&cid=540&u=ap/20050409/ap_on_re_mi_ea/iraq…>, 9 April 2005.

## SYRIA AND LEBANON

The assassination of the former Lebanese Prime Minister Rafik Hariri has shifted Lebanon to center stage; Syrian forces that were deployed there in 1990 to assist in quelling the Lebanese civil war, are now withdrawing under international pressure.[16]

The Syrians pulled out their forces in two phrases—all the 14,000 troops have now moved back via Bekka Valley to Syria. After the movement of troops started, anti– and pro-Syrian rallies jostled with each other; the situation without doubt has the potential of dividing the Lebanese society both vertically and horizontally.

The Lebanese population comprises Maronite Christians, Sunni Muslims, and a Shiite sect, Druze. All thee sects had been jointly agitating under the leadership of Rafik Hariri against Syria. If the assassination of Hariri was carried out with the aim of breaking up the movement against the established pro-Syrian government, the results have been just the opposite.

"Whoever orchestrated Hariri's assassination imagined the explosive event would produce results in accordance with a master plan. It is unlikely, however, that the master plan included strengthening the bonds between the United State and France…"[17]

If some one in Syria planned and executed the assassination of Rafik Hariri, he has clearly lost out because after hundreds of anti-Syrian demonstrators took to the streets, international pressure forced Syria to withdraw its army from Lebanon. This sudden withdrawal of Syrian troops has left a vacuum that will create serious security problem unless the UN or some other neutral troops are deployed in Lebanon to look after the security of the country. If the vacuum created by the withdrawal of the Syrian troops continues, it will pose a serious danger and the country may gradually slide into utter chaos.

[16] Reuters, 'Shiites Mark Anniversary of Baghdad's Fall,' 9 April 2005.

[17] Nicholas Blanford, After Syria, a UN role in Lebanon?' <http://www.csmonitor.com/2005/0315/p06s01-wome.htm>, 15 March 2005.

President Bush and his administration have been urging the Syrian regime to "remove its military and intelligence personnel from Lebanon and cede any political role there."[18] The US administration believes that after withdrawal of Syrian troops and intelligence agencies, a pro-US government may be formed, a regime that would not be hostile to Israel and help in increasing US influence. Many in the US administration believe that such a course would set the stage for the eventual collapse of the Syrian regime thus removing a 'Baathist' rogue state without directly employing force. In the meanwhile, the Bush administration plans to coerce Syria to "sustained improvements in its behaviour on Iraq and terrorism."

Any attempt to establish a pro-American government in Lebanon will, however, be resisted by Hezbullah, the largest party in Lebanon's parliament.[19] The situation in Syria and Lebanon is fluid and fraught with dangerous possibilities. Hezbullah will play a crucial role in any future setup in the region, while collapse of the Syrian regime can throw the entire region into chaos and prove a safe haven for radical Islamist groups and al-Qaeda-led terrorists . Even the National Security Adviser to Mr. Sharon recently observed, "An overly precipitous Syrian withdrawal from Lebanon could pose a threat to Israel."[20]

'Hezbullah' whose main objective so far has been to establish an Islamic state in Lebanon is yet to open its cards; presently they are waving Lebanese flags instead of their own 'Kalashnikov holding fist'; moreover the usual virulent attacks on the US and Israel are missing in their slogans. "The scene encapsulated a seminal question for Lebanon, the Middle East and the US security: can Hezbullah be

[18] 'A shift in the war on terrorism,' <http://toledoblade.com/apps/pbcs.dll/article?Date=20050219&Category=COLUMNIST14...>, 19 February 2005.

[19] Flynt L. Leverett, Senior Fellow, Saban Center for Middle East Policy, *The New York Times*, <http://www.brookings.edu/views/op-ed/fleverett/20050302.htm>, 2 March 2005.

[20] Ibid.

transformed form a terrorist organization into a political party."[21] It is yet to be seen if the situation that is developing in the Syria-Lebanon region is a strategic opening for the US or opening of a new area of chaos and conflict.

## IRAN

If Iran is invaded, it is likely to prove a tough nut to crack and the coalition forces, whatever their composition, might face unacceptable attrition if they invade Iran. Attaining political or military objectives in Iran may not be possible by the use of force without unleashing uncontrollable chaos in the Middle East as Iran is unlikely to give up its nuclear ambitions without a fight. In the prevailing circumstances, the US should attempt to come to an agreement with Iran rather than starting a new conflict in the region.

'Building a regional coalition against Iraq will not be easy because there is now a deep resentment against the US in the Arab world. Many countries now consider the US a 'rogue cop' and are apprehensive that there is nothing to be no change in the aggressive policy of George Bush towards the Arab world. They are more concerned about their sovereignty and safety because of the aggressive designs of the US rather than Iran's nuclear ambitions. Most Muslim countries resent the double standards of the US administration in ignoring the possession of nuclear weapons by Israel besides its many violations of various UN resolutions regarding treatment of the Palestinians."[22]

Militants in the Middle East are not unduly concerned about the current Iranian predicament. They believe that a close US-Arab security arrangement against Iran would further their ends, as it would embitter people against their own governments and weaken US hold on the region in the long run. They do not mind the

[21] Ibid.
[22] Ibid.

politico-strategic costs of driving these governments into the ambit of the US plans that aim to undermine Iran's nuclear plans.[23]

'From Washington, the rhetoric calls for diplomatic solutions to the nuclear standoff with Iran. But Tehran also hears a growing drumbeat for war that echoes the b uild up to US invasions of Afghanistan and Iraq. In preparation for any strike on its budding nuclear facilities, Iran is making clear that the price will be high, burnishing its military forces, boosting its missile program, and warning of a painful response against US ad Israeli targets in the region.' "They see a fight coming, regardless of what they do, so they are getting ready for it," says a European diplomat in Tehran, referring to ideologues who think a US invasion is a "very real prospect." Even moderate conservatives fear the "Iraqization of the Iran dossier." Says the diplomat. The result is that Iran is "constantly trying to project strength" and is developing a new doctrine of asymmetric warfare.[24]

It is generally accepted that Iran is a strong country and it will neither accept coercion nor will it be dissuaded by threats despite the known US potential of destroying or neutralizing its nuclear capability without putting boots on the ground.

In case of a war, Iran would not let American troops in Iraq and the targets in Israel go unpunished, and in these environments the entire region, Syria, Turkey, Iraq, Iran may go up in flames much to America's disadvantage. It seems that in the long run, it will be more prudent for America to address the causes of proliferation rather than destruction of nuclear capabilities of Iran . A peaceful solution may emerge with the co-operation of Arab States, EU, and the UN, A US-led invasion of Iran will prove an unmitigated disaster for the Middle East regardless of who gets the upper hand in the region.

Israel says it cannot live with a nuclear Iran under any circumstances; yet, there is hope that certain measures can dissuade Israel from

[23] George Perkovich, Vice President for Studies, Carnegie Endowment for International Peace, Policy Brief, February 2005.

[24] Ibid.

taking recourse to a disastrous military confrontation with Iran. A strategy that addresses the regional concerns and takes the interest of Iran into account in procuring nuclear weapons may be able to diffuse the situation.

A policy brief issued by the Carnegie Endowment states: The only way to create a zone free of weapons of mass destruction, which Israel and Iran and most Arab states say that support, is for every state in the region and, in the future, a Palestinian state-to implement policies that do not threaten the security of their neighbors... The United States should pursue these bold changes in Israeli policies and actively support the EU approach to Iran because both countries have merit in and of themselves. The added benefit of these moves would be to create solid footing for pushing Egypt and other Arab states to join in tough diplomacy to pressure Iran.[25]

## AFGHANISTAN

Three years have passed since the establishment of a secular government in Aghanistan, but the insurgency has not died down completely specially in the countryside, which is not quite under the control of the Central government. The military at best can hut down the Taliban insurgents, but it is in no position to influence events beyond that. The first Afghanistan Human Development report released recently shows remarkable progress in many spheres since 2001, but also clearly states that there was room only for 'cautions optimist' because Afghanistan faces serious security problems. Low life expectancy, poor conditions of women and children, and very low literacy rates continue to create major socio-political problems. The UN paints a gloomy picture of conditions in Afghanistan and warns in a statement accompanying the report that if peoples' grievances were not addressed, Afghanistan may rapidly slide into chaos. The report says, unless grievances such as

[25] 'Behind Diplomacy, Iran Sees A Fight Coming,' *Christian Science Monotor*, Tehran, Iran, 31 March 2005.

'lack of jobs, health care, education and political participation were addressed the fragile system would easily tumble back into chaos.' If that happened, Afghanistan will 'collapse into an insecure state, a threat to its own people as well as to the international community' the statement adds.[26]

Violence and terrorism have escalated in recent months in Afghanistan – whether this is due to general discontent or because of a deliberate plan of Islamic groups based in the Pakistan-Afghanistan belt to keep the pot boiling is a moot point. Recent bomb explosions in Spin Boldak near the Pakistan border and another opposite a government office in Jalalabad, a pre-dawn attack in Helmand province that resulted in several casualities indicate escalation in violence. A convoy of US troops was ambushed recently; car bombs at Kandahar, Masar –I-Sharif, and Jalalabad show that the Taliban are still active in these areas and can pose serious challenges to the Karzai regime. According to Lt. Gen. David Barno, who is presently the commander of the US forces in Afghanistan, 'Osama bin Laden and al-Qaeda are making fresh efforts to stage a come-back and regain a personal foothold in the country.[27]

The fact is that several religious and political organisations in Pakistan are still providing bases, arms, and explosives to the Taliban-al-Qaeda combine and Pakistan government is either unable or unwilling to act decisively against them. These developments cannot be very reassuring for the US administration or to the countries in the Central and South Asian region.

## THAILAND

Thailand's first car bombing in February 2005 was a signal that international terrorism has arrived, and it is going to spread and

[26] Ibid.

[27] David Brunnstrom, 'UN Warns of New Chaos if Afghan Grievances Not Met,' <http://www.reuters.com/newsArticle.jhtml?type=topNews&storyID=7688493 &src=eDialo...>, 21 February 2005.

become progressively more lethal in the future. Islamic terrorists have opened a new front here and have delivered a message that their objective is creation of a separate homeland for the Thai Muslims in Yala, Pattani, and Narathiwat, which are the Muslim majority areas in Thailand. Car bombing near a hotel, in a crowded street in the border town of Sungai Kolok sent a sinister message that Islamic insurgents are willing to up the ante and disturb the communal harmony that had prevailed in the country. During several attacks in the preceding few months, terrorists have made extensive use of remote-controlled devices to blow up their targets and cause maximum casualties on innocent bystanders and security forces. The use of sophisticated explosive devices and tactics that are being used the local terrorist groups point to their links with international Jehadi terrorism. At least 600 civilians and military personnel have been killed in terrorist attacks since January 2004.[28] Thailand that has been one of the quieter areas in Southeast Asia has apparently been selected by the Jehadis for establishing new bases for spreading terrorism and chaos in Muslim-majority areas of Thailand and other parts of the country.

The strategy of al-Qaeda after the American invasion of Iraq has been to exploit discontent among Muslims and create bases for future operations in new areas. If the government takes harsh measures to suppress the Muslim population, it suits al-Qaeda all the way. The Thaksin government's reaction has been exactly as the al-Qaeda wanted it to be. The Thai army's brutality against Muslims during the Tak Bai riot when at least 85 protestors were brutally murdered was an example of state violence that has increased alienation and discontent among Muslims.

It has been reported that al-Qaeda and its associated groups are organizing and training local groups with a view to widen the conflict by attacking targets in Bangkok and other cities of Thailand.

[28] 'Bombings, attacks rock Afghanistan,' <http://www.isn.enthzch/news/sw/details.cfm>id=11041>, 5 April 2005.

At this rate, terrorism is likely to grow both in intensity and size in Thailand and neighbouring areas. Al-Qaeda seems all set to engineer communal violence and ethnic strife to achieve its ends. The government of Thailand is not equipped to counter international terrorism of this kind and will require international assistance to bring back normalcy to the country.

After the current escalation of terrorist activities, the government of Thailand has warned the Bangkok residents to be on the alert against terrorist attacks, as Islamic terrorists intend to widen the area of their operations right up to the national capital region. The US state department has also warned Americans against travel in the region because of increasing terrorist threats. It seems that eventually Americans will have to assist Thai authorities to counter international terrorism threatening that country.

## XIII

# War on Terrorism: Confusion Prevails

*Maj. Gen. (Retd.) Afsir Karim*

*The White House has persistently refused to enter into a dialogue with Iran or Syria; on the other hand, by all indications, the US plans to use force against those countries. This will expand the conflict beyond Iraqi borders, and spread violence to several new areas. The tough rhetoric followed by the second military raid involving Iranian officials in Iraq is a sign of escalation in the US-Iran confrontation that could further complicate rather than calm the situation in the region.*

*In Somalia a combination of Ethiopian and Somalian government forces managed to drive away the Islamists but the problem is that the interim government of Somalia lacks popular support, while the Islamists enjoy immense popularity among the people. The Ethiopian troops have provided only a temporary reprive to the Somalian government. The Islamist militias have not been defeated, and the resentment caused by external intervention will undoubtedly increase the influence of the radical elements who will bide their time till Ethiopian forces leave.*

*Various subnational groups who are using unconventional tactics have been able to frustrate the nearly laid down operational plans of the conventional forces in several parts of the world. The dynamics of emerging asymmetrical strategies that have the potential to render the superior military capability of an adversary redundant must be fully understood for adopting the method of warfare that should be used against them.*

## ENLARGEMENT OF CONFLICT IN IRAQ

The American vision of establishing democracy in Iraq proved basically flawed. The fragmented verdict in the elections intensified the ethnic and religious confrontation between the Shiite majority and its Sunni and Kurdish groups (Non-Arab Sunnis). Soon after the parliamentary elections, sectarian violence erupted, a kind of violence never seen in Iraq before. Inevitably, it gradually assumed the shape of a civil war. The new political system sought to be introduced by the Americans in Iraq has proved a zero-sum game—as expected by all discerning observers of the Arab political culture. In 2006, militias wielded the real power, Americans failed to control the situation and the rule of the gun prevailed causing large number of civilian deaths. Most estimates put the Iraqi civilian death toll between 30,000 and 35,000.[1]

President Bush's plan to send 21,500 additional troops to Baghdad to subdue Sunni insurgents and Shiite militias is likely to be the last push by the US administration and a decisive phase of the war in Iraq. It is unlikely to result in victory for the American forces because saturating the battle field with troops for fighting in the lanes and by-lanes of Baghdad will only increase the number of civilian casualties and create greater chaos. There is little doubt that the operation will make the conflict more bloody and violent.

The prospect of fierce internecine battles in the Iraqi capital is on the cards, which could involve the US military in prolonged messy operations in this urban jungle. The plan for US and Iraqi forces to fight jointly in heavily built up areas will push American troops to rely very heavily on the ramshackle Iraqi army, whose ability and loyalty to the American cause is at best uncertain. In these environments, US forces will fight under serious disadvantages in this war. The US defense secretary Robert M. Gates recently said that the so-called surge will actually be a gradual increase of US troops

[1] Martin Sieff, "Another Year in Iraq," UPI Senior News Analyst.

that are now about 1,35,000. "The increase in military forces will be phased in. It will not unfold overnight. There will be no D-Day. It won't look like the Gulf War," he said. "Absent a threat of withdrawal, that phased addition of troops could be critical leverage, possibly the only leverage, the United States has over the Iraqi government which has so far demonstrated either an unwillingness or inability to quell the violence and reach the political compromise needed to draw the fractured country together."[2]

It is widely believed in the Arab world that the US plan of troop increase in Iraq will fail and it will, on the other hand, increase sectarian violence if American forces and the Iraqi troops fail to disarm Shiite militias. Some observers believe that US military action against Shiite militias may lead to a clash of interest, souring the ties between Washington and Shiite-led government in Iraq. "The al-Maliki government might be the first victim of the new strategy," read an editorial of the *Al-Quds Al-Arabi* newspaper. How would such a sectarian government accept liquidating its major base of support—the al-Sadr group and its militia?[3]

The raid on the Iranian Embassy in Baghdad and seizure of five Iranians there soon after President Bush declaring his much publicized strategic 'surge' in Iraq is an indication that the US administration has begun to take recourse to measures that will widen the conflict. It is evident that US forces plan to take on Iranian and Syrian supporters of Iraqi insurgency without delay. It appears that the American forces will make a major thrust to defeat the Sadr militia that has close ties with Iran. Military action against the Sadr's Mahdi Army can be a prolonged and costly operation. Al-Maliki has resisted any action against the Mahdi Army in the past, but Iraqi officials now say that he has warned al-Sadr that under the new strategy no armed faction "would escape attack."[4]

[2] Thomas E. Ricks and Ann Scott Tyson, *Washington Post*, Updated: 8:35 a.m. ET 11 January 2007.

[3] *Al-Quds Al-Arabi*, (Pan-Arab) UK newspaper.

[4] Op cit, n.2.

It seems that President Bush is determined to confront Iran and Syria, as his recent statements indicate. He declared: "These two regimes are allowing terrorists and insurgents to use their territory to move in and out of Iraq. Iran is providing material support for attacks on American troops," Bush said. "We will disrupt the attacks on our forces. We will interrupt the flow of support from Iran and Syria. And we will seek out and destroy the networks providing advanced weaponry and training to our enemies in Iraq."[5]

Forces going to Iraq region include Patriot missile batteries and equipment to counter antiship mines. None of these weapon systems would be useful against Iraqi insurgents. Many analysts believe that the US administration has another task for them in mind—Iran. This threat has highlighted by Democratic senator Dennis Kucinich, 2008 presidential aspirant. He said, "President Bush appears to be setting the stage for a wider war in the region,— He has blamed Iran for attacks on America. The president is vowing to disrupt Iraq. He is going to add an aircraft carrier to the shores off the coast of Iran. He has promised to give Patriot missiles to 'our friends and allies.' Isn't one war enough for this president? It is time the media and the Congress began to pay attention to this president when he talks aggressively about Iran and Syria."[6]

Even after waging four years of a disastrous war, the White House seems to have no intention of accepting responsibility for creating the present chaotic conditions in Iraq. Americans do not even acknowledge their failure to provide basic amenities such as electricity, water or gas, which they had so thoughtlessly destroyed during the invasion; lack of basic amenities actually ignited the spark among people that helped fuelling of insurgency by extremist groups. Yet when asked if he owes the Iraqi people an apology for botching the management of the war, President Bush said "Not at all. We

[5] Bush address on Iraq on BBC news, 11 January 2007.

[6] Matt Renner, "Bush's Speech Sets Stage for Showdown with Congress," Truth out/ Report.

liberated that country from a tyrant. I think the Iraqi people owe the American people a huge debt of gratitude."[7]

After five years of operations in Afghanistan and Iraq, the American forces, given their vast resources and superior equipment, have been unable to stabilize these countries: is this failure only due to lack of sufficient number of troops on the ground, as is being made out, or because of employment of blatantly wrong strategies? What will the long-term implications be if this new surge fails to change the situation and violence continues unabated in Iraq, is not clear. As it has happened in the past, American administration will work overtime to claim victory and prove that the operational objectives have been fully achieved, much to the astonishment of the rest of the world.

## SOMALIA

Ethiopian troops supported by tanks and bomber aircraft recently went into action in neighbouring Somalia in support of the Somalian government in their fight against the Islamists. The Islamists have not been defeated; they have merely retreated. They can reassembly in the thickly forested areas of southern Somalia and strike back at the government that is being kept afloat with the help of external forces. The terrain and unstable conditions in several areas of northern Kenya and southern Sudan also provide well concealed safe havens to terrorist groups. The Somalis are traditionally suspicious of the Ethiopians, and if the Ethiopian army does not leave Somalia very soon, it will become extremely difficult for the government to gain legitimacy in the eyes of the people. The situation is still fluid, and the conflict is not likely to end soon.[8]

The American air strike in Somalia that is reported to have killed at least ten suspected terrorists but failed to kill the three most

[7] Bush dares Democrats to stop Iraq troop surge, www.chinaview.cn 2007-01-15 18:11:20.

[8] Michael McClennen, "Somalia Tragedy and Opportunity," Truth out/Guest Contributor, 27 December 2006.

wanted al-Qaeda operatives, is likely to increase popular resentment towards the US. The American air strike was the first overt US military action since the withdrawal of the US troops from Somalia in 1993. The Horn of Africa, and particularly Somalia, has been the focus of the US planners who oversee the global campaign against al-Qaeda. After ousting al-Qaeda from Afghanistan, the US had established a base for a special group in Djibouti to coordinate counterterrorist operations with Ethiopia, Kenya and other neighbouring countries.[9]

The US intelligence has kept a close watch on al-Qaeda groups operating in the Horn of Africa, but the air strike has heralded resumption of military operations by the United States in this region; US warships deployed off the coasts of Somalia and Kenya are kept in readiness to take on fleeing Islamists. American sources maintain that the leaders of the Islamic Courts movement, which have been controlling most parts of Somalia since last year, include prominent al-Qaeda operatives. While doubts persist about the extent of al-Qaeda's hold over the Islamic Courts, the phenomenal rise in popularity of the fundamentalist movement is a fact of life.

"We're concerned about the al-Qaeda threat worldwide, but the fundamental way to address that threat is to give stability to Somalia (and) not Somalia be a safe haven for terrorism," a top US official for Africa Jendayi Fazer said.[10]

Horn of Africa comprising Djibouti, Eritrea, Ethiopia, is a region of porous borders and restive Muslim populations; it provides tailor-made areas for al-Qaeda to regroup. To counter the threat, the US military set up a 1,500-member counterterrorism unit in 2002—the Combined Joint Task Force Horn of Africa—in a former French foreign legion outpost in Djibouti, just north of Somalia.[11]

[9] Somalia Airstrikes Mark New Foray, Associated Press, <Military.com>, 10 January 2007.

[10] US sees Somalia as key front in war on terror, Zill-Haj 24, 1427, A.H. International, the News Pakistan, 15 January 2007.

[11] Ibid.

Once the Islamic Courts were on the verge of being overrun by Somalia's interim government's beleaguered headquarters in Baidoa. Washington gave its nod for the Ethiopian offensive, which succeeded in routing the Islamists. But, it is evident that they have not driven out the Islamist militias for good. Gayle Smith, a long-time observer of Somalia, who is now with the Centre for American Progress, cautioned against a US approach that focuses more on combating terrorism than dealing with the underlying frailty of Somalia, which allowed the radicalism to take root in the first place.[12]

The US-Ethiopian search for certain key Islamic Coruts leaders includes Hassan Dahir Aweys who carried out attacks on Ethiopia in the 2990s and has continued to make "irredentist claims on Ethiopian territory," said David Shin, a former US ambassador of Ethiopia.[13]

The quick response of US military forces to attack retreating Islamists signifies the importance Washington gives to the unstable Horn of Africa region in its war on terrorism. The United States has also been feeding intelligence gained through spy satellites to Ethiopian units who were pursuing retreating Islamist leaders.[14]

An Africa and Middle East expert Marina Ottaway said, "Today, what makes it [Somalia] important is the fear of the spread of the influence of al-Qaeda to Muslim areas outside the Middle East," "Somalia and the Horn of Africa in general are prime targets for that."[15]

Ken Menkhaus, a Horn of Africa specialist at Davidson College in Charlotte, North Carolina, has warned of a new kind of war in the Horn of Africa. "This could be the beginning of a new kind of war," he told Reuters. "One in which the Islamists are going to fight

[12] Ibid.
[13] Ibid.
[14] Ibid.
[15] Ibid.

their kind of war…as asymmetrical war involving a combination of hit-and-run guerrilla attacks, car bombings, assassinations and possibly even selected acts of terrorism on other parts of East Africa."[16]

The fall of Mogadishu came after a ten-day offensive by government troops, backed by Ethiopian tanks and fighter jets. They reclaimed most of south and central Somalia, seized by the Somalia Islamic Courts Council since June. While Somali prime minister Ali Mohamad Gedi celebrated a triumphant return to his home village outside Mogadishu for the first time since 2002, he acknowledged the chaotic country was far from stable. Mr. Gedi, said parliament will declare martial law to gain control of the country. "This country has experienced anarchy and in order to restore security we need a strong hand, especially with freelance militias," Gedi told reporters in Mundul Sharey, a dusty village some 40 km southwest of Mogadishu.[17]

Ethiopia's prime minister Meles Zenawi said his troops' mission was restricted to removing the threat of the Islamic Courts. "The idea that the Ethiopians can just bring this government from outside, plonk it down in the capital and walk away and everything will be solved – I think that's very, very unrealistic," Richard Dowden, director of the Royal African Society, told Sky News in London.[18]

Meanwhile, a serious humanitarian crisis is in the offing as thousands of people are fleeing the war zone. According to the UN relief agency, the fighting has caused the displacement of approximately 34,000 Somalis who sought refuge in neighbouring Kenya.[19]

[16] New Vision (Kampala), "Vision Reporter Kampala," 29 December 2006, posted to the Web on 30 December 2006.

[17] Ibid.

[18] Ibid.

[19] War Looms in the Horn of Africa by Claude Salhani UPI International Editor Washington (UPI) 27 December 2006.

Military operations in Somalia by American commandos and the use of the Ethiopian army as a surrogate force to root out operatives for al-Qaeda in the country are a blueprint that Pentagon strategists say they hope to use more frequently in counterterrorism missions around the globe.[20]

The military action of the kind visualized by the Pentagon that includes bombing of towns by jets that mostly kills civilians, causes great resentment among the people and strengthens the indigenous fundamentalist movement and Islamist groups in the long run.

Threat from Asymmetric Strategies

American administration has been regularly making predictions of al-Qaeda attacks in the United States. Sine 2003, those who specialize in unconventional threats and terrorism have been declaring that a terrorist strike far more devastating than 9/11 could occur before the end of 2004. Americna attorney general John Ashcroft declared that al-Qaeda could "hit hard" in the next few months and that 90 percent of the arrangements for an attack on US soil were complete. That fall, *Newsweek* reported that it was "practically an article of faith among counterterrorism officials" that al-Qaeda would strike in the run-up to the November 2004 election.[21] Department of Home and Security in its manifesto warned, "Today's terrorists can strike at any place, at any time, and with virtually any weapon."[22]

It appears that all such warnings are speculatie and far removed from realities as no such attack has come since 2001. If al-Qaeda is unable to mount a major attack despite the provocation of Guantanamo Bay or other actions by the US against al-Qaeda

[20] "Pentagon Sees Move in Somalia as Blueprint Mark Mazzetti," the New York Times, 13 January 2007.

[21] John Mueller, Is there Still a Terrorist Threat?: The Myth of the Omnipresent Enemy, From Foreign Affairs, http://www.foreignaffairs.org/2006901facomment85501/john-mueller/is-there-still-a-terrorist-threat.html, September/October 2006.

[22] Ibid.

operatives, it is not as active as the apprehensions in America would suggest.

Since long, al-Qaeda's top leaders are supposed to have threatened catastrophic attacks on Australia, India, Bahrain, Egypt, Italy, Japan, Saudi Arabia and the United States, but a major attack is yet to be mounted by al-Qaeda anywhere in the world. Should the absence of al-Qaeda catastrophic attacks be taken as a sign that alarmists in America are barking up the wrong tree or spreading fear for benefit of other strategic agendas; is al-Qaeda really lurking in dark shadows, waiting for chance to mount a far more devastating attack than 9/11?[23]

In Iraq and Afghanistan, terrorism is not the main weapon of war; it is the irregular shadowy fighter who, taking advantage of the resentment caused by the presence and activities of foreign troops is in the forefront. It will be a mistake to underestimate this particular kind of belligerent fighter who has limited military capability but the capacity to cause great psychological and material damage. They take recourse to innovative and unconventional methods for neutralizing military superiority of the US and NATO forces. In normal course, it would be impossible for a weaker adversary to challenge a more powerful one unless the strong military infrastructure and constitutes the strength of the stronger adversary is first neutralized or paralyzed. The so-called "fourth generation warfare" that challenges conventional military wisdom and war-fighting methods, is being successfully waged by non-state actors by marshalling fanatics, extremists, and mercenaries of several nationalities, operating through secret networks.

The potential of conventional forces to defeat an enemy that employs asymmetrical strategies, which invariably include terrorism, has been found to be rather limited. Surprisingly, many military theorists still believe that such an enemy can be defeated by

[23] Ibid.

conventional methods; they maintain that the war is eventually won by the stronger military power. They forget that an enemy who discards high-technology, even cell phones, and employs unconventional tactics annuls most 'advantages of sophisticated technologies, which conventional armies employ to defeat the enemy. The strongest military apparatus of the world was unable to preempt or stop the 9/11 attacks because they were launched by an adversary "who used box cutters and ceramic knifes" to render American defence apparatus incapable of anticipating or stopping attacks on the American mainland.

In the recent past, asymmetrical wars have taken the shape of slow-moving conflicts waged by subnational ethnic or religious entities that are shadowy and formless, who generally operate from several regions, transcending national boundaries. Asymmetric strategies are diverse and numerous and can take various forms such as insurgency, guerrilla warfare and terrorism. It is the role of al-Qaeda in conjunction with unconventional forces operating in Afghanistan and Iraq, Africa and other parts of the world that needs to be explored rather than its capability to mount sporadic terrorist attacks in isolation.

# XIV

# South Asia: Scope of Nuclear Terrorism–Policy Imperatives

*Vijai K Nair*

*"Bioterrorism, like the anthrax threats currently rattling America, is horrific. But perhaps the ultimate horror in our newly uncertain world is the prospect of terrorists with nuclear weapons."*[1]

*The dimension and nature of the 11 September 2001 attack on the World Trade Center heralded a quantum jump in the qualitative and quantitative approach to terrorist action by a calamitous magnitude that shocked the West out of their misplaced belief of their invulnerability to the phenomenon of terrorism.*

*"The head of the International Atomic Energy Agency (IAEA) says that the ruthlessness of the September 11 attacks has alerted the world to the potential of nuclear terrorism–making it "ar more likely" that terrorists could target nuclear facilities, nuclear material and radioactive sources worldwide."*[2] *Curiously, the approach of the West to this new and hitherto neglected threat churned out numerous theories regardless of past history and experience amongst the developing world, which resulted in strategies and tactics that contrasted fundamentally with the understanding of and approach to terrorism in developing countries such as India.*

[1] Bruce G. Blair, "President Ceter for Defense Information. The Ultimate Hatred Is Nuclear," *The New York Times Dateline—Washington*, 22 October 2001.

[2] "Calculating the New Global Nuclear Terrorism Threat," Press Release, IAEA Press Centre, 1 November 2001.

## INTRODUCTION

The Indian government has always viewed militancy from within its indigenous people as a law-and-order problem and, therefore, to be suppressed by the use of 'minimum force' as they were misguided state subjects. Military resources can only be used at behest of the government in the role of 'aid to civil power,' and control over these forces and their operations has always been delegated to civil authority.

However, terrorism as perceived by the US and its allies has a totally different connotation. President George W. Bush's was against terrorism is predicated on the application of unrestricted military force against non-American peoples. This has not only altered the definition of terrorism but has also freed the hands of terrorists to match forces in an asymmetrical manner to achieve their ends. The major difference in this Western concept of waging war against militants with that governs India's concept is that the latter draws a line in the use of force against its own citizens no matter what. The unrestricted and indiscriminate use of military forces against the Afghan and Iraqi people has led to a search to acquire weapons of mass destruction (WMD) for clandestine use to deliver maximum destruction on the invading forces and their logistical infrastructure.

The definition of terrorism on which the Gilmore Commission, that was set up the assess the threat from terrorists is, "Terrorism is violence or the threat of violence, calculated to create an atmosphere of fear and alarm, through acts designed to coerce others into actions they otherwise would not undertake or in refraining from actions that they desired to take."[3] This captures the very essence of the concept of terrorism as it has emerged at the turn of the century. The

[3] "Assessing the Threat," The first annual report to the president and the Congress of the Advisory Panel to assess domestic response capabilities for terrorism involving WMDs, 15 December 1999. Also known as the Gilmore Commission, Washington: RAND Publications, 1999, p. i.

target population must be convinced either by demonstration or other means that the terrorist organisation/state sponsor has a confirmed capability to inflict unacceptable punishment through discrete or indiscrete weapon systems that would overwhelm the protective cover of legislated authority. The intention is to generate sufficient levels of fear to convince the targeted populace that there is no other option but to acquiesce to the terrorist demands. It is a conceptual framework to meet specific conditions by which this instrument operates. The resources available are either self-generated or facilitated by a state sponsor as in the case of the proxy war being waged by Pakistan for two decades in Jammu and Kashmir (J&K).

## CHARACTERISTICS PECULIAR TO TERRORISM

What is most menacing about terrorism is the unpredictability of their strikes, which does not abide by the logic imbued in the science of modern military warfare, but gains its impetus through random targeting—time, space, weaponry and intensity—that is not directed to breaking down a perceivable military threat, but to psychologically undermining the collective psyche of the populace to bend to the larger objective, which the terrorists aspire for. The spin off of these attacks is not measured in military gains but in terms of their effect on the targeted populace by wide publicity of the perceived lethality of their operations through changing devices of annihilation, the latest being a resort to chemical attacks that affected hundreds of people.

Terrorism is an evolving phenomenon that has its genesis in individuals who covet resources of others to enhance their personal power quotient within the prevailing socio-economic status. Terror has always been one of the instruments of human interaction and, as such, is not a new phenomenon.

T he second obvious manifestation of this phenomenon lies in the shadow of the evolving means for conflict between states—i.e. the increasing lethality of means available to perpetrate destruction of property or human life. The percolation of these means, usually confined to the states, to non-state actors is a consequence of the diffusion of Industrial capacities that fabricate production of lethal systems and subsystems, thereby facilitating access to individuals and groups with ulterior motives.

The third tangible signature of terrorism is that techniques and means used to incapacitate the human mind through fear are denigrated by constant repetition and the capacities to develop mitigating countermeasures. This has brought about a dynamic that causes an incremental character to the means of inducing fear. The mere 'threat' of WMD attack generates exponential fear amongst hapless population.

The fourth feature is the need by the advocates of terrorism to bring about imbalances within the tactical application of force by state law-and-order agencies that follow predictable patterns, through random actions that break that continuity, and demoralize the state machinery, thus reducing the confidence of the public in the state to provide them security.

And fifthly, terrorism is not a new factor nor is it of a constant nature. Evolution to more effective means to instill fear either in the individual or the collective community is a pre-requisite to effectively subjugate the target body in keeping with the desired objectives of the predator.

From the turn of the century, terrorists around the world (Iraq, Afghanistan, Pakistan, India, Russia, Philippines, Thailand, Indonesia, the Middle East and South America) have acquired and put to use modern weapons systems that are usually in the domain of security forces of states and beyond the capacity of non-state players to acquire in the general market. Furthermore, terrorist groups are clandestine organizations that do not have the facilities to develop and produce complex weapon systems of their own. These resources are obviously being made available by sponsor states that have a vested interest in supporting dissenting groups in selected states. Two glaring examples of state sponsorship are:

- American support to the Chechens to undermine the erstwhile Soviet Union when President Carter sanctioned $500 million to fuel disgruntled Islamic Groups amongst the Caucasians.[4]
- Pakistan's military support to Muslim malcontents in J&K. Through the Inter Services Intelligence (ISI), Islamabad facilitated military training of Kashmiri youth and infiltration of indigenous Kashmiri terrorists and Pakistanis including military personnel, funds, arms and munitions, and state of the art communication systems to fuel militancy in J&K. Pakistan has used this ploy to wage a *proxy war* short of an outright military offensive against India's superior military potential.[5]

The current status of the American war against terrorist has fast developed into a stalemate in Iraq where terrorists have successfully held the world's most powerful military forces at bay for over four years. In J&K militancy continues but greatly restrained by the sustained counterterrorism operations by Indian security forces and, to a degree, Pakistan's preoccupation with militant forces on its Western borders, which has soaked up over 80,000 troops and President Musharraf's efforts to achieve Pakistan's aspirations vis-à-vis assimilating J&K through political means.

Pakistan is a nuclear weapon state that hosts the Taliban and al-Qaeda on its soil[6] despite its so-called alliance with the US in the war against terrorism to defeat these two entities in Afghanistan. Add to this the current instability in Pakistan generated by fundamentalist groups;[7] its wide-ranging n uclear infrastructure, past interaction between Osama bin Laden and significant personnel of its nuclear

[4] Terrorism Watch, Magoo Strategic Infotech, Disclosures by Brezinski.

[5] Syed Jamaluddin, *To Eliminate Terrorism: Divide Pakistan*, New York, Lincoln, Shanghai: iUniverse, Inc., 2006, pp. 50–51.

[6] "Terrorist Havens: Pakistan," Council on Foreign Relations, December 2005, <http:/www.cfr.org/publications/9514/>.

[7] Syed Saleem Shahzad, "Waziristan Jihadis Wage War On Each Other," *Asia Times Online*, 23 March 2007.

establishment;[8] the capture of 'two top nuclear scientists of the Pakistan Atomic Energy Commission' from a nuclear facility in the NWFP, by the Taliban about six months ago;[9] and evidence of al-Qaeda's determination to acquire nuclear weapons;[10] and we have an extremely dangerous environment across India's western borders. More about this later.

## US WAR ON TERRORISM: ESCALATION BEYOND CONVENTIONAL MEANS

The wars being fought against terrorism by the US in Iraq, NATO in Afghanistan, Russia in Chechnya, Pakistan in the North West Frontier Province (NWFP) and Balochistan, India in J&K, all have some things in common: the involvement of nuclear weapon states (NWS) in each case; slow but evident increments in the weapons being used by the terrorists; and a general state of stalemate that portents long dawn out conflicts.

With the diffusion of chemical, biological and radiological means in the existing global socio-economic scenario, there is a need to address the possibilities of terrorists escalating their offensive by introducing chemical, biological, radiological and nuclear weapons (CBRN)[11] in the evolving phenomenon of terrorism, either now or in the foreseeable future.

The characteristics of biological and chemical weapons make them the most likely candidates to spearhead the advent of CBRN weapons in terrorist arsenals. The nerve gas attack in a Tokyo subway in 1995, resulting in 12 fatalities with a further 5,500 being incapacitated was seen as a wake-up call to the world's large cities. It

[8] Subodh Atal, "Extremist, Nuclear Pakistan: An Emerging Threat?" *Policy Analysis*, no. 472, 5 March 2003.

[9] "Top Pakistan Nuclear Scientists in Taliban Custody," *Zee News*, 7 March 2007.

[10] David Albright, "Al Qaeda's Quixotic Quest to go Nuclear. Nautilus Institute for Security and Sustainable Evidence," reproduced by *Asia Times Online*, 22 November 2002.

[11] Op cit, n. 3, p. iii.

served as a warning of just how vulnerable they are to attacks from terrorists who are prepared to use WMDs.[12]

In the past two weeks, insurgents have created and employed a number of chlorine bombs. "In Falluja, west of the capital Baghdad, suicide bombers driving tankers filled with chlorine targeted two separate locations. There were at least three such attacks in Iraq during February 2007. The chemical is easy to obtain. It is widely used as a cleaner and a water purifier.[13]

Acquisition of these weapons by terrorist groups would have to be done through off-the-shelf purchases from commercial sources, theft from laboratories or hospitals, development of required agent from natural sources by the terrorist group, or procurement from a rogue state, a disgruntled government scientist, or a state sponsor.[14] However, the focus of this paper is on the nuclear-cum-radiological aspect of CBRNs.

### Nuclear weapons and Radiology Dispersal Devices

These can be used either as fission weapons (standard nuclear weapons) or as crude radiological dispersal devices (RDD) that do not activate a chain reaction but disperse radioactive isotopes, which if ingested by the targeted population can cause death or illness, depending on the curies of the isotope.

"Nuclear Knowledge, materials and weapons are oozing out of control. Nuclear weapons technology and knowledge continue to spread. Nuclear explosives themselves, and nuclear materials, are spreading into hands hostile to the US."[15]

What needs emphasis is that this is a global phenomenon that casts its web far beyond the North American shores and in particular

[12] Andrew Silke, "Bioterrorism: It's only a question of time," *Times of London*, 18 October 1999.

[13] Hugh Sykes, "Iraqis killed by chlorine bombs," BBC Report, 17 March 2007.

[14] Op cit, n. 3, p. 22.

[15] Edward R. Royce, Chairman of the Subcommittee on International Terrorism and Nonproliferation of the Committee on International Relations House of Representatives, 14 April 2005.

has its genesis in India's own backyard. Therefore, while all studies on nuclear terrorist are related to country-specific national security interests, each state must understand the totality of this occurrence as it evolves, its systems, structures and players, and formulate national policy to suit its own specific requirements.

When President George W. Bush's declared 'war on terrorism,' he also enunciated the policy of pre-emptive attack, which extended the use of nuclear weapons to *non-state players* (terrorists) that had or aspired to acquire a potential for WMDs. "Now, shadowy networks of individuals can bring great chaos and suffering to our shores for less than it costs to purchase a single tank. Terrorists are organized to penetrate open societies and to turn the power of modern technologies against us. … We will cooperate with other nations to deny, contain, and curtail our enemies' efforts to acquire dangerous technologies. And, as a matter of common sense and self-defense, America will act against such emerging threats before they are fully formed."[16]

The doctrine of pre-emptive attack is based on the concept that WMDs in the hands of 'rogue states' or transferred to terrorist groups, are so threatening to the security of the US and its allies that it is justifiable to use armed force to deal with this especially dangerous form of WMD proliferation. Moreover, as happened in Iraq, it is justifiable to launch an anticipatory military attack on the state believed to be producing these weapons; the attacks can take place early on, even before the weapons are produced, used or transferred to terrorist groups.[17]

The policy of pre-emptive attack has a risky spin-off in that states that are party to the Non Proliferation Treaty (NPT) whom Washingtom has loudly declared enemies of the US such as Iran and North Korea, and proven proliferate—Pakistan—have demonstrated

[16] George W. Bush, The National Security Strategy of the United States of America, The White House, 2002.

[17] "The US Doctrine of Preemptive attack—Real Problem, Wrong Answer," Report of the Task Force on Peace and Security United Nations Association, National Capital Area, 17 June 2003.

to others the impotence of an overstretched US military to convert the president's threat into action that would actually eliminate the ongoing nuclear programme of a 'rogue state' successfully.

Consequently, proliferation of radiological materials continues unabated with some possibly landing in the hands of terrorist organizations such as al-Qaeda. Policymakers need to scrutinize the dimension of nuclear weapons for three basic reasons that are intractably embodied into the philosophies driving conflict at the turn of the century.

First, nuclear weapons are an integral part of the war fighting doctrines and military structures of at least five of the countries involved directly in the conflict in Afghanistan: the US, Russia, Pakistan, the UK and France. Added to this, there is no guarantee that the conflict will not spill over across the territories of two other concerned regional states that are plagued by indigenous terrorist activities and are also NWS in their own rights—China and India. Each of these states can be expected to reconfigure their nuclear strategies in keeping with the dynamics of the conflict and threat perceptions. For the first time in the past half-century, we see all NWS closely engaged in a military conflict in a geostrategic location that can appropriately be described as a 'nuclear hornet's nest.' The possibility is that any one of the NWS involved in the fight against terrorists in Afghanistan could trigger a nuclear strike would have serious repercussions vis-à-vis other nuclear armed military forces in the region and exact colossal environmental damage on the central and south Asian landmass.

Second, all known NWS have problems with terrorist of their own. The means to terrorise selected population centers have progressed incrementally along the curve of the destructive capacities built into weapons hitherto restricted to waging war, and their utility is limited to the diminishing returns of repetitiveness. Recent manifestations suggest that these means have peaked at the threshold of WMDs. The ongoing conflict lends itself to a WMD conflagration.

Third, the diffusion of hitherto restricted technologies to a number of 'third world' countries and the growing propensity amongst weaker protagonists to sponsor non-state terrorist groups to wage war against their more powerful protagonists has brought CBRN weapons within reach of terrorist groups. This, in turn, has led to fundamental changes in the doctrine of nuclear deterrence, in states such as the US, being widened to include targeting options in response to attacks by CBRN. Thus affecting an enormous increment in the variables on which military conflict is managed, lowering the threshold for 'nuclear use' dangerously.

Fourth, but not the least, is the possibility that al-Qaeda may have acquired nuclear weapons from the Russian black market in the 1990s, or sufficient radiological inventories to initiate RDD attacks on invading states either in the battlefield or against population centers on the enemy's home land.

Therefore, to fully appreciate the commonly bandied label 'nuclear flash-point' that Western analysts tend to ascribe to the acquisition of nuclear weapons in South Asia, there is a need to understand the role of nuclear weapons as propagated by NWS; the doctrines, structures and systems that their militaries have created to employ nuclear weapons within the larger political objectives; and, most importantly, the nature and likelihood of the WMD threat from terrorist groups and sponsor states and the probably responses.

The problem lies in the fact that the increased potential to develop nuclear devices amongst the hitherto non-nuclear weapon states (NNWS) who cannot challenge the military and nuclear supremacy of the primary NWS—US, Russia and China—are expected to look to asymmetric strategies to exploit their clandestinely augmented capabilities. What has now become abundantly clear is that some of the prospective proliferates realised that the prevailing nuclear deterrence theology was predicted on psychological captivation of 'state players' and could be effectively undermined by sponsoring non-state players to project the threat of WMDs. The lack of geographic and identification characteristics of the perpetrators would make it impossible to direct the psychological or material elements at a recognised target. The very utility of nuclear deterrence against a non-state player (terrorist group) armed with nuclear, biological or chemical weapons was voiced as early as 1993 by the then British secretary of state for defence, Malcolm Rifkind, who opined, "(I)t is difficult to see deterrence operating securely against proliferators."[18]

The mechanisms that worked to facilitate strategies of deterrence between states are near impossible to replicate vis-à-vis terrorist groups. For instance, deterrence rests on the ability to influence the decision-making process of those individuals in the terrorist group who may aspire to acquire WMDs and carry out a strike against an inimical state. But these are not within a recognisable framework of hierarchically organised groups as exist in the states that have hitherto been the targets of deterrence. Because a deterrence strategy is a function of inducing exception levels of fear to freeze the target's decision-making process, it is imperative that a clear and effective means of communication is established between the deterrer and the target—which would demolish the very concept on which 'terrorism' works.

In 1995, a study group under the deputy assistant secretary of defense for counter-proliferation, Dr. Michael Wallerstein, examined the role of US nuclear weapons in relation to the spread of WMD. This group concluded that the US "nuclear posture has minimal impact on terrorist unless state sponsored." Furthermore, the assistant secretary of defense, Dr. Ashton Carter, posited that "non-state actors [are] not deterred by [the US] nuclear posture."[19]

Despite these conclusions, two years later, in February 1996, the Joint Chiefs of Staf included 'non-state actors' as likely targets for

[18] Robert Green, "Deterring War Responsibly: Better, Lawful Alternatives To Trident," Nuclear Age Peace Foundation, June 1998.

[19] Hans M. Kristensen, Research Associate, Nautilus Institute, "Nuclear Weapons Against Terrorism," British American Security Information Council [BASIC], 28 August 1998.

nuclear strikes,[20] which amounted to "general broadening of the target horizon for nuclear forces" authorising the US forces to plan on responding to an attack by chemical and biological weapons (CBW). This resulted in the broadening of the nuclear target options as a part of a changing deterrence strategy extended to cope with the situation in which the US or allied forces were attacked with CBWs, which in this case amounted to directing use of nuclear weapons against shadowy indistinguishable non-state actors suspected to be armed with WMDs.

This strategy has since been mimicked by the French Defense minister Alliot Marie.[21] The current war on terrorist is being waged by at least two NWS professing a nuclear deterrence strategy that encompasses nuclear response to non –state players who may resort to CBRN attacks against them and, the opposition, Osama bin Laden's al-Qaeda, has repetitively issued threats to use CBRN means to defeat the US. In a background briefing, Admiral Craig R. Quigley clarified US military forces in Afghanistan would be expected to respond to a CBRN attack, if it were perpetrated, in accordance with the Doctrine for Joint Theatre Nuclear Operations.[22]

Coalition forces' sensitivity to this danger was apparent by the deceptive clips released on TV during the highly publicised operation to capture al-Qaeda's headquarters at Tora Bora. While approximately 3,00 Special Forces personnel from the US, Britain, Germany and Russia scoured the caves of Tora Bora, not one of them appeared in the TV clips. Instead, these clips depicted elements of the Northern Alliance and post-strike smoke plumes on targets five to six mountain ranges away. This gives credence to the report that "The

[20] Joint Chiefs of Staff publication, Doctrine for Joint Theater Nuclear Operation.

[21] President Jacques Chirac, "Chirac threatens nuclear weapons against 'terrorist' states," Ile Longue Military Base, France, 19 January 2006, *Agence France Presse*, <http:www.turkishpress.com/news.asp?id=104067>.

[22] Background briefing on Afghanistan by two defence officials, introduced by Rear Admiral Craig R. Quigley, deputy assistant secretary of defence for public affairs, United States Department of Defence News Transcript, 12 October 2001.

Special Forces personnel operating in the region are attired in NBC suits and carry protective equipment against radiation and biological or chemical agents. It has been declared a no-go zone for journalists, even those attached to the US military."[23]

According to DEBKA-Net-Weekly's intelligence sources, the priority of the Coalition military operation in the Tora Bora mountains was to locate al-Qaeda's WMD—including nuclear devices—in a desperate race against the clock.[24]

This generated an extremely volatile situation—a nuclear 'flashpoint,' which could lead to a cascading domino effect in a region where military forces of the world's nuclear weapon powers had converged, some of which were organised and equipped to enforce the strategies of deterrence expounded by their governments.

In the words of Secretary Rumsfeld, "… we know of certain knowledge that the nations on our terrorist list have weaponised CBWs, and we know that a number of them are seeking nuclear capabilities. And we know that they have close linkages with terrorist networks, and that in many cases, they have sponsored terrorism. Therefore, it doesn't take a leap of imagination to expect that at some point those nations will work with those terrorist networks and assist them in achieving and obtaining those kinds of capabilities."[25]

From UN Secretary General Kofi Annan[26] down to all and sundry, the threat of terrorists acquiring a capability to institute a CBRN attack was being portrayed as the 'greatest danger' facing the world. Osama bin Laden's statement, "The Nuclear Bomb of

[23] "Nuclear Chase in the Tora Bora Complex," Copyright © 2001, Debkafile net weekly, *Intelligence Journal*.

[24] Ibid.

[25] Secretary Rumsfeld, interview by Tim Russert, *Meet the Press*, NBC, 30 September 2001, United States Department of Defense News Transcript.

[26] Mark Riley, "Nuclear Or Chemical Attack 'Our Biggest Threat' – Mr. Anna," the *Sydney Morning Herald*. Mr. Annan made the remarks when he opened a weeklong session of the UN General Assembly.

Islam,"[27] declaring "it is the duty of Muslims to prepare as much force as possible to terrorize the enemies of God," and Madouh Mahmud Salim's endeavours to acquire a 'suitcase bomb' from Chechen mobsters,[28] were being revisisted out of context creating hysteria in Western societies.

Barely a week after the WTC outrage, US diplomatic sources disclosed that the Defense Department had recommended to President Bush the use of tactical nuclear weapons (TNWs) as a military option to retaliate for 9/11 terrorist attacks in the US. The *Japan Times* reported that ever since the attacks on Libya and Afghanistan failed analysts suspect that US officials "may be mulling the use of TNWs, which can cause much greater destruction than conventional weapons."[29] Sam Cohen, the scientist who invented the n eutron bomb, has urged officials in the Bush administration and in Congress "to use a small neutron bomb to wipe out Osama bin Laden in a quick first strike in the war on terrorist."[30] General Alexander Haig, former NATO supreme commander, secretary of state and White House chief of staff, is reported to have said in an interview "to prevent the use of weapons of mass destruction by terrorists, the President should give 'a firm warning in advance that we would retaliate in kind and in a devastating manner."[31] And,

[27] Bin Laden Endorses the Nuclear Bomb of Islam: On or about 29 May 1998, bin Laden issued a statement entitled "The Nuclear Bomb of Islam," under the banner of the "International Islamic Front for Fighting the Jews and Crusaders," in which he stated that "it is the duty of Muslims to prepare as much force as possible to terrorize the enemies of God."

[28] Elizabeth Neuffer, Boston Globe. Dateline, New York, 9/16/2001. 'Bin Laden Sought Nuclear Matter-Officials Have not Confirmed The Purchase'; and 'Bin Laden Has History of Trying to Acquire Nuclear, Chemical Weapons,' Washington, 17 September 2001, source: azcentral.com.

[29] "Pentagon Said To Eye Nuclear Attack Against Terrorists," the *Japan Times*, Washington (Kyodo), 20 September 2001.

[30] Wes Vernon, "Father Of Neutron Bomab: Use It on Osama," Washington, 25 September 2001, source: NewsMax.com.

[31] Alexander Haig to Newsmax, "Warn Rogue States Of 'Devastating' Response," John Douglas Browne, 25 September 2001, Source: NewsMax.com.

Senator Jon Kyl proposed that the US should retaliate with nuclear weapons if terrorists launch chemical or germ warfare against the nation,[32] while Rep. Steve Buyer, R-Ind, supported "limited use of a nuclear device under certain specific circumstances"[33]

Nuclear weapons theologies had transcended Cold War limitations of use against NWS as a deterrent or as a war-fighting tool and were being re designed to fit the post Cold War security environment. As for the "War on Terrorism," it has dangerously lowered the nuclear threshold—which if activated by one of the NWS players—would generate unforeseen consequences from unforeseen quarters, and would give impetus to the highly organized international terrorist organization such as the al-Qaeda to acquire nuclear weapons of the fission type or RDDs to inflict massive casualties on the homeland of attacking states.

## EVIDENCE OF TERRORIST ORGANISATIONS' EFFORTS TO ACQUIRE NUCLEAR WEAPONS/RDDS

Having left a discernible train leading from Afghanistan to the Middle East and onto the American mainland, al-Qaeda is the prime terrorist suspect that aspires to develop crude first generation nuclear weapons and RDDs. Needless to add that for a non-state actor to get its hands on the knowledge—and possibly—materials to develop any form of nuclear device in the wilds of Afghanistan indicates complicity with the power on whose territory such a programme is managed, and a sponsor state willing to part with this knowledge. As evidence will show, the finger of suspicion points to the Afghani

[32] "Kyl Refuses To Rule Out U.S. Nuclear Retaliation," *Associated Press*, Tucson, 30 September 2001.

[33] "Congressman Suggests Limited Nuclear Retaliation," *The Indianapolis Star*, 1 October 2001. Rep. Steve Buyer, R-Ind, member of the House Veterans Affairs Committee, in an interview with Indianapolis television station WRTV said, "he would support limited use of a nuclear device under certain specific circumstances ... if the United States can prove a causal link between the anthrax and bin Laden's organization, I would support the use of a limited precision tactical nuclear device."

government under the Taliban that was supported monetarily and militarily by the al-Qaeda, and Pakistan, a NWS whose nuclear scientists were known to be in touch with Osama bin Laden before the US mounted their attack on Afghanistan.

Following the fall of the Taliban government in late 2001, according to an exhaustive review of documents, booklets, personnel records, videos, equipment, materials, computer hard drives that were discovered in houses, caves and training camps in Afghanistan by Western and Northern Alliance intelligence officers and journalists of all Western media, was indicative of WMD programmes.[34]

Mike Boettcher and Ingrid Arnesen of CNN reported, "The al-Qaeda terrorist organization was building a serious weapons program with a heavy emphasis on developing a nuclear device, according to an exhaustive review of documents discovered in Afghanistan." Amongst the documents, a 25-page document filled with information about nuclear weapons included a design for a nuclear weapon that would require hard-to-obtain materials like plutonium to create a nuclear explosion. It is, however, doubtful that al-Qaeda had laid hands on bomb-grade fissile material before their eviction from Afghanistan. The CNN team concluded, "if easier-to-acquire radioactive materials are used—like discarded nuclear power plant fuel rods—the design could become a radiological dispersal weapon or 'dirty bomb.' The device would not create a nuclear explosion, but instead would blow radioactive debris over a wide area, rendering it uninhabitable."

In December 2001, after CIA director George Tenet's visit to Islamabad to meet Musharraf and authorities in Kabul, US intelligence officials told CNN that during a meeting of senior al-Qaeda leaders in Afghanistan within the last year, a member of the terrorist network displayed a cylinder and said it contained radiological material that could be used in a dirty bomb.[35]

[34] Op cit, n. 10.

[35] Mike Boettcher and Ingrid Arensen, source: CNN, http://archives.cnn.com/2002/US/01/24/inv.al.qaeda.documents/index.html.

But Albright cautioned there is no indication that al-Qaeda's nuclear work has gone beyond theory. To create a nuclear weapon, Albright said a designer must learn a whole set of manufacturing steps not mentioned in al-Qaeda's manual and develop confidence in the weapon's design.[36]

We on the subcontinent are familiar with the reports that confirmed that at least six Pakistani scientists reportedly met with Osama bin Laden and Ayman al-Zawahiri in Kabul along with Bashir ud-Din Mahmood and Abdul Majeed,[37] who under interrogation admitted that they had had discussions with both Laden and Zawahiri on a visit to Afghanistan in August 2001. They are reported to have observed that Osama bin Laden was "intensely interested in nuclear, chemical and biological weapons,"[38] and that Bin Laden indicated to them that he had obtained, or had access to, some type of radiological material that he said had been acquired by the radical Islamic Movement of Uzbekistan.[39] Mahmood and Majeed reportedly told bin Laden that it would not be possible to manufacture a nuclear weapon from that material.

Both are known to have fundamentalist beliefs and also ran a charity in Kabul called Ummah Tameer-e-Nau, which is on the US 'Terrorist Watch List.' Mahmood was reported to have attended the annual conference of the Markaz-ul-Dawa-wal-Irshad, the parent organization of the Laskar-e-Toiba (LET), along with ex ISI chiefs, Generals Hamid Gul and Mahmood Ahmed.[40]

[36] Ibid.

[37] Rajesh Kumar Mishra, "Nuclear Safety and Security in Pakistan: Under the Shades of Terrorism," South Asia Analysis Group Paper, no. 520, 20 September 2002. And, "Nuclear Scientists Interrogated Over Possible Bin Laden Link," CNN, 26 October 2002.

[38] Kamran Khan and Molly Moore, "2 Nuclear Scientists Briefed Bin Laden, Pakistanis Say," the *Washsington Post*, 12 December 2001.

[39] The *Washington Post* reported on 11 June 2002, that the US government had concluded that al-Qaeda controls enough radioactive cesium, strontium, or cobalt to mount a radiological attack on the United States.

[40] Op cit, n. 8.

Another document showed these scientists had plans to explore the mining of minerals—including uranium, inside Afghanistan. Two others amongst these six scientists, Suleiman Asad and Mohammed Ali Mukhtar, that the US had asked to be interrogated, had been hastily dispatched to Myanmar soon after 11 September 2001 and were provided asylum allegedly at the behest of General Pervez Musharraf. They were not recalled and cannot be extradited as Pakistan does not have an extradition treaty with Myanmar.[41] Both these scientists "are directly related to the country's nuclear programme, and have been working in the Kahuta Research Laboratories for the last few years."[42]

The willingness of Pakistani scientist to work with al-Qaeda's supreme and the ease with which they could access war torn Afghanistan suggests that with or without formal government blessings (does not rule out maverick elements in the ISI), Pakistan nuclear technology is likely to have found its way to Osama bin Laden—the leader of al-Qaeda who continues to be shielded by Pakistan from capture by the US.

However, they claim they provided no material or specific plans to bin Laden, but rather engaged in wide ranging 'academic' discussions. Other Pakistani officials familiar with the interrogations told the *Washington Post* that the scientists provided detailed responses to bin Laden's technical questions about the manufacture of nuclear, biological and chemical weapons.[43]

In summation, these scientists are believed to have provided al-Qaeda a blueprint for making nuclear weapons. They are suspected of providing classified information about producing nuclear weapons to al-Qaeda or the Taliban or of facilitating access to others in the Pakistani nuclear program who had that knowledge.[44]

[41] David Sanger, "Nuclear Experts in Pakistan May Have Links to Al Qaeda," *New York Times*, 9 December 2001.

[42] Op cit, n. 5, p. 87.

[43] Kaman Khan, "Pakistan Released Nuclear Scientists for Ramadan's End," the *Washington Post*, 16 December 2001.

[44] Op cit, n. 10.

"An al-Qaeda videotape obtained by CNN shows a level of sophistication in bomb making that would allow terrorists to arrive in a target city unarmed and easily put together high-explosive devices to carry out destructive attacks, experts who saw the tapes say … Essentially a training video for select al Qaeda recruits, the tape shows the steps needed to make pure TNT and bomb components using easy-to-obtain materials to make powerful explosives from scratch."[45]

Tony Villa, a consultant for the US government on terror tactics and bomb making opined, "… the video confirms his fear that al Qaeda's techniques are now so sophisticated that its bomb makers can cheat detection … The overarching point here is that they can pick any venue or target city—with nothing on them—arrive in that city."[46]

While the lack of bomb-grade fissile material may thwart al-Qaeda's nuclear weapons aspirations, the confirmed ability to make trinitrotoluene (TNT) gives on site, through locally acquired ingredients, al-Qaeda the core for its dirty-bomb project and the abundance of locations where radioisotopes are also locally available substantially increases the threat of an RDD attack.

David Ensor of CNN reported on 4 December 2001 that according to US officials, one hand-drawn diagram found either in a Taliban or al-Qaeda facility showed a design for a dirty bomb.[47]

At a Defense Department briefing on 16 January 2002, Secretary of Defense Rumsfeld stated, "We have found a number of things that show an appetite for WMD." A claim he supported by citing evidence from the collective analysis of evidence acquired from Afghanistan in November 2001.

CIA director George Tenet told Congress in late January 2001 that the US had uncovered rudimentary diagrams of nuclear

[45] Nic Robertson, "Bomb Making Videos Reveal Scope of Al Qaeda Threat," CNN, <http:/archives.cnn.com/2002/US/08/21/terror.tape.main/index.html>.

[46] Op cit, n. 10.

[47] Op cit, n. 10.

weapons in a suspected al-Qaeda house in Kabul. According to a CIA report released publicly on 30 January 2001, these "diagrams, while crude, describe the essential components—uranium and high explosives—common to nuclear weapons."

All this evidence confirms that Osama bin Laden was putting together a serious programme to develop, produce and employ nuclear weapons to enhance capacities to strike terror in the minds of the enemies of al-Qaeda anywhere in the world in general and the US in particular. It shows that al-Qaeda "was creating a quasi-state nuclear weapons programme with the tacit or direct approval of the Taliban government."[48] Which in turn was the creation of Pakistani support, both militarily and politically.

Pakistan's Inter-Service Intelligence service provided management for Taliban operations and Islamabad had nearly nine army brigades deployed to consolidate the Taliban and to project operations against the Northern Alliance in attempts to control the country with a view of enhancing strategic depth for Pakistan vis-à-vis India. Nothing could escape the notice of the Inter-Service Intelligence service network in Afghanistan, least of all this ongoing clandestine nuclear weapons programme.

Added to this vast collation of evidence of al-Qaeda nuclear programme, two pieces of fresh and definitive nuclear intelligence sent US Special Forces in the last week of November 2001 into intensified action in the Tora Bora cave complex in Eastern Afghanistan and triggered a major terror alert inside the US, the third since September 11.

First was the intelligence report in US hands claiming that al-Qaeda chiefs removed their WMD arsenal from secret hideouts in Kabul to Tora Bora six days in advance of the September 11 attacks. That information persuaded Russian, Pakistani and Northern Alliance intelligence that bin Laden and al-Zawahiri went somewhere

[48] Op cit, n. 10.

else, anxious to remove themselves from harm's way anywhere near a site where WMDs might explode.

Second, a piece of alarming intelligence reaching Washington on 27 November primarily from Pakistan was Pakistan was that bin Laden and al-Zawahiri were now reported to be planning to take advantage of the slowdown in US air activity forced by the inclement weather to complete their preparations for massive pre-Christmas terrorist strikes in the US, including a possible nuclear or radiological weapon attack. The target period referred to was between 5 and 20 December. Al-Qaeda's operational teams were described at standing by at the various departure points, some waiting only for the delivery of explosives, others just for their last order to go.[49]

The credence of this intelligence was reinforced by an alarming incident that occurred in New Jersey in October 2001. A very sick Pakistani national without valid entry papers was admitted to a hospital complaining of bleeding gums and pain, symptoms of gingivitis. The hospital diagnosed that the patient was suffering from a massive dose of radiation sickness and reported the incident to the Federal Bureau of Investigation who took him into custody for further investigation. A reporter at the hospital reported this in the New Jersey media. The Pakistani died three weeks later. Though the cause of death was not released, medical experts note that the bleeding gums the anonymous Pakistani was treated for are a symptom of radiation poisoning, suggesting that he might have been a 'mule' transporting nuclear materials or devices into the US. Was he the only carrier or are there others employed by al-Qaeda to smuggle nuclear materials or devices tasked to plant their deadly burdens in pre-arranged secret locations, ready for activation. He remained in FBI custody for three weeks and considering the record of US 'interrogation techniques' he must have provided considerable actionable information on possible terrorist efforts to mount a

[49] Debka-Net-Weekly, Third Week November 2001.

nuclear weapon/RDD attack on the American mainland before he died.

Concurrently, another Pakistani national was apprehended crossing from Jordan to Israel. According to initial published reports, he was caught trying to smuggle in a 'dirty' nuclear device. Then came a news blackout. He was handed over to the US after which the Washington initiated a demand that Pakistan take six more nuclear scientists into custody for interrogation.

This made President George W. Bush decide to send CIA chief George Tenet urgently to Islamabad to try and establish the credibility of this intelligence data with Pakistani leader Pervez Musharraf and the heads of Pakistan's Inter-Service Intelligence service.

According to DEBKA-Net-Weekly's sources, Musharraf showed Tenet documents and first-hand witness accounts collected in the past two weeks by Pakistani military intelligence officers who had discovered and entered underground stores around Kabul, in which high levels of nuclear radiation were detected. The Pakistani agents also spent large sums of money to buy from Kabul locals, descriptions of the men in charge of the stores and anything they may have picked up about the type of goods cached there.

They came up with a description of dark-colored, cone-shaped, ultra-heavy containers, about four feet long, which they were given to understand were radioactive. The guards, identified as a special al-Qaeda unit of foreigners, Egyptians, Saudis and Chechens, spoke to no one. Their commanders communicated directly with bin Laden and al-Zawahiri.

According to DEBKA-Net-Weekly's sources in Islamabad, Musharraf advised the CIA director to go to Kabul himself and verify the information at first hand. They report that Tenet took this advice and paid a secret visit to the Afghan capital on Sunday, 2 December 2001 under the protection of US and Russian Special Force units.

With the help of interpreters, he and his assistants interrogated the Pakistani agents' sources directly. After six hours in Kabul, Tenet called the White House to confirm the Pakistan report, adding that it tied in with previous intelligence attesting to nuclear activity in the Tora Bora complex.

Washington's order to switch the objectives of the Tora Bora offensive went out accordingly at the beginning of the week. A nuclear terror alert was declared in the US on 4 December 2001. And NEST teams scarred New York and Washington for possible nuclear devices through the Christmas and New Year holidays.

Pakistan is perceived to be a potential source of diversion of its nuclear materials, technology and its arsenal. According to the Center of Defence Information, "the weapons are probably assembled at Wah [50 miles from Afghanistan], and are stored at Sargoda near a missile complex."[50] With its proximity to the NWFP, the province where the kidnapping of a Pakistani nuclear scientist by the Taliban six months ago—acknowledged by the Pakistani government—could put a dangerous twist to the recorded attempts by al-Qaeda to advance its own nuclear weapons progrmme. Even the storage site of the Pakistani nuclear arsenal was shifted, after Deputy Secretary of State Armitage visited Musharraf in September 2001, from Sargoda to an undisclosed location Chitral district, which lies in close proximity to South East Afghanistan where Hekmatayar's Mujahideen are the dominant force fighting against Afghani forces. In the current state of upheaval in Pakistan, both these locations are extremely vulnerable to fundamentalist forces in both Afghanistan and Pakistan. "The Pakistani situation, in particular, deserves careful monitoring—using surveillance and intelligence assets in the region … In fact, the U.S. government should be prepared to provide arsenal security even without Islamabad's permission if emergency circumstances dictate."[51]

This accumulative evidence leaves little grounds to deny al-Qaeda's aspirations to employ nuclear devices, fission type or RDDs,

[50] "What If Terrorists Go Nuclear?" CDI Terrorism Project, 1 October 2001.

in their war against its enemies and that it acquired much of its knowledge from Pakistan. The most targeted states would be the Western Coalition fighting Islamic insurgency in Iraq and the prime enemy of its mentor—Pakistan—namely secular India that is under siege by terrorists such as the LET and Jaish-Mohammed, long time allies of the Taliban and al-Qaeda. Osama bin Laden's fixation on the Middle East notwithstanding, we cannot lose sight of the fact that he heads the Pan-Islamisation movement and is on record that the Eastern front of this movement had reached Jammu and Kashmir in India.

### ATTACK BY RADIOLOGICAL DISPERSAL DEVICES ALSO KNOWN AS THE 'DIRTY BOMB'

As recently as the first half of March 2007, the Director Defense Intelligence Agency, Lieutenant General Michael Maples told the Senate Armed Services Committee, "We also judge that Al Qaida and other terrorist groups have the capability and intent to develop and employ a radiological dispersal device." He said, "At this time, we do not believe that Al Qaida has a nuclear weapon capability, although acquisition remains a goal; the acquisition of sufficient weapons usable nuclear material remains Al Qaida's key obstacle to an improvised nuclear capability."[52]

A dirty bomb/RDD combines a conventional explosive, such as dynamite, with radioactive material. Most RDDs would not release enough radiation to kill people or cause severe illness—the conventional explosive itself would be more harmful to individuals than the radioactive material. However, depending on the scenario, an RDD explosion could create fear and panic, contaminate property, and require potentially costly prevent the panic sought by

[51] Ibid.

[52] Lt General Michael Maples, "DIA reviews threat of nuclear terrorism by 'non-state actors,'" Geo-Strategy Direct, 14 March 2007, http://www.geostrategy-direct.com/geostrategy-direct/secure/2007/03 14/ba.asp.

terrorists.[53] It is far cheaper and comparatively simpler and safer to produce than a nuclear fission device. It combines explosive destruction and radiation damage. "The problem is wider in scope than often acknowledged, and the stakes are enormous: It takes only a few grams of a deadly radioactive substance such as cesium-137 or strontium-90 to make a dirty bomb."[54]

The aftermath of a dirty-bomb attack in a metropolis and the news of radioactive contamination would generate mass panic amongst the populace leading to a stampede to evacuate the city and could actually cause more casualties than the bomb itself. Even more debilitating would be the direct adverse effect on the economy by disrupting critical infrastructure across the country. This is exactly why dirty bombs are such an attractive weapon for terrorists whose objective is to draw the attention of the public and inspire mass terror across the widest possible area beyond even the targeted city.

The most accessible nuclear materials for any terrorist group that has mastered the techniques to develop TNT—such as al-Qaeda—are locally available of-the-shelf purchases that would be the core of the dirty bomb. This bomb would consist of radiological materials available in the form of waste by-products from nuclear reactors that are usually not secured as well as nuclear weapons, wrapped around a conventional explosive device, which would eject deadly radioactive particles into the environment. Yet another vulnerable source is during the transportation phase of spent fuel rods to and from reprocessing plants and storage sites. Also accessible are the by-products of nuclear blasts at nuclear weapon test sites, which are not properly secured or are abandoned and have abundant unburnt radioactive isotopic substances. Large amounts of unsecured radio isotopic substances are also available in abandoned ex-Soviet military bases in Georgia and other Central Asian States.

[53] "Dirty Bombs," Fact Sheet, United States Nuclear Regulatory Commission, Office of Public Affairs.

[54] Alex Rodrguez, "Radioactive, Unprotected: A Dirty Bomb Nightmare," *Chicago Tribune*, 15 February 2007.

But this is not the sole gamma ray emitting radioactive material available to an enterprising terrorist group. Equally effective and possibly more accessible because of their extensive use in the civil domain are:

- Cesium-137—a fission product that is widely used for industrial radiography, nuclear medicine in hospitals, in universities for experiments, and a by-product of underground nuclear testing.
- Strontium-90—a potent fission product available at nuclear waste storage sites and used as an energy source in thermo electric portable generators (each has a sizeable amount of this potent isotope). Many of the nuclear batteries lie abandoned around the former Soviet Union with questionable security. Strontium-90 is also a by-product of underground nuclear testing.
- Cobalt-60—commonly used for radiological treatment for cancer therapy and in food irradiation plants to kill harmful bacteria, etc.
- Iridium-192—used in industrial radiography such as checking welding of pipes and structures.
- Americium-242—Alpha emitters limited in availability and recorded in the Register of Bhabha Atomic Research Centre.
- Natural radioactive uranium isotopes available at all uranium mines around the world.

Accumulated inventories of fissile materials that have been successfully smuggled over the years could contribute to terrorist inventories for their dirty bombs. According to the IAEA, over the period 1993-2004, there were 662 confirmed cases of radioactive materials smuggling around the world. More than 400 involves substances that could be used in dirty bombs.[55] These figures indicate successful interception of smuggled fissile materials excluding that part of this

[55] Ibid.

trade that has gone undetected. This excludes fissile material losses in other nuclear energy dependent countries.

Having tabulated the means available to terrorists to put together an RDD, we need to examine the kind of damage it could cause, the different methods by which a dirty-bomb attack could be executed and the options available to the Indian government to defend its population and mitigate the consequences as efficiently as possible.

A dirty bomb has more in common with ordinary explosive devices such as the ones used in the recent train bombings in India than with the widespread destruction that accompanies a classical nuclear weapon. Blast and thermal effects caused by the RDD would be equivalent to traditional explosive devices currently in use by terrorist organizations. The primary difference lies in its projection of pulverized radioactive pellets and particles that would spread radiological contamination to a comparatively restricted area. Immediate human casualties would be proportionate to the intensity of the conventional device and the density of people in the immediate blast zone. Radiological contamination would depend on the direction and velocity of wind that would carry a radiated dust cloud beyond the blast zone.

"High explosives inflict damage with rapidly expanding very hot gas. The gas expansion is the means of propelling radioactive material over a wide area … The long term destructive force of the bomb ionizing radiation, from the radioactive material which includes alpha particles, beta particles, gamma rays and X-rays, is radiation that has enough energy to knock an orbital electron off of an atom. Losing an electron throws off the balance between the atom's positively charged protons and negatively charged electrons, giving the atom a net electrical charge (the atom becomes an ion). The free electron may collide with other atoms to create more ions. … In a dirty bomb, the ionizing radiation would come from radioisotopes … simply atoms that decay over time … In other words, the arrangement of protons, neutrons and electrons that make up the atom gradually changes, forming different atoms. This radioactive decay releases a lot of energy in the form of ionizing radiation."[56]

If it enters a human body ionizing radiation, it can cause a lot of serious problems such as breaking the DNA chain, which would lead to cancer, or malfunction of cells resulting in radiation sickness. This is not necessarily fatal as the average human is normally exposed to very small doses of ionizing radiation from outer space, X-ray machines, etc. Exposure within the damage radiation of a dirty bomb would boost the prevailing radiation levels sufficiently to increase the risk of cancer and radiation sickness to some degree. Depending on the exposure and ingestion levels, not many immediate fatalities may occur—other than those killed by the conventional explosion. However, there is a real danger of exposed pèople dying in the following years. The long-term threat of the dirty bomb is worrisome.

A nuclear scientist interviewed in Delhi is skeptical of the damage potential of a dirty bomb when used in the traditional manner of high explosives covered by radioactive isotopic substances, though he does agree with international opinion that such a device would generate immediate fatalities but limited, if any, through ingestion of radioactive dust and continuous exposure in the restricted contaminated zone. He sees a long-term potential of varying degrees of radiation sickness where the authorities may fail to clean up properly. However, he is of the opinion that mass panic would be the most debilitating affect with magnitude of the evacuation having serious repercussions on the economic being of the targeted metropolis. The costs of the cleanup of residual radioactive substances would be exorbitant and time-consuming. It would require specialist trained manpower, materials and equipment to be readily available, a network of instant communications to facilitate and limit evacuation of the people, to issue directions on how they should

[56] Tom Harris, "How Dirty Bombs Work," source:How Stuff Works, http://science.howstuffworks.com/dirty-bomb.htm.

respond to the event and where they should report for suitable medical advice and assistance. The government would have to establish suitable rehabilitation facilities for evacuees to mitigate their state of affairs.

However, he is of the view that the effects of a dirty bomb can be exponentially magnified to horrendous levels if the terrorists were to exploit the storage sites of radioisotopes commonly used in hospitals, educational institutions and industrial facilities in major cities that are licensed to use radioactive materials. By overcoming the limited nongovernmental security manifest at these sites, terrorists could blow up these storage facilities by planting huge quantities of conventional explosives that would result in immediate destruction and fires creating a ball of radioactive dispersion that would extend its dispersal over a radius of between 500 metres to a kilometer. There are numerous such targets available in the midst of all major metropolises in India and worldwide. The fallout of the radioactive dust would extend over residential areas and centres of economic activity and nodal governmental offices. One such dirty bomb could effectively close down the socio-economic being of an entire city immediately and the affected radius of the real estate, after it is established by designated expert teams, for many years. The most visible fallout of such an attack would be mass immigration to other cities with a debilitating effect on the national economy.

He views the threat of an attack on the transportation system for nuclear waste and depleted radioactive fuel rods where it passes through or in the vicinity of large population or industrial centres to have equally disastrous consequences.

There is an urgent need for the Indian government to assess the threat, from a singularly Indian perspective, in its entirety, create specialist facilities for immediate and long-term responses and a host of other means to cope with such a dirty-bomb attack. In other words, the government must lose no time to evolve a comprehensive policy to tackle such an event, create appropriate structures and systems, trained human resources, integration of the print and electronic media to facilitate government emergency bulletins and information critical to the affected population, and integrate this policy directive into the national disaster management policy that is currently being formulated.

Some of the critical actions required without any delay would include:

- Create a national register with details of government and civilian institutions that are licensed to use and store radioactive materials and strengthen material accounting, control and physical security.
- Review security systems to safeguard all radioactive inventories and institute a standardized government controlled security system with stringent regulations and appropriate equipment to secure all possible sources of radioactive materials with civilian institutions.
- Place the security of uranium mines and nuclear testing sites under security forces responsible to the government.
- Enhance the counterterrorism and intelligence agencies' capacities to detect radioactive material and substances in order to prevent illicit trafficking, pre-empt their falling into the hands of terrorist groups, and to search for and confiscate unlawfully held radioactive materials with unauthorized individuals/groups.
- Enhance ongoing operations to deny terrorists secure bases and access to monetary resources to limit their potential to acquire radioactive substances.
- Improve national technical means to identify radioactive materials that are used in a dirty-bomb attack to facilitate responses by the medical infrastructure, and cleanup operations in the event of such an attack.
- Put into place suitably equipped radiation detection, identification and cleanup teams.

- Ensure a real-time workable system of sharing intelligence amongst all agencies entailed in defence against a dirty-bomb attack and concerned local law enforcing agencies.
- Screen all personnel and electronic devices involved in security of radioactive sites at random intervals.
- Deploy radiation detecting equipment at all ports of entry and devise improved systems to secure India's porous land borders to detect smuggling of radioactive sources.

# XV

# Terrorism and Nuclear Deterrence Theory

*Nishikant Tiwari*

*The central theme of this article contradicts the conventional wisdom that nuclear deterrence cannot work against contemporary terrorist groups. The author argues that terrorists could be deterred and convinced for inaction. It takes a holistic view of nuclear deterrence to include both of its deterrent mechanisms—deterrence by punishment and deterrence by denial. The application and scope of deterrence by threat of retaliation against nonstate groups has been examined while considering various factors like rationality, motivation and return address problem. This article suggests that deterrence by denial is always helpful when states seek to communicate a deterrent message to terrorist groups. Terrorists could be also deterred via regimes that provide active or passive support to them. However, deterrence could also fail. This necessitates a twin military strategy of deterrence and coercion as complementary to each other to persuade terrorist groups from contemplating and executing plans that could lead to mass casualties. If a regime or nonstate group is already involved in terrorist activities, then coercion or compellence is the only way to undo the current situation. Later, when a situation of no terrorist activity appears, then the role of deterrence would be to continue with this status quo situation while dispatching a sufficient and credible deterrent message to them. Deterrence and coercion are just two facets of military strategy to tackle terrorism.*

*This paper has been framed as follows. First, a brief understanding of the nuclear deterrence theory with its two deterrent mechanisms—deterrence by punishment and deterrence by denial—have been revisited in the context of terrorist threats in the post-cold war era. Second, the applicability of deterrence by punishment has been explored in the context of terrorists' rationality, motivation and target of retaliation. Third, while discussing the efficacies of threat of retaliation, it also seeks to examine the potential of denial capability of a state in dissuading terrorist groups from executing actions leading to mass casualties. Fourth, a brief conclusion has been given at the end.*

Terrorist has emerged as a major security threat for Westphalia states in the post-cold war. Terrorist threats are also changing in ways that make it more dangerous and lethal in the dynamic context of technology and strategy. Some terrorist groups like al-Qaeda are known for their tactical innovation. 9/11 is a classic example of such tactical shocks, which brought international terrorist into focus as a global issue to be fought globally. A worse situation could be assumed in the near future if terrorist groups somehow manage to acquire weapons of mass destruction (WMD) and missile systems.[1] The rapid proliferation of such weapons and missile technology gives rise to the danger that future terrorist attacks might involve such weapons. Terrorist's access to more powerful techniques could endanger our 'vital national interests.'[2] According to Kydd and Walter, the different strategy of their 'costly signalling'[3] is finally coming to be recognized as a 'strategic threat.'[4]

[1] WMDs were defined by a Resolution of the United Nations Commission for Conventional Armaments dated 12 August 1948 as: "atomic explosive weapons, radioactive material weapons, lethal chemical and biological weapons, and any weapons developed in the future which have characteristics comparable in destructive effect to those of the atomic bomb or other weapons mentioned above." WMDs are also called 'CBRNE' weapons (Bowen: 2004).

[2] David Omand, "Countering International Terrorism," *Survival*, 47(4): 2005, pp. 107–116.

[3] Andrew Kydd and Barbara Walter, "The Strategies of Terrorism," *International Organization*, 31(1): 2006, pp. 49–80.

[4] Ely Karmon, "The Role of Intelligence in Counter-Terrorism," *The Korean Journal of Defense Analysis*, XVI(1): 2003, pp. 119–139.

Kydd and Walter define terrorist as "the use of violence against civilians by nonstate actors to attain political goals."[5] Lake sees it as "the irregular use of violence by nonstate groups against non-military targets and personnel for political ends."[6] For Cronin, terrorism is an illegitimate tactic that by its very nature is purposefully and ruthlessly employed.[7] However, this use of violence is getting newer forms. For example, suicide bombers who are mobile choose the best moment to wreak the greatest havoc. It is argued that they are the most sophisticated smart bombs ever designed.[8]

There exists a general belief that terrorists are fanatical, apocalyptic, irrational, highly motivated for some divine cause and mobile bombers who may not care for their life and consequently, may not fear retaliation. Further, some transnational terrorist groups have no single host, sponsor or homeland. A few apocalyptic terrorists believe that they have a direct divine mandate and they are not accountable to any earthly authorities. For them, self-preservation has no value. Other religious terrorist groups like al-Qaeda claim a religious justification for their actions and killing 'infidels' (enemies of Islam) is a religious duty for them.

These nonstate groups looking for mass casualty terrorist have emerged as a serious threat for state actors in the context of their growing activities in quantitative and qualitative terms in the contemporary era. Different tools and tactics have been developed and deployed by states against terrorist groups as part of their counterterrorist strategies—for example, persuasion like winning hearts and minds, economic empowerment, democratization, and appeasement. However, these could be time-consuming and might

[5] Op cit, n. 3, p. 52.

[6] David A. Lake, "Rational Extremism: Understanding Terrorism in the Twenty-first Century," *Dialog-IO*, vol.1: 2002, pp. 15–29.

[7] Audrey Kurth Cronin, "How al-Qaida Ends: The Decline and Demise of Terrorist Groups," *International Security*, 31(1): 2006, pp. 7–48.

[8] Doron almog (2004–05), "Cumulative Deterrence and the War on Terrorism," http://www.carlisle.army.mil.usawc/parameters/04 winter/almog.pdf, 26 March 2007.

prove to be ineffective in the short term. Military means are the most readily available to deter and coerce these groups.

Military strategy has two components—coercion, i.e. use of force to coerce terrorist groups, and deterrence to prevent these groups and persuade them for inaction. However, it is important to theoretically differentiate deterrence from coercion. Deterrence is the threat to take hostile actions if the adversary acts. It demands inaction. So, deterrenceis about preserving the status quo. Compellence or coercion is the threat to take hostile actions unless the adversary acts. It demands actions so that the present position could be altered. Thus, it is about altering the status quo. For example, US air strikes against Libya in 1986 sought to alter the Libyan policy of sponsoring terrorist activity against American targets in Western Europe. So, if a regime is already involved in some form of terrorist-related activities, any threats to influence its behaviour would be coercion and not deterrence in pure theoretical terms because the aim would be changing the status quo (i.e. to change the regime's behaviour). Consequently, a strictly deterrent strategy would only be relevant to regimes not currently implicated in any form of terrorist support but which might contemplate becoming involved in the future. The crux of this study is to examine deterrence strategies in preventing terrorist's hostile actions.

But, did deterrence strategies have any role in the confrontation against radical Islamic terror and asymmetric warfare and help the world community face up to the new dangers highlighted by the events of 9/11? Can contemporary terrorists who are faceless and having no return address be subjected to deterrence logic? Scholars disagree. There are two different views in the scholaristic debate on the matters of deterrence applicability against terrorist groups. Many scholars and strategic analysts such as Davis and Jenkins[9] as also

[9] *Paul K. Davis and Brian Michael Jenkins (2002), *Deterrence and Influence in Counterterrorism; A Component in the war on al-Qaeda*, Santa Monica, Califpersuade: RAND, <http://rand.org/pubs/monograph_reports/2005/MR1619.pdf>,10 October, 2006.

Kamp[10], Almog[11] and Rajain[12] see classical deterrence as nonfunctional and ineffective against contemporary terrorists. They argue that deterrence has no significant role to play in countering the new terrorist threats. The National Security Strategy of the United States of America (2002) also notes that the traditional concept of deterrence will not work against a terrorist enemy.[13]

The preceding viewpoint regarding the ineffectiveness of deterrent strategies against nonstate actors like terrorists, according to Trager and Zagorcheva, rests on three broad assumptions.[14] First, the irrationality of these groups and their unresponsiveness to any cost-benefit calculation which is vital for deterrence. Second, their high motivation and deterrence by punishment strategy, which targets their nonpolitical ends like life, liberty and property are insufficient. Their resolve also remains high to perpetrate extreme violent activities without any hesitation. They love to die and, therefore, are not deterred by fear of retaliation. Third, the lack of return address, which makes any retaliation difficult. Scholars argue that if terrorists cannot be found, the use of force against them is ineffective.

However, some scholars such as Steinberg,[15] Bowen,[16] Trager and Zagorcheva[17] express different views that suggest that deterrence strategies can be applied against nonstate adversaries also to prevent them from executing certain actions. They argue that it is wrong to

[10] Karl-Heinz Kamp, "Nuclear Stability, Deterrence and Terrorism," in P.R. Chari et. Al. *Nuclear S tability in Southern Asia*, New Delhi: Manohar, 2003.

[11] Op cit, n. 8.

[12] Arpit Rajain, *Nuclear Deterrence in Southern Asia: China, India and Pakistan*, New Delhi: Sage Publication, 2005.

[13] The National Security Strategy of the United States of America (September 2002) , White House, http://www.whitehouse.gov/nsc/nss.pdf, 31 March 2007.

[14] Robert G. Trager and P. Dessislava Zagorcheva, "Deterring Terrorism: It Can Be Done," 2005–06.

[15] Gerald M. Steinberg (2001), "Rediscovering Deterrence After September 11, 2001," Jerusalem Letter/Viewpoints, http://www.jcpa.org/j1/vp467.html, 2 March 2007.

[16] Wyn Q. Bowen, "Deterrence and Asymmetry: Non-State Actors and Mass Casualty Terrorism," *Contemporary Security Policy*, 25(1): 2004, pp. 54–70

[17] Op cit, n. 14.

consider members of terrorist groups as irrational and unresponsive to cost-benefit calculations. Also, they note that motivation factor is not equal for all members of the group. The very make up of the group entails whether or not they are susceptible to deterrence logic. They also note that regimes who are contemplating to extend any sort of support to terrorist groups can be straightway subjected to deterrence logic. In fact, terrorists have no territory of their own. Proper intelligence gathering and analysis and, also, modern technology enables state actors to locate terrorist groups. Specially, they argue that it is always helpful to build denial capabilities, which strengthen deterrence by denial, which in turn have dissuasive effect on the opponent.

This study seeks to examine the application and scope of nuclear deterrence theory in deterring nonstate groups from executing a particular course of action that leads to destruction of life and limb at mass level. While investigating the interplay between state actors and nonstate actors, it seeks to investigate deterrence strategy and its two principal mechanisms applied to deter mass casualty terrorism—deterrence by punishment and deterrence by denial. The absence of a detailed study analyzing the applicability of nuclear deterrence theory in the interaction between a state actor and terrorist groups is the primary rationale for this study. The objective is to contribute to the understanding of how states could deter the threats posed by nonstate actors with focus on an integrated approach to deterrence theory for meeting this asymmetric threat.

## UNDERSTANDING NUCLEAR DETERRENCE

Deterrence is meant for preventing a real/potential adversary from initiating a particular course of action. It is a 'psychological exercise' that demands inaction from the opponent to remain with the status quo condition.[18] Prevention of an aggression is sought by two principal deterrence mechanisms—deterrence by punishment and

[18] Bown, n. 16, p. 58

deterrence by denial—originally noted by Snyder.[19] The punishment mechanism involves a dissuasive effect based on threat of retaliation to harm something the adversary values. It persuades the opponent to seriously consider the impact of an action, which would significantly outweigh the potential gains associated with it if it executes the same. This is done by convincing and influencing calculations of an opponent's possible and probable costs and gains.[20]

Deterrence by denial focuses on denial strength where the possession and development of certain types of capabilities could potentially deter an opponent from pursuing a given objective. According to Trager and Zagorcheva, denial strategy involves 'hardening targets' in the hope of making an attack on them too costly to be tried.[21] Thus, this strategy seeks to influence the behaviour of the adversary and create a credible doubt of getting success in case an attempt is undertaken.

During the cold war, strategic stability was achieved primarily through strategic deterrence based on threat of retaliation and the fear of mutual assured destruction. However, looking into the unpredictability, asymmetric context and different challenges in the post-cold war era, a holistic view of deterrence is seen as vital for securing national objectives. Denial capability in this respect has become an unavoidable means and is complementary to deterrence by punishment. The current Bush administration in its national strategy (2002) has devised a deterrence strategy based on punishment and denial to get the desired result.[22]

A credible deterrent strategy requires certain things on behalf of the deterrer like possession of the requisite capability and also intent

[19] Glen n H. Snydr (1961), *Deterrence and Defense: Towards a Theory of National Security*, quoted in Rajagopalan, *Second Strike: Arguments about nuclear war in South Asia*, New Delhi: Penguin Viking, 2005.

[20] Op cit, n. 18.

[21] Op cit, n. 14.

[22] Op cit, n. 13.

and resolve to fulfil the deterrent message. Robert Powell notes that the context of resolve between a state actor and nonstate adversary is vital for the sake of deterrence.[23] If a state demonstrates a very high level of resolve to tackle terrorism, then it signals a clear resolve to the opponent. If there is some uncertainty about the state's levels of resolve, then the opponent may doubt the deterrent message.

This message regarding the deterrer's credibility and resolve to impose unacceptable punishment should be credibly communicated by the deterrer as also clearly understood by the opponent to produce intended effects. However, such a message, as Steinberg notes, could be complicated by ethnic, national, religious and linguistic differences.[24] This may be vital in an asymmetric context when deterrence is sought against nonstate adversaries like terrorists.

This communication is linked with the issue of rationality, which assumes that parties involved in deterrence interaction would be the cost-benefit calculator. An irrational actor may not understand the explicit-implicit threat imposed by the deterrer. Rationality is defined as the ability to weigh options on the basis of likely costs and benefits. It demands that the decision-making by the adversary should be sufficiently influenced by cost-benefit calculations. However, what is rational for one actor may not be the same for another.[25] This is because it is influenced by culture, value systems and the processes through which decisions are reached. In this context, Bowen argues that it is important to see inside an 'opponent's black box' to understand what is rational in the target's mind set.[26] This could be again an important issue for deterring terrorists.

The success of deterrence, as Trager and Zagorcheva note, also depends upon certain other things.[27] For example, the deterrer must

[23] Robert Powell, "Nuclear Deterrence Theory, Nuclear Proliferation and National Missile Defense," *International Security,* 27(4): Spring 2003, pp. 86–118.

[24] Op cit, n. 15.

[25] Op cit, n. 16.

[26] Ibid.

[27] Op cit, n. 14.

be able to hold something the adversary values at risk and the adversary must value what is held at risk over the expected value of taking action. If the deterrer executes the threat owing to provocation by the opponent, then deterrence no longer remains an option.[28] Also, the preferences of both sides over states of the world should not be precisely opposed. In an adversarial relationship, deterrence is possible when the preferences are nearly opposite but deterrence is not possible when preferences are precisely opposed (then, relations are zero sum).[29] There should be some overlap in the preferences to make deterrence work, as Schelling notes, "if his pain were our greatest delight and our satisfaction his greatest woe, we would just proceed to hurt and frustrate each other."[30] Viewed in this way, deterrence resembles a bargain where both sides agree to cooperate on a state of affairs that both prefer to alternatives.[31] They argue that deterrence is not only threat or action imposed by the deterrer designed to increase an adversary's perceived costs of engaging in a particular behaviour, it is also an implicit/explicit offer of an alternative state of affairs if the adversary refrains from that behaviour.[32]

Bowen notes three asymmetries between nonstate actors and state actors for applicability of the deterrence theory.[33] The first asymmetry is about the relative balance of interests at stake involved in any conflict scenario. The greater the interest an actor perceives to be at stake, the greater the resolve to prevail over an adversary. The second asymmetry is about the existence of political, social, economic and cultural differences, which result in varied value systems and mind sets. The deterrer has to keep in mind these factors while deterring

[28] Ibid.

[29] Ibid.

[30] Thomas Schelling (1963), *Arms and Influence,* quoted in Trager and Zagorcheva, "Deterring Terrorism: It Can Be Done," *International Security*, 30(3): 2005–06, pp. 87–123.

[31] Op cit, n. 14.

[32] Ibid.

[33] Op cit, n. 16.

a state or nonstate adversary and to be also aware of the lens through which such actors are likely to perceive a deterrent message. The third asymmetry is about technological gap in conventional military capabilities between some state actors and nonstate adversaries. As these groups cannot fight face to face, this situation leads to asymmetric warfare where a state faces constraints in dealing with the situation. This interest/resolve; perceptional variables like mind, rationality, etc.; and asymmetric context of the battle-field determine the applicability of the deterrence strategy against non state adversaries.

The classical understanding of the nuclear deterrence theory was built on the assumption that deterrence would take place among state actors. However, this state-centric strategy and inter-state relations in the post-cold war era were complicated with the advent of powerful nonstate groups like al-Qaeda whose efficacy to disturb calculations for state actors was widely noted. The terrorist attack of 9/11 was seen as challenging the classical notion of deterrence theory as a primary mechanism to prevent potential adversaries from executing a particular action. This event clearly demonstrated that these groups have both the motivations and capabilities to conduct a devastating attack on territory, citizens and infrastructure of any state. This unexpected terrorist assault on the United States attracted the strategic community to redevise the military strategy to deter and coerce these groups in the dynamic context.

To combat terrorist in this context became a priority, and different counterterrorist measures have been devised and applied to deal with the current pace of terrorism. States adopted coercive measures to coerce these groups from achieving their local and global objectives. Apart from coercion, deterrence was one prime tool to prevent these actors from pursuing terrorist activities.

## TERRORISM AND DETERRENCE BY PUNISHMENT

Deterring terrorist groups from prosecuting mass casualties requires an understanding of the interplay between state actors and nonstate actors. Rationality and motivation factor along with return address problem have been examined in the specific context of terrorist groups. The potential of punishment and denial strategies have also been dealt with for their application in deterring terrorists. A possibility has been also considered when threat of retaliation fails to stop terrorist groups. Though, coercion is different from deterrence, it reinforces deterrence in case it fails to preserve the status quo. Susceptibility to deterrence logic and a deeper understanding of terrorist's resolve, making of their system and role of state in assisting these nonstate groups have been also explored in the subsequent paragraphs.

## TERRORISTS' RATIONALITY AND THEIR SUSCEPTIBILITY TO DETERRENCE LOGIC

It is argued that deterrence assumes a level of rationality on behalf of the target.[34] On the issue of rationality and deterring terrorist groups, there exists a mistaken belief that terrorists are not rational and they seldom make cost-benefit calculations. Hence, they cannot be subjected to deterrence logic. However, some scholars such as Crenshaw,[35] Schachter,[36] Trager and Zagorcheva[37] show that terrorist groups often have different goals in preference and they devise strategies based upon costs-benefits calculation. It is argued by Sprinzak,[38] Lake,[39] Kydd and Walter,[40] and Pape[41] that terrorist is

[34] Ibid.

[35] Martha Crenshaw, "The Causes of Terrorism," *Comparative Politics,* 13(4): 1981, pp. 379–399.

[36] Jonathan Schachter (2002), "The Eye of the Believer: Psychological Influences on Counter-Terrorism Policy-Making," RAND dissertation, http://www.rand.org/pubs/rgs_dissertations/RGSD166/, 1 March 2007.

[37] Op cit, n. 14.

[38] Ehud Sprinzab (2000), "Rational Fanatics," *Foreign Policy* No. 120:66-73, http://www.foreignpolicy.com/Ning/archieve/archieve/120/rationalfanatics.pdf, 27 March 2007.

[39] Op cit, n. 6.

[40] Andrew Kydd and Barbara Walter, "Sabotaging the Peace: The Politics of Extremist Violence," *International Organization*, 56(2): 2002, pp. 263–296.

[41] Robert A. Pape, "The Strategic Logic of Suicide Terrorism," *American Political Science Review,* 97(3): 2003, pp. 343–361.

strategically rational and strategic tactic, which works.[42] Lake argues that terrorist activities are rational extremism. The move of terror tactics itself is a strategic choice of weaker actors because they cannot fight with powerful forces face to face. While examining the strategic logic of suicide terrorism, Pape argues that they (suicide terrorists) are giving up their lives because it has been proved successful in coercing liberal democracies.

Further, Quinlan notes that only the truly insane have no sense of weighing consequences and to have a different value system does not mean having none.[43] He argues that it is hard to think of any instance in the history of a state or similar power grouping that had no assets, which it wished to retain, no collective concern for the lives of its members, and no interest in the survival of its ruling regime.[44] Traditional terrorist groups like groups motivated by nationalist goals such as Irish Republic Army (IRA) and LTTE seem to impose self-restraint and in this respect, they calculate costs and benefits of a particular action up to some extent. Such groups are self-deterrers when it comes to mass casualty terrorism, as Brian Jenkins notes, "a lot of people watching, not a lot of people dead."[45]

As discussed above, deterrence is about prevailing the status quo. To work it successfully, the target must believe or be made to believe that status quo is preferable to the costs of acting, at least in the short term if the goal of deterrence is to buy time for other approaches to take effect. However, if an opponent is well determined to alter the status quo, this could make deterrence unworkable, as Achen and

[42] Max Abrahams, "Why Terrorism Does Not Work," *International Security,* 31(2): 2006, pp. 42–78.

[43] Sir Michael Quinlan, "Deterrence and Deterrability," *Contemporary Security Policy,* 25(1): 2004, pp. 11-17.

[44] Ibid.

[45] Brian Michael Jenkins (2001), statement on 'Terrorism: Current and Long Term Threats' before the Senate Armed Services Subcommittee on Emerging Threats (15 November 2010), quoted in Bowen, "Deterrence and Asymmetry: Non-State Actors and Mass Casualty Terrorism," 2004.

Snidal note, "not all conceivable opponents are deterrable."[46] The more fanatical a terrorist's organization, the stronger the resolve of its members and as a result, they are likely to be less susceptible to deterrence.

The susceptibility of nonstate actors to deterrence logic requires concerted and targeted intelligence collection and analysis. For example, specific groups or individuals within those groups could be focused to assess their cost-benefit calculations. Are they risk prone or risk averse, or do they think in terms of minimizing losses/ maximizing gains? Also, a preliminary examination regarding how important are nonpolitical goals like survival, security, recognition, wealth, power or accomplishment to them would decide their approach to deterrence logic. Robert Jervis argues that in almost no interactions do two adversaries understand each other's goals, fears, means-end beliefs and perceptions.[47] He further notes that while the commitments of the deterrer may appear "objectively clear and credible," to a disinterested third party, they may not be perceived that way by the target.[48]

Howev er, Trager and Zagorcheva note that the decision-making processes in terrorist organizations consist of both rational and nonrational elements.[49] They argue that deterrence requires only that terrorists be sufficiently influenced by cost-benefit calculations. In this context, Bowen maintains that a terrorist system, different actors will calculate possible and probable costs and gains differently, and this will be influenced by context-specific variable such as the target's value system, mind set and decision-making processes.[50] Examining these variables determines whether a target is deterrable.[51]

[46] Christopher H. Achen and Duncan Snidal (1989), "Rational Deterrence Theory and Comaprative Case Studies, *World Politics,* 41(2): 1989, pp. 143-169.

[47] Robert Jervis, "Rational Deterrence: Theory and Evidence," *World Politics*, 41(2): 1989, pp. 183–207.

[48] Ibid.

[49] Op cit, n. 14.

[50] Op cit, n. 16.

[51] Ibid.

However, perfect rationality is not required for the deterrence mechanism and it is not expected also as Robert Jervis argues. "Much less than full rationality is needed for the main lines of deterrence theory to be valid."[52]

## TERRORISTS' NETWORKS AND THREAT OF RETALIATION

Gerald Steinberg refers to the mistaken belief that terrorists such as bin Laden and members of groups such Hamas, Hizbullah and Islamic Jihad are suicidal and cannot be deterred.[53] According to him, it is possible to identify 'high value targets' including family members and supporters that would cause even the most radical leaders to calculate the possible and probable costs and benefits of particular courses of action.[54] He argues that unlike suicide bombers, terrorist leaders are not so quick to sacrifice their own lives and to risk the destruction of their supporters and the end of any legacy.[55] So, attention needs to be focused on examining the extent to which such leaders and their supporters and lieutenants, will respond to retaliatory threat. According to Kydd and Walter,[56] a 'targeted retaliation' against terrorists could have a better result.

Understanding terrorist's susceptibility to retaliatory threats requires a careful survey of various elements of the terrorist system and an understanding of the processes that lead to attack. According to Trager and Zagorcheva, terrorists maintain "system of actors which comprises leaders, lieutenants, financiers, logisticians and other facilitators, foot soldiers, supporting population segments, and religious or otherwise ideological figures."[57] Davis and Jenkins also break down the actors or targets in a terrorist system into top leaders,

[52] Robert Jervis, "Deterrence Theory Revisited," *World Politics,* 31(2): 1979, pp. 289–324.

[53] Op cit, n. 15.

[54] Ibid.

[55] Ibid.

[56] Op cit, n. 3.

[57] Op cit, n. 14.

lieutenants, foot soldiers, recruites, external suppliers and facilitators and heads of supportive states. In this context, the most direct approach would be targeting the eladers and members of terrorist organizations like al-Qaeda.[58]

Some elements like financiers of terrorist system are less motivated than other elements and thus easier to deter. It is argued that if a state makes a priority to trace those financiers, then flow of resources to terrorist's system could be checked and this would in turn have a deterrent effect.[59] State sponsors are also part of the terrorist network. They are considered less motivated than other elements of terrorist network and could be easily located also.

Concentrating on individual elements of terrorist networks and their different channels of processing a particular activity is also vital to understand their vulnerability against deterrence logic. According to Trager and Zagorcheva, terrorist activity is seen as a process or series of actions culminating in violence.[60] Each stage in this long process presents an opportunity for detection by intelligence networks. The risk of detection and consequent punishment outweighs the benefits of a successful attack as also the probability of success.

Terrorist Motivation and Application of Deterrence

Problem of terrorist motivation refers to some ideological and religious beliefs, which call terrorists to unite for their common cause. Trager and Zagorcheva define motivation as "the extent to which terrorists value their political goals over non political ends like lie, liberty, property, etc. the intensity of terrorist motivation determines the scope of deterrence application against terrorist groups.[61]

For terrorists who are highly motivated and who place top priority on their political objectives, holding at their nonpolitical ends will not be sufficient to influence their behaviour. This means

[58] Op cit, n. 9.
[59] Op cit, n. 14.
[60] Ibid.
[61] Op cit, n. 14.

that there exists little scope for overlapping in the preferences between them and deterring states. However, as Trager and Zagorcheva argue, the political goals for which they are ready to die and willing to run any risks can be held at risk for the cause of deterrence.[62] So, if they are convinced that their very objective would be eclipsed by a particular course of action, they may respond to the threat of retaliation. In this case, an offer is made to the terrorist group by the deterring state in the event it refrains from the undesired behaviour. Even a little overlapping in the preferences is imperative to exploit deterrence possibility.[63] Trager and Zagorcheva highlight the importance of the offer made to the challenging terrorist group if it complies with the deterrer's demands, and the possibility of using leverage over one political end for leverage over the actions a group takes in pursuit of another.[64] By altering the offer, such as by refraining from intervening in local conflicts or even tacitly permitting lower-level violence, states can wholly or partially deter even highly motivated groups.[65]

A lower level of terrorist motivation implies that terrorists value nonpolitical ends also apart from political goals. In this case, deterrence by punishment would apply against them by holding both nonpolitical ends and political goals at risk. But if the preferences are precisely opposed between terrorist groups and deterring states, then deterrence may not be working against terrorists. However, according to Davis and Jenkins,[66] Trager and Zagorcheva,[67] they can be influenced. They can not be deterred because their high level of motivation means that no matter what threat is leveled against them, they will always pursue their

[62] Ibid.

[63] Trager and Zagorcheva, A detailed analysis of such overlapping in the preferences has been discussed, 2005–06.

[64] Ibid.

[65] Ibid.

[66] Op cit, n. 9.

[67] Op cit, n. 14.

objectives, and because their preferences are precisely opposed, no bargaining space exists.

### TARGETING TERRORISTS AND THE PROBLEM OF RETURN ADDRESS

The issue of return address is also linked with the problem of targeting terrorists. Terrorists against whom retaliation could be visited are usually difficult to be found. Lack of return address reduced the degree of coercive leverage of a particular threat against them. Members of terrorist groups are mobile and diverse. Trager and Zagorcheva argue that the more important issue is whether states can make certain demands from particular terrorist groups with a credible threat imposed against them. They argue that states can find members of terrorist organizations if this becomes a priority and intelligence and other resources are sufficiently used for the same.[68] Also, they operate in certain areas controlled by some states. Though the states giving refuge to members of a terrorist group, the deterring state can make a threat. Though targeted states cannot find every terrorist and terrorist facilitator, they almost always have the ability to increase the costs to terrorist groups of achieving their political goals. Pape notes that "military action can disrupt a terrorist group 's activities temporarily."[69] It is not necessary that the use of force would result in the capture of every terrorist. Still, it can hurt the interests of the group and its members.

### State Sponsors/Vulnerable Regimes and Deterrence by Punishment

Regimes could be also targeted whose territory might be used to organize and operate terrorist activities by nonstate adversaries. A regime or state sponsor is said to be a less-motivated element of any terrorist network and can also be easily located. A deterrent message backed by the threat of retaliation would persuade a regime(s) not

[68] Ibid.

[69] Robert A. Pape (2005) , *Dying to Win: The Strategic Logic of Suicide Terrorism*, New York: Random House, chapter-wise summery available on Wikipedia, http://en.wikipedia.org/wiki/Dying to Win the strategic logic of suicide terrorism, 1 February 2007.

to provide or sponsor any sort of terrorist activities in their territories. Even neutrality in this respect could be considered as passive sponsoring of terrorist activities. In other words, a would-be state sponsor could be deterred by powerful states from harbouring terrorists in their territory. It persuades regimes for inaction and remains with the status quo.

Steinberg argues that the world is divided into states, and all terrorist groups need territory from which to operate, controlled by states.[70] Thus, the chain of responsibility ultimately lies with identifiable and vulnerable regimes and political leaders and they can be deterred by threatening their own survival. He further argues that if regimes are targeted selectively, then it could have dissuasive effects.[71]

Quinlan notes that terrorists seldom exist and operate in isolation from organizations and these organizations rarely in isolation from states and deterrence can be brought to bear by that route.[72] States responsible for providing implicit or explicit support or even those that are neutral to terrorist activities in their territory, place themselves at risk of penalty. The experience of the Taliban government in 2001, ac cording to Quinlan, transmitted this message vividly.[73] Robert Frost puts fourth similar arguments.[74] He maintains that white terrorist groups themselves might not be directly deterred by the threat of massive retaliation, host or sponsor states might be, which could have an indirect or secondary deterrent effect on militant groups.[75]

However, if a state or regime is already involved in tolerating and sponsoring terrorist groups, then deterrence will not persuade them

[70] Op cit, n. 15.

[71] Ibid.

[72] Op cit, n. 43.

[73] Ibid.

[74] Robert M Frost, "Nuclear Terrorism after 9/11," Adelphi Paper 378, Chapter 4: 20 04, pp. 63–68.

[75] Ibid.

to undo the present situation. Only coercion could alter this situation. Coercion in this context involves actual use of military force to punish regimes if they are already involved in assisting these groups by sponsoring, harbouring or merely tolerating them. For example, the US-led campaign against the Taliban in Afghanistan was an example of coercion that sent a clear message that they (the US and allies) possess the intent, resolve and capability to punish and unseat regimes who are found to be sponsoring terrorist groups like al-Qaeda. Gerald Steinberg wonders that if the costs of hosting al-Qaeda had been made clear to Taliban leaders in the months and years prior to 11 September, then this could have resulted in the eviction of Osama bin Laden from Afghanistan.

Once a new situation (a condition of no terrorist activities) by means of coercion is achieved, then maintaining this status quo becomes a priority for states. Now, deterring state would keep such vulnerable regimes and states on alert by convicting them that any fresh contemplation in this regard would lead to retaliation and unacceptable damage for them.

Byman argues that at times, the greatest contribution a state can make to a terrorist's cause is by not acting.[76] He notes, "A border not policed, a blind eye turned to fundraising, or even the toleration of recruitment all help terrorists build their organizations, conduct operations and survive."[77] Such passivity in the face of terrorism can be deadly. In conducting the 11 September attacks, al-Qaeda recruited and raised money in Germany with relatively little interference, enjoyed financial support from many Saudis unobstructed by the government in Riyadh, and planned operations in Malaysia. None of these governments are active sponsors of al-Qaeda, but their inaction proved vital to al-Qaeda's success.

[76] Danial Byman, "Passive Sponsors of Terrorism," *Survival,* 47(4): 2005–06, pp. 117–144.

[77] Ibid.

A state could be an active or passive sponsor.[78] Active state sponsorship involves a deliberate regime decision to assist a terrorist group, often in the form of arms, money, training or sanctuary.[79] A regime can be said to be guilty of passive support if it knowingly allows a terrorist group to raise money, enjoy sanctuary, recruit or otherwise flourish without interference, but does not directly aid the group itself.[80] Such passive support is tolerated primarily because of the low level of perceived threat and relatively low cost of inaction. Bowen argues that the majority of terrorist groups often get perennial support of state sponsors or enjoy sanctuary or protection of states. In this respect, it is to be noted that the UN Security Council Resolution 1373[81] mandates states to patrol their territories to prevent terrorists from organizing, thinking and executing terrorist plans.[82] Robert Frost maintains that states should be aware about terrorists in their homeland.[83] Kydd and Walter note that states should seek to deny terrorists access to the most destructive weapons, especially WMD. Any weapons that can inflict enormous costs will be particularly attractive to terrorists pursuing a war of attrition.[84]

However, Phillip Heymann asks several questions here: to what extent does a regime have control over a terrorist group, what degree of support is a regime giving to a group, is territory being made freely available, is it providing resources such as money and weapons, and is a regime merely providing sanctuary and nothing else?[85] A supporting regime may believe that retaliatory strikes could have a

[78] Op cit, n. 76.

[79] Ibid.

[80] Ibid.

[81] Op cit, n. 16.

[82] Adopted on 28 September 2001, this resolution focuses on a state's responsibility in refraining from "providing any form of support, active or passive, to entities or persons involved in terrorist acts."

[83] Op cit, n. 74.

[84] Op cit, n. 3.

[85] Phillip B. Heymann, *Terrorism and America: A Commonsense Strategy for a Democratic Society,* Cambridge, MA: MIT Press, 1998.

beneficial effect in the local politics. Here, Hey mann's focus is on regimes that are already involved with terrorist entities in one way or another. However, as Bowen argues, any threat in this context would be coercive in nature because the aim would be no "change the status quo."[86]

## TARGETING TERRORISTS AND DETERRENCE BY DENIAL

A denial-based approach, according to Bowen, involves demonstrating that the capability existed to ward off, or to minimize damage in the event of attack thereby mitigating the desired effects.[87] According to Trager and Zagorcheva, deterrence-by-denial strategies have the potential to be effective against all types of terrorist groups.[88] By hardening targets (e.g. fortifying embassies, reinforcing cockpit doors, upgrading border security, and tightening immigration controls) and demonstrating the resolve not to make concessions, the deterring state can lessen a terrorist's motivation by reducing the benefits of terror tactics.[89] Though defensive strategies cannot protect every target, they can minimize the terrorist's power to hurt, thereby lessening the coercive power of terrorist action. Thus, although defensive strategies are inadequate in themselv es, they form an important component of a deterrence approach. Kydd and Walter also argue that a state can harden likely targets to minimize the costs the terrorist organization can inflict.[90]

A good intelligence could be the best weapon against international terrorism. Karmon argues that intelligence is essential in countering terrorism, in diminishing its tactical effects and strategic importance.[91] Kydd and Walter note that at the tactical level, the available tools of

[86] Op cit, n. 16.
[87] Ibid.
[88] Op cit, n. 14.
[89] Ibid.
[90] Op cit, n. 3.
[91] Op cit, n. 4.

intelligence gathering along with target defence make sense no matter what the terrorist's strategy is.[92]

Thus, developing specific denial capabilities could have a vital dissuasive effect as part of a deterrent message for an opponent, a state could develop the following denial capabilities:

- Build active and passive defensive systems (alert systems in land, sea and air wings), including force protection assets.
- Ensure operational readiness of military to defeat adversary's objectives, including readiness of fighter aircraft and anti-aircraft systems to defeat the enemy's intrusion.
- Develop a national will to demonstrate the state's capability to locate the interdict nonstate actors before they can act.
- Enhance law enforcement capabilities.
- Increase intelligence and counter intelligence (gathering, analysis and reporting), a comprehensive disaster control mechanism.
- Prevent the proliferation of materials, technology and expertise required to manufacture WMDs through tight export control.
- Develop specific preparations and capacity against specific terrorist weapons like a biochemical shield against biologic al and chemical weapons (comprehensive vaccination programme, first aid system, readiness of first respondents, mask, emergency systems, etc.) and missile defence system to intercept incoming missiles from an adversary.

However, there are certain limitations of denial strategies. If the goal is to buy time to frustrate an adversary who is strongly motivated to change the status quo, as George and Smoke note, the consequences of succeeding are not always predictable and favourable to the deterring party.[93] It is argued that deterrence success because an adversary may become increasingly desperate to mount a challenge

[92] Op cit, n. 3.

[93] Alexander George and Richard Smoke, "Deterrence and Foreign Policy," *World Politics*, 41(2): 1989, pp. 170-182.

and may proceed to acquire greater resources to do so.[94] There is another facet of hardening terrorists' targets. If high-value targets are hardened, then terrorists could strike against soft targets. This has been taken as a sign of the futility of defensive strategies. However, terrorist motivation and terrorist actions would be likely to increase if the terrorists were able to strike higher-value targets more easily. Hence, developing such capabilities need not be avoided as according to Trager and Zagorcheva what is important is to be aware of the interactive nature of strategy and potentially negative consequences of developing a specific posture.[95]

## ALMOG'S CONCEPT OF CUMULATIVE DETERRENCE

Almog provides a different conceptualization of deterrence called 'cumulative deterrence' in the context of terrorist threats.[96] This notion is based on the application of threats and military force on the one hand and incentives for the adversary on the other, to finally persuade the enemy for inaction. According to him, cumulative deterrence would involve a multilayered, highly orchestrated effort to inflict the greatest damage possible on the terrorists and their weapon systems, infrastructure, support networks, financial flows, and other means of support. Also involved would be intelligence gathering and analysis, a broad coalition and a globalised network that would facilitate the exchange of vital information and encourage transparency. It would also require cutting-edge technology and highly trained military forces.

Cumulative deterrence, according to Almog. Has several key features. Its effectiveness is measured in terms of the number of victories accumulated over the duration of the conflict, which could be seen as 'assets in a victory bank.' Over time, these victories produce increasingly moderate behaviour on the part of the adversary

[94] Ibid.
[95] Op cit, n. 14.
[96] Op cit, n. 8.

and a shift in his strategic, operational, and tactical goals until there is a near-absence of direct conflict. This moderation may eventually result in political negotiations and perhaps even a peace agreement. Almog gives evidence of the success of cumulative deterrence in the case of the Arab-Israeli conflict. Through a string of Israeli victories and recognition among Arab states of their growing inability to counter Israel's ever-increasing military capabilities, Israel's cumulative deterrence strategy has succeeded in fostering Arab moderation and improving Israel's overall strategic position in the region. One particularly noteworthy reflection of this change in the dramatic reduction in calls from Arab leaders for Israel's destruction, which for so long served as one of the most powerful rallying cries within the Arab world.

## CONCLUSION

After examining both the deterrent mechanism i.e. deterrence by punishment and deterrence by denial and the nature and very make up of terrorist groups, this study concludes that the notion of deterrence is not only meant for deterring state actors in preventing a particular course of action, but it could also be useful against nonstate actors who are contemplating mass level terrorist attacks on civilian and military targets. From the military point of view, deterrence would figure as a vital aspect of any broader and comprehensive antiterrorist strategies. Deterrence by denial, as Bowen argues, appears most applicable when the target is a nonstate actor and deterrence by punishment is best suited when the target is a regime contemplating whether or how to support a terrorist group.[97]

Both rationality and motivation are crucial when deterrent strategies come into play. As argued, terrorists are not as irrational as generally considered. They often calculate cost-benefits of pursuing a particular action. Accordingly, they plan and move ahead very

[97] Op cit, n. 16.

carefully towards attaining their political objectives. Understanding different constituent elements of a terrorist system as also their different stages of processing a particular planning are vital to deter them.

The intensity of motivation is also not the same for each individual terrorist member. Less motivated terrorists could be deterred like a normal criminal. Threat of retaliation could be applied while holding their nonpolitical ends and also the very political objectives at risk. Highly motivated terrorists could also be deterred by fear of punishment if their political objectives are held at risk. As argued in this study, some overlapping in the preferences between the deterring states and terrorist groups could be exploited for the deterrence purpose because accommodation and offers are also communicated along with threat. But for those highly motivated message because of precisely opposed preferences, relations becomes zero sum and deterrence would not work against them. However, this could be a very rare situation of terrorist groups who are apocalyptic/fanatical and driven by some divine mandate.

States are directly responsible for sponsoring any sort of terrorist activities in their territory. They have to patrol their territory and to ensure that no terrorist activities are being carried out from their end. Through states, terrorists could be subjected to deterrence logic. If a state is found to be already involved in terrorists activities, then coercion could be used to undo the situation. And, for future, deterrence would perform the task to ensure that no fresh contemplation regarding sponsoring terrorist groups is being made.

Denial strategy, based on enhanced denial capabilities and hardening targets, is always useful in lessening the coercive power of terrorist action and, therefore, the motivation to carry out attacks. Soft terrorist targets could be hardened. A good intelligence could be the best weapon to deal with terrorist groups. Human intelligence is key in generating the necessary understanding of a real or potential adversary's motives, resolve, culture, internal workings, decision-making process, resources, capabilities, locations and conflict techniques. It requires concerted efforts for gathering, sharing, analyzing and reporting in a coordinated way to communicate and convince and adversary for inaction. However, denial strategy, though very effective in dissuading terrorist groups, could be at best a delaying option. It is considered vital in the sense that it provides temporary deterrence for other strategies to take place.

As Bowen notes, deterring terrorists would also depend upon the three aspects of asymmetries between the deterring states and terrorist groups.[98] They are the relative balance of interest/resolve at stake; value system, mind sets and perceptions; and finally, conflict strategies, techniques and capabilities. He further argues that priority should be placed on getting inside an opponent's 'black-box' to understand what is rational in the target's mind set.[99] For deterrence to be successful, and according to Lebow and Stein, one needs to understand where the frame of reference for the actor's thinking comes from, how it is evoked, and the set of alternatives considered by an opponent in the choice process.[100]

Deterrence and coercion are two different things in theoretical terms. Deterrent strategy is one which targets those groups by means of threat of retaliation and denial capabilities to defeat and deny them from achieving their operational objectives. If nonstate actors and also state actors are seriously contemplating mass casualty terrorism, the role of deterrence would be to persuade them from further moving and to be with the status quo. Thus, it is aimed to persuade the adversary for inaction. Coercion is different from deterrence in the sense that it coerces the enemy to do something. This is not aimed to preserve the status quo but to change it.

However, they should be seen as integrated and complementary to each other and as dual facets of broader counterterrorist military strategies. They could be used alternatively also. Deterrence is meant

[98] Ibid

[99] Ibid.

[100] Richard Ned Lebow and Janice Gross Stein, "Rational Deterrence Theory: I Thinl, Therefore I Deter," *World Politics,* 41(2): 1989, pp. 208–224.

for preserving status quo, i.e. a situation of no terrorist activities. If terrorist activities start, then coercion could be used to go back to the previous status quo. So, in a practical sense, coercion and deterrence back each other. In this respect, as Almog argues, cumulative deterrence, which comprises both coercion and deterrence, could be effective against terrorist groups.[101] As said earlier, the efficacy of cumulative deterrence is measured on the basis of success achieved in the victory bank. Resolve and demonstrated capability not to back down in any conflict context would be vital in balancing these nonstate groups. Steinberg in this respect notes that the United States and allies demonstrated a clear resolve to militarily coerce terrorist groups in Afghanistan after 9/11, which has had a dissuading effect on the adversary.[102]

[101] Op cit, n. 8.
[102] Op cit, n. 15.

# Index